WITHDRAWN

D1159827

Russian Versification

RUSSIAN INSTITUTE
OCCASIONAL PAPERS

491.76
Si32r

Russian Versification

THE THEORIES OF

Trediakovskij, Lomonosov, and Kantemir

by RIMVYDAS SILBAJORIS

COLUMBIA UNIVERSITY PRESS

New York and London 1968

THE RUSSIAN INSTITUTE of Columbia University sponsors the Studies of the Russian Institute and the Occasional Papers in the belief that their publication contributes to scholarly research and public understanding. In this way the Institute, while not necessarily endorsing their conclusions, is pleased to make available the results of some of the research conducted under its auspices. A list of both series appears at the back of the book.

Copyright © 1968 Columbia University Press
Library of Congress Catalog Card Number: 67-13777
Printed in the United States of America

Preface

GAI Aug 13'73

The translation of each of the treatises is preceded by a brief bibliographical note. In addition, each treatise is provided with notes which elucidate certain passages, compare by means of cross references the views of the authors on a number of specific points and, where possible, trace the origins of their views either to foreign theory and practice or to native developments before the reform.

A number of passages omitted from Trediakovskij's treatise of 1735 are referred to in brackets in the body of the translation. These omissions constitute lengthy original poems which Trediakovskij included in his treatise essentially as a means of publishing them, but they are not needed to illustrate the principles of versification. There seemed no point in reproducing or translating them, since this would contribute nothing to the understanding of Trediakovskij's metrics; moreover, any literary value the poems may have is outside the scope of the present work. The omitted poems may be found in a recent Soviet edition of Trediakovskij's works: Trediakovskij, *Izbrannye proizvedenija*, Moscow-Leningrad, 1963. The 1735 treatise is also included in this edition on pp. 365–420.

In most instances the examples of metrics quoted by the authors under discussion are given in Cyrillic as they were in the original texts. A separate metric analysis of the quoted examples is frequently provided. At such times the x-marks indicate syllables of the Russian words; the stress is shown by a ' sign, and the underlined x-marks indicate word boundaries.

v

201325

Acknowledgments are due, first and foremost, to Professor Leon Stilman, of Columbia University, whose creative and scholarly mind has left its imprint on many of the following pages and who guided me carefully through the complexities of the work when it was still a dissertation. I would also like to thank Professors Nathan Greenberg, Vinio Rossi, and Andrew Bongiorno of Oberlin College, who were of great help in matters concerning Greek, Latin, French, and Italian versification. Miss Louise E. Luke, of *The Slavic Review*, gave generously of her time and her lucid intelligence during the initial stages of preparation of this manuscript for the press. I am also grateful to Professor Leon Twarog, of Ohio State University, for his constant concern and encouragement while the work was proceeding to its conclusion.

February, 1968   Rimvydas Silbajoris

Contents

The transliteration system used here is as follows:

А а	A a	К к	K k	Х х	X x
Б б	B b	Л л	L l	Ц ц	C c
В в	V v	М м	M m	Ч ч	Č č
Г г	G g	Н н	N n	Ш ш	Š š
Д д	D d	О о	O o	Щ щ	ŠČ šč
Е е	E e	П п	P p	Ъ ъ	"
Ж ж	Ž ž	Р р	R r	Ь ь	'
З з	Z z	С с	S s	Ѣ ѣ	ě
И и	I i	Т т	T t	Ю ю	Ju ju
Й й	J j	У у	U u	Я я	Ja ja
		Ф ф	F f		

I

Introduction

IN THE second quarter of the eighteenth century, a system of versification was introduced in Russia which was based on regular alternations of stressed and unstressed syllables. That system is traditionally referred to by Russian scholars as the "syllabo-tonic" system.[1] Its name is rather inadequate, however, because by themselves its two component parts describe two different kinds of versification: the "tonic" (or accentual) pattern of Russian folk poetry comprising a more or less constant number of accents per line, but a variable number of unstressed intervals; and the "syllabic" system of the "learned" poetry of the seventeenth and early eighteenth centuries which required a fixed number of syllables in a line of verse, but no regular alternation of accented and unaccented syllables. It might therefore appear that the syllabo-tonic system was a synthesis of these two kinds of versification. Actually, the two basic measuring units—the number of stresses and the number of syllables—were used in working out Russian equivalents of an entirely different system, namely, of Greek and Latin metrics.[2]

The syllabo-tonic system, evolved by 1740, remained practically unchallenged in its basic principles until the early years of this century. It is still very much alive in Russian poetic practice despite the important departures, innovations, and experiments of the last fifty or sixty years.

There has been considerable discussion among Russian scholars as to who among the poets and theoreticians in Russia deserves the honor of having introduced the syllabo-tonic system. Certain scholars even

1

tend to minimize the role of the individual reformers and to present the transition from syllabic to syllabo-tonic versification as a gradual, spontaneous, "natural" process. There can be no doubt, however, that a major part in the development of the new system was played by the treatises written by Vasilij Trediakovskij (1703–69) and by Mixailo Lomonosov (1711–65). The first of these treatises was Trediakovskij's "New and Brief Method for Composing Russian Verse," written in 1735. This work provided the initial stimulus to which Lomonosov and Antiox Kantemir (1708–44) responded with their own theoretical discussions of Russian versification: Lomonosov with his "Letter on the Rules of Russian Versification" (1739), and Kantemir with the "Letter of Xariton Makentin to a Friend on the Composition of Russian Verse" (1743). A detailed summing-up of the new syllabo-tonic versification theory was made by Trediakovskij in 1752, when he published a substantially revised version of his "Method."

Trediakovskij introduced the concept of verse feet, based on a systematic arrangement of stressed and unstressed syllables. He applied this concept to the eleven- and thirteen-syllable lines of the earlier syllabic versification. Lomonosov's statement of 1739 was in part a critical reaction to Trediakovskij, since he advocated a broadening of the reform to include lines of any length and to move away altogether from the syllabic system. The treatise by Antiox Kantemir was also formulated in reaction to Trediakovskij's work: not only did he oppose the reform; he also introduced certain refinements into the theory and practice of syllabic verse. Thus, the new theory was elaborated in the course of a three-cornered dialogue, as it were, which Trediakovskij initiated in 1735. The concluding statement was made by Trediakovskij in 1752, with the publication of his revised treatise; the revisions tended in general toward the acceptance of Lomonosov's views.

Syllabic versification developed in Russia in the seventeenth and early eighteenth centuries. Some attempts were made to formulate a theory of versification before the syllabic system had established itself; these must be discussed briefly, since both Lomonosov and Trediakovskij were concerned with them in their own treatises on versification. The main feature of these early theories was the attempt to work out an exact imitation of Greek and Latin versification patterns. In 1596 L. Zizanij's Slavonic grammar was published; according to the custom of the time, it included a section on prosody.

His system was based on an arbitrary classification of certain Russian vowels as long and others as short.[3] The old Cyrillic alphabet contained various symbols for vowel sounds modeled on letters of the Greek alphabet. In Russian usage, groups of two or even three symbols took on identical sound values. They were differentiated only by their orthography, which, in Zizanij's days, was not too strictly normalized. Zizanij quite arbitrarily attributed quantitative values to symbols representing the same sound. He then used these distinctions to describe the heroic meter as a six-unit verse consisting of dactyls and spondees, and the elegiac meter (a variation of the heroic) and the iambic meter—also as a six-unit line, but consisting of iambs and spondees; the foot consisted in each case of syllables arbitrarily regarded as long or short.

The second attempt to devise a purely quantitative versification system was made by Meletij Smotrickij, a poet writing in southwestern Russia in the sixteenth and early seventeenth centuries. Smotrickij's Slavonic grammar, which first appeared in 1619, contained an elaborate system of quantitative metrics. It became known as "Maksimovskaja prosodija" (Maximian prosody), due to a mistaken attribution of the prosodic sections of Smotrickij's grammar to Maxim the Greek, a monk famous for his learning who wrote and taught in Russia early in the sixteenth century.[4] Smotrickij elaborated on Zizanij's classification of Russian vowels into long, short, and common, and extended it to include what he considered Russian diphthongs.[5] He also postulated the lengthening of vowels in certain positions according to an intricate system which followed the Greek patterns, and mentioned all of 124 possible verse feet based on various combinations of long and short syllables. Finally, he presented definitions with examples of various types of verse. Smotrickij's system, like Zizanij's, was almost wholly theoretical; hence, there are not many traces of attempts to put these theories into practice.[6]

In addition to the "quantitative episode," mention should be made of the so-called presyllabic verse,[7] an adaptation of Russian spoken verse. Rhyme was the only functional element of versification found in these imparisyllabic lines, and it usually formed rhymed couplets. Similar poetic endeavours were appearing at that time in the Ukraine and had also been found in earlier, presyllabic, Polish poetry. No attempt was made to observe any regularity in the syllabic length or in

the number of stresses common to these verses. Below is an example
from the "Povest' ot" prežnix" let"'" (Story of former years), commonly
attributed to Prince I. M. Katyrev-Rostovskij, written in 1626:

> Начало виршемъ,
>
> мятежнымъ вещемъ
>
> ихъже разумно прочитаемъ
>
> и слагателя книги сеи потомъ уразумѣваемъ.
>
> Изложенна бысть лѣтописная книга
>
> о похожении Чюдовского мниха,
>
> понеже бо онъ бысть убогии чернецъ
>
> и возложилъ на ся царскии вѣнецъ,
>
> царство великие Росии возмутилъ
>
> И диядиму царскую на плещахъ своихъ носилъ.[8]

A syllabic type of verse was destined to play a more important role
in the history of Russian prosody. Syllabic verse arrived in Russia
from Poland about the middle of the seventeenth century, having first
been adopted in the Ukraine and Belorussia—countries which had
previously been a part of Poland.[9] The Polish heroic line, the most
important element in the development of Russian syllabic verse, was a
line of thirteen syllables, divided at the seventh syllable by a feminine
caesura and having a feminine clausule. This form was achieved after
Polish word stress became stabilized on the penultimate syllable, in
the sixteenth century; before this Polish verse had been based on
imparisyllabic intonational groups.[10]

One of the first Polish poets to write syllabic verse was Mikołaj
Rej (1505–69). Obligatory stresses on the sixth and twelfth syllables in
the heroic verse line, and enjambement, are rare in Rej's poetry. The
fully developed use of these elements represents the major contribution
to Polish versification of Poland's greatest sixteenth-century poet—Jan
Kochanowski (1530–84). His influence was most decisive in developing
strictly syllabic verse and in establishing a fixed rhyme scheme.[11]

Historically, this Polish 13-syllable verse line developed from
medieval Latin models, after Latin verse had become essentially
syllabic. Maria Długska explains its genesis as follows:

> Syllabic verse has the oldest tradition among our contemporary systems
> of versification. . . . It was transplanted to our soil from Latin verse, at
> first in the form of relative syllabism, that is, one in which the count of
> syllables was not adhered to very rigorously. The first meter of this type
> known to us was our later epic meter—the 13-syllable line.[12]

There is also a certain similarity between the Polish epic line and the French alexandrine. The alexandrine consists in principle of twelve syllables with a thirteenth syllable added for feminine rhyme. Masculine and feminine rhymes can alternate. In Polish, however, there is no alternation of feminine and masculine rhymes, since the fixed stress on the penultimate syllable of Polish words does not permit masculine rhymes, unless, of course, the final word in the line is monosyllabic. For this reason Polish heroic verse came to resemble the French alexandrine consisting of thirteen syllables. It should be added that the caesura of the French alexandrine fell after the sixth syllable, whereas in Polish heroic verse, because of the penultimate word stress, the caesura had to be "feminine" and follow the seventh syllable, as in the following lines from Kochanowski's "Muza":

> Sobie śpiewam a Muzom!// Bo kto jest na ziemi,
> Coby serce ucieszyć// chciał pieśniami memi?[13]

In this form the Polish 13-syllable line was borrowed by the Ukrainian and Belorussian poets and then by the Russian syllabic poets. The major poet of the syllabic epoch in Russia before Kantemir was Simeon Polockij (1629–80), a Kievan monk and graduate of the Mohila Academy in Kiev—a school modeled on Polish Jesuit academies in which the study of the theory and practice of poetry was based on Polish example. He was extremely prolific and wrote on a variety of topics in various genres: epic, lyric, ode, elegy, etc. Polockij was also highly skilled in syllabic versification. According to I. P. Eremin, "he demonstrated almost all of the meters of syllabic 'verse making' that were used in his time, beginning with short six-syllable [lines] and ending with awkward and long fourteen-syllable lines."[14] It was also characteristic of Polockij in his later verse to use masculine caesurae, which were not common in Polish poetry.

As for the other Russian syllabic poets, one should mention Feofan Prokopovič (1681–1736), a high dignitary of the Russian Orthodox Church and an active participant in the reforms of Peter the Great. Like Polockij, Prokopovič was a Kievan by origin and a graduate of the same Mohila Academy. He was a close associate of Antiox Kantemir and had some influence on the latter's development as a poet, Among his other works, Prokopovič wrote a number of lyric poems in short lines, remarkable for their regularity of stress distribution.

Many of Prokopovič's lines, composed long before the syllabo-tonic reform, seem to have been written in almost regular trochees, iambs, etc. The following example may be described as lines in trochaic tetrameter (with rather frequent substitutions of pyrrhic feet for trochees):

За могилою рябою
Над рекою Прутовою
Было войско в страшном бою[15]

In general, it should be said that Russian syllabic verse did not consist of long 13- and 11-syllable lines alone. The variety of forms in Polockij's verse has already been mentioned. Below are a few more examples of syllabic verse from which it can be seen not only that the line length varied, sometimes within a single poem, but also that the rhyme scheme was not necessarily limited to paired rhymes.

From "Plačet pastušok" (The shepherd's lament) by Feofan Prokopovič:

Коли дождусь я весела ветра
И дней красных?
Коли явится милость прещедра
Небес ясных?

From Trediakovskij's "Pesenka ljubovna" (Love song):

Красной умильна!
Паче всех сильна!
Уже склонивши,
Уж победивши.
Изволь сотворить
Милость мя любить.
Люблю драгая
Тя сам весь тая.

And finally, from Trediakovskij's "Stixi poxval'nye Rossii" (Verses in praise of Russia):

Начну на флейте стихи печальни,
Зря на Россию чрез страны дальны:
Ибо днесь мне ее доброты
Мыслить умом есть много охоты.

Russian syllabic poetry survived well in to the eighteenth century, and some of the later poets—for instance, Petr Buslaev, who lived and wrote between 1700 and 1755—acquired great skill in mastering the syllabic rules. However, at the very time when this poetry was achieving its fullest development in Russia, it was being replaced by the new syllabo-tonic system. The codification of the Russian syllabic system by Antiox Kantemir, the most outstanding syllabic poet in Russia, already contained features, to be discussed later, which did not exist in traditional syllabic verse.

Vasilij Kirilovič Trediakovskij was born on February 22, 1703, to a clergyman's family in Astraxan, in southeast Russia, on the Volga near the Caspian Sea. He received his primary education from Roman Catholic monks, mostly of Polish origin, who had established residence and a school in this remote province in the wake of a large Armenian immigration to the city.[16] In 1723 Trediakovskij left his home town and family to study at the Slavo-Greco-Latin Academy in Moscow. Although originally a theological academy, this school later expanded its curriculum to include more general subjects and changed its language of instruction from Greek to Latin. Trediakovskij soon realized that a better education could be acquired in Western Europe, particularly in Paris, and he went abroad at the beginning of 1726. At the end of 1727, after a short stay in Holland, he proceeded on foot to Paris to take up studies in mathematics, philosophy, and linguistics at the University of Paris, and in theology at the Sorbonne.[17]

On his return to Russia in 1730, Trediakovskij learned that during his sojourn abroad his parents had died in an epidemic and the family home in Astraxan had been destroyed by robbers, He went to St. Petersburg and found a position there as translator in the Academy of Sciences. While doing various translations for the Academy, Trediakovskij published a prose version of Paul Tallemant's erotic pastoral allegory, *Voyage à l'ile d'amour*, which caused a sensation among the Russian reading public. It was the first important attempt to approximate spoken Russian as a vehicle of secular literature to replace the more or less Russified Church Slavonic in use at that time.

In 1733 Trediakovskij became a member of the Academy and was given the title of secretary. While his main task still centered on translations from French and German, the duty which Trediakovskij himself considered most important was his work in the "Russian Assembly," established in 1734 by order of the new president of the Academy, Baron Korff. The main function of this organization, to which all the translators of the Academy belonged, was to purify and develop the Russian literary language. Trediakovskij apparently hoped that this group might eventually grow in importance to become the Russian equivalent of the Académie Française.[18] It was under the auspices of this Assembly that Trediakovskij wrote, in 1735, his "New and Brief Method for Composing Russian Verses," which established his reputation as a linguist and theoretician of Russian versification.

A series of misfortunes began to plague Trediakovskij about 1740. The first setback was literary. Lomonosov's "Ode on the Taking of Xotin" together with his "Letter on the Rules of Russian Versification," which had been sent to the Academy, eclipsed everthing that Trediakovskij had done as a poet and expert in versification.[19] Even worse, he was soon to suffer personal indignities. In February, 1740, Trediakovskij was cruelly beaten and mistreated by Artemij Volynskij, a minister in the cabinet of Empress Anna Ioanovna.[20] Soon afterwards Trediakovskij became involved in sharp controversies with Lomonosov and Sumarokov over literary questions, disputes that were to ruin his reputation completely.

These debates began calmly enough in 1743, with a discussion on the meter best suited for exalted poetry in Russian, the iamb and the trochee being considered. Trediakovskij maintained that trochees and iambs per se were neutral as vehicles for emotional expression, while his two opponents insisted that iambs portrayed nobler feelings, while trochees were better suited for light verse.[21] Gradually, the pride and vanity of all three disputants, added to their divergent views on literature and their different social backgrounds, exacerbated literary differences into furious personal quarrels which reached their peak about 1755. Satirical epigrams of a highly personal character were exchanged among the three writers in rapid-fire succession. Trediakovskij even went so far as to accuse his enemies of atheism and political unreliability. Lomonosov, then a very powerful figure in the Academy, persecuted Trediakovskij relentlessly until the Academy stopped printing the latter's works without even deigning to explain its position.[22] This forced Trediakovskij to express his opinions either under pseudonyms, in the lengthy prefaces he wrote to his various translations from the French, such as Barclay's *Argenis* (1751), or in prefaces to his collected (previously published) works, as in 1752. The persecution, the extreme poverty he had suffered all his life, the failure of his publishing ventures, and such additional misfortunes as the several fires in his home in which many of his manuscripts perished[23] finally broke Trediakovskij's spirit. He became more and more depressed and withdrawn, ceasing even to attend the meetings of the Academy. His mood at that time can be judged by the conclusion of his letter to Sumarokov, written in 1755, in answer to the latter's attack on Trediakovskij's views concerning the Sapphic stanza: "Please forget about me; leave alone a man who has fallen in love with solitude, silence and the peace of his soul."[24] When Razumovskij, then president of the Academy, addressed an official inquiry to Trediakovskij asking why he had stopped coming to meetings and threatening him with suspension of his salary, the latter's answer included the following remarks: ". . . hated in person, despised in words, thwarted in affairs, gored by satirical horns, represented as a monster, even in my morals (what could be more shameless than that?) . . . I have lost my strength and this is why it has become necessary for me to seek solitude."[25] In 1758 Trediakovskij asked to be retired from the Academy; his request was granted in March, 1759.

The last years of his life were spent in continued labor over the translations of Rollin's *Histoire ancienne* and *Histoire romaine* (1761). In 1766 Trediakovskij published his *magnum opus*—a verse adaptation of Fénelon's *Les Aventures de Télémaque* (in his adaptation, *Tilemaxida*); he had to print it at his own expense. The meter he chose, dactylic hexameter, was an important innovation. However, the immediate reaction to this work again served as the basis for ridicule. There is a story that Empress Catherine II punished her courtiers by making them memorize sections from the *Tilemaxida*. Nevertheless, later scholars have found considerable merit in the work, not the least of which lies in the skillful handling of the Russian hexameter.[26] On April 6, 1769, not long after the completion of the *Tilemaxida*, Trediakovskij at last succumbed to his prolonged illness.

While he admitted that his terminology had been borrowed from the French, an interesting feature of Trediakovskij's "New and Brief Method for Composing Russian Verses" is his insistence that the "substance" of the new system derives from Russian folk poetry; employing a Russian proverb, he says, "I owe French versification the purse and ancient Russian poetry the whole thousand rubles" (See below, p. 53.) Trediakovskij does not explain exactly what he meant by the "substance" or the "thousand rubles," but from the context of his treatise one may surmise that the "thousand rubles" referred to the organizing role of stress as the main principle of the new versification, the stress being, in his opinion, the distinguishing feature of Russian folk verse. Later in his life Trediakovskij maintained the same opinion, and even went so far as to ascribe to Russian folk verse all the features of the syllabo-tonic system. In an essay entitled "An Opinion on the Beginning of Poetry and Verse in General," published in 1752, he said, concerning the metrics of Russian folk verse, that "Its feet were mostly trochees, or trochees and dactyls, or else dactyls alone; also the iamb, or iamb with anapest, or again the anapest alone, and, as a poetic license, the pyrrhic foot was used instead of the iamb and the trochee."[27]

In 1755, in his essay "On the Ancient, Middle, and New Russian Versification," Trediakovskij repeated the same assertion and went on to say that he based his opinion on the testimony of "living witnesses who are above suspicion."[28] In 1735, however, Trediakovskij could not have had in mind such a wide range of metric patterns in the folk verse, for, even though he named folk versification as his model, he refused to admit trisyllabic meters into his new system, and was reluctant to admit the iamb.

There is no evidence that Trediakovskij ever made a serious study of Russian folk versification beyond citing a few samples of Russian folk songs in which he claimed to have found specimens of various syllabo-tonic meters (see below, p. 158). Nevertheless, the studies of Russian folk verse made in the nineteenth century by such scholars as A. F. Hilferding,[29] A. X. Vostokov,[30] and P. D. Goloxvastov,[31] and in our day by Kiril Taranovski,[32] Roman Jakobson,[33] and others indicate that word stress plays an important organizing role in Russian folk versification and that, moreover, the distribution of stress is often quite regular and, on the whole, manifests a pronounced trochaic tendency. Nevertheless, it is difficult to relate Trediakovskij's formal organization of the 13-syllable line, with its trochaic feet, masculine caesura after the seventh syllable, and feminine rhyme, to any particular model from folk verse.

In seeking other sources of Trediakovskij's new system, attention has been drawn to the fact that a metric structure resembling the syllabo-tonic can be found in some seventeenth- and eighteenth-century verse written in Ukraine, especially in the so-called leonine verse. This verse had internal rhymes, often feminine, and a rather regular distribution of stresses. Here is an excerpt from the eighteenth-century Ukrainian poet G. Konisskij:

> Čísta ptíca/ Golubíca/ Tákov nráv iměet
> Búde město/ Gdě nečísto,/ Támo ne počíet,
> Nó gdě trávy/ Í dubrávy/ Í sěn ést' ot znója
> Tó prilíčno,/ Tó obíčno/ Město éj pokója.[34]

In Ukrainian the symbol transcribed here as *ě* stands for *i*, and therefore in the above excerpt *město* rhymes with *nečisto*, and *iměet* with *počiet*.

It is true that Trediakovskij was familiar with the Ukranian and Russian poetry of his time and could have borrowed ideas from it for his new system. However, Trediakovskij's heroic line and the leonine verse have only two elements in common: feminine rhyme at the end of the line, which also existed in classical syllabic poetry, and a regular distribution of stress. The differences, on the other hand, are more significant. First of all, Trediakovskij, in his "Method" of 1735, strongly opposed internal rhymes because of their tendency to split the line (see Rule VII, p. 45), whereas this was the principal device of the leonine verse, obvious from the above example. Second, instead of having a caesura in the middle of the line, a leonine verse line breaks into three metrical fragments of two plus two plus three trochaic feet. The word beginning each fragment is capitalized, and the rhyme pattern is as follows:

$$
\begin{array}{ccc}
----\,/\,----\,/\,------ \\
\text{a} \qquad \text{a} \qquad \text{b} \\
----\,/\,----\,/\,------ \\
\text{c} \qquad \text{c} \qquad \text{b}
\end{array}
$$

Nevertheless, the example of leonine verse may have contributed to Trediakovskij's conviction that Russian verse rhythm can be organized on the basis of stress distribution.

Another possible source of Trediakovskij's ideas which has been frequently cited is the poetry written in Russian according to the rules of German versification by Germans and other foreigners living in Russia. Perhaps the earliest examples of such poetry were written by

the German pastor Johann Gottfried Gregori (1631–75), who lived
in "Nemeckaja sloboda"—the district of Moscow assigned to foreign
residents. In 1672 Gregori wrote in German, and then translated into
Russian, a Biblical drama, *The Play of Artaxerxes* (*Artakserksovo
dejstvo*).[35] The first act was translated with the obvious intention of
reproducing the iambics of the German original. Another foreigner, a
Swede, Johan Gabriel Sparwenfeld (1655–1727), wrote in 1704 a
dedication in Russian dactylic tetrameters to a doctoral dissertation on
the Russian Church.[36] Lyrical poetry in Russian, imitating German
meters, was written by Johann Ernst Glück (1652–1705) and Johann
Werner Paus (1670–1735), Lutheran churchmen who came to Russia
at the beginning of the eighteenth century to spread learning and the
Evangelical faith, and by Wilhelm Mons (1688–1742), a Russian-born
adventurer and soldier of fortune.

Since in some cases this poetry was either older than Trediakovskij's
or at least contemporary with it, it has been suggested (especially by
V. N. Peretc) that these foreigners should be considered the real
reformers of Russian versification. However, our primary concern
here is not with chronological priority in the use of syllabo-tonic verse
in Russian, but rather with the elaboration of those theoretical foundations upon which Russian poetry actually developed. It is therefore
important to see whether there was any continuity between the efforts
of Trediakovskij and those of his foreign predecessors.

Potentially the most important of these was Paus, since he appears
to have been the only one to leave a written record of theoretical considerations on Russian verse structure. In an unpublished manuscript,[37] composed when Paus was working at the Academy as a translator and containing translations of several psalms from German to
Russian, he included, under the heading "De Prosodia Russica," a
few remarks on how to adapt German metrics to Russian verse. His
two most important ideas were that live pronunciation, and not Greek
and Latin quantity, must be the guide in devising Russian prosody,
and that monosyllabic Russian words could be considered long or
short, as the occasion demanded. Trediakovskij could certainly have
seen these notes as well as Paus's poetry, for he worked at the Academy
at the time of Paus's death and, according to Peretc, could have had
access to Paus's papers which the Academy took over after the latter's
death in 1735.[38] But be that as it may, the verses written by Paus as

well as by the other Germans were, in their main metrical features, entirely unrelated to the versification proposed by Trediakovskij in his "Method." First of all, Paus wrote mostly in iambics, while Trediakovskij in his treatise objected to the iambic meter as altogether inferior (see Rule I, p. 42). This opposition to the iamb might indicate that Trediakovskij knew Paus's work but, far from desiring to imitate him, was strongly opposed to Paus's principles. Second, Paus and the other Germans wrote only in short lines, and it is precisely these lines that Trediakovskij excluded from his reform.[39] Thus, in developing his theoretical formulations Trediakovskij by-passed Paus's verses, and the syllabo-tonic verses by written the Germans are even less relevant to the elaboration of Trediakovskij's theory than is the Ukrainian leonine verse.

On the other hand, there is a real possibility that the syllabo-tonic principle was suggested to Trediakovskij not by the verses of Paus (and others), but by the German scholars with whom he worked at the Academy. One of Trediakovskij's tasks was to translate into Russian the various odes written by the German academicians on festive occasions, and it is very likely that these translations were discussed with the authors of the originals, leading to deliberations of a general nature concerning the possibility of syllabo-tonic poetry in Russian. Direct documentary proof of this is not available, but some scholars have made this surmise. To quote one of them, Pumpjanskij:

> In academic St. Petersburg, Trediakovskij got into a German atmosphere. This and the political role of Germans (*Bühren*), and the forced participation in the academic writing of poetry (translations of German odes, especially those of Junker) led Trediakovskij to the thought of seriously learning the German language and versification. For a linguist like Trediakovskij this was not a difficult matter. The talks with Junker led him into the literary background of German classicism (*Schule der Vernunft*); it turned out that the German school was a colony of Boileau's French classicism. Thus the study of German poetry was the first example for Trediakovskij of syllabo-tonic poetry. Just at this time he also wrote his first syllabo-tonic poem—congratulations to Baron Korff.[40]

A more direct piece of evidence is Trediakovskij's letter to academician Stählin concerning the new Russian versification. A. Kunik reports this circumstance as follows:

In 1735 he [Trediakovskij] actually reverted to the former syllabic meter. This evoked disapproval on the part of the "experts" on the Russian language and gave occasion for the letter (Lettre d'un Russien à un de ses amis, écrite au sujet de la nouvelle versification Russienne) to Stählin, on Oct. 11, 1736, concerning the new Russian versification. (M. Trediakoffski la [the reference is to an ode by Stählin] traduisant en Vers Russien sans scansion entendit de plusieurs connoisseurs que dans l'original allemand reignait infinitement plus d'harmonie que dans la Traduction Russe. Il s'en entretenoit sur les raisons avec Mr. Stehlin et fut convaicu que la Langue Russe étoit assez propre pour cette harmonie.)[41]

To be sure, this particular letter was written after the "Method" had been published, but a conversation similar to that between Trediakovskij and Stählin, during which he "became convinced" that syllabo-tonic "scansion" was suitable for Russian verse, could have easily taken place on more than one occasion before 1735.

Finally, there is the opinion advanced by L. I. Timofeev that Trediakovskij's reform was really only a written codification of partial results of a natural process of "tonization" of the long lines in Russian syllabic verse. In his article "Syllabic Verse,"[42] Timofeev presents a statistical analysis of stress distribution in Russian syllabic verse, concluding that this verse clearly manifested: a) an increasing tendency to distribute stresses in a trochaic pattern); b) an opposite tendency to distribute them in an iambic pattern; and c) a tendency to combine the above two meters. Consequently, according to Timofeev, when Trediakovskij in his "Method" sanctioned the trochaic meter, he was in effect taking note of the "trochaic tendency" and giving it a theoretical formulation.[43]

Timofeev's concept of the "evolutionary development" of syllabic verse toward metrical regularity may have some validity. In a very general sense it is probably true that Trediakovskij was working with, rather than against, "natural" trends, and his treatise would probably have passed unnoticed had it been in disagreement with "the nature of things." Nevertheless, the fact remains that, whatever the "trends," syllabic poetry assumed a metrically definable regularity only as an exception.[44] And it was most certainly an important innovation to make the regularity in the distribution of accents the central principle of versification. Trediakovskij, it may be added, strongly insisted that the old syllabic verse, because of its lack of regular stress distribution, did not differ essentially from prose (see p. 38).

Trediakovskij's "Method" of 1735 was essentially a reform of the old syllabic 13-syllable (and, by extension, the 11-syllable) line. There was never any question in Trediakovskij's mind that the heroic line should preserve the traditional number of syllables: "Our hexameter can have neither more nor less than thirteen syllables" (see p. 51). This is perhaps the best explanation for his essential indifference to such "trifles" as short verse lines, and for his lack of interest in the leonine verse which was, after all, a *tour de force* of formal virtuosity. According to Trediakovskij, serious poetry was written in the syllabic heroic line; consequently that line had to be improved because the old syllabic system, which neglected word stress, failed to describe adequately the properties of verse.

The main features of Trediakovkij's reformed 13-syllable line were: 1) verse measurement by feet, and not, as previously, by syllables; 2) a trochaic cadence as best suited for Russian verse; and 3) a masculine caesura on the seventh syllable (not a feminine one, as in Polish verse). The feminine rhyme adopted in Trediakovskij's new "Method" already existed in the old syllabic verse. The fact that Trediakovskij proceeded from the old syllabic line can perhaps best be demonstrated by the changes made by Trediakovskij in a line from Kantemir's first satire which he quoted many times in his own, emended version in the treatise. Kantemir's original line read as follows:

Уме слабый, плод трудов// не долгой науки

The stress pattern was:

$$\acute{x}\,x \quad \acute{x}\,x \quad \acute{x} \quad x\,\acute{x}// \quad x \quad \acute{x}\,x \quad \acute{x}\,x\,x$$

This is a 13-syllable line with a more or less accidental trochaic pattern in the first hemistich, but no pattern in the second. Trediakovskij changed the line to read:

Ум толь слабый плод тру/дов// краткия науки

The resulting metric pattern

$$\acute{x}\,\underline{x}/ \quad \acute{x}\,x/\acute{x} \quad \acute{x}/\,\acute{x}// \quad \acute{x}\,x/\,x\,\acute{x}/\,\acute{x}\,x$$

fulfills all the requirements of Trediakovskij's new heroic line:

trochaic feet (except for the pyrrhic in the fifth), a stressed seventh "caesura syllable" not counted in the total number of feet, and a feminine rhyme. This demonstrated the whole substance of the reform, by moving two accents. The example, it is true, was chosen deliberately to show that he was not breaking with earlier practice, but merely improving on it.

In his treatise Trediakovskij emphasized that only a few small changes were needed in order to obtain his new line from the old syllabic one (see p. 66). However, in the context of the history of Russian versification up to that time these "small changes" actually involved new theoretical concepts which had not previously been formulated in Russia. The most important changes concerned the notion of word stress, and it may be useful to discuss them briefly here.

First of all, Trediakovskij adapted the terminology of ancient Greek and Latin versification to his new system in a manner consistent with the realities of the Russian language. In order to explain the meaning of the classical Greek and Latin terms, "length" and "brevity" of syllables, as used in his own system of versification, he substituted opposition based on stress for the classical one based on length. This he asserts in Corollary 2, stating that the length and brevity of syllables understood in this new Russian versification is not the same as what the Greeks and Latins used in their versification; but only *tonic*, that is, consisting of voice stress alone (see p. 40). His solution was the same as that adopted by other Western languages having a strong word stress. All European theories of verse adapted the classical terminology to a completely new tonic verse system which had developed from various sources in medieval Latin, English, and German poetry.[45]

Second, Trediakovskij introduced the concept of rhythm or cadence in verse, adding it to the requirement of a constant number of syllables in syllabic verse. B. Tomaševskij describes this innovation in the following manner:

The basic thought of Trediakovskij is that together with meter—the canonized system of sound elements of verse—there exists rhythm—the cadence, that is, the trend toward organization of other, noncanonized, forms of sound (for the syllabic versification of a system of stresses in a verse line). In borrowing his terminology from France, Trediakovskij gave this term—the cadence—an expanded interpretation apparently because the question of the role of stress in Russian versification had matured by that time and a system of stresses was naturally advanced as a new artistic format, supplementing the canonized principle of syllabic verse— the count of syllables.[46]

Most of Trediakovskij's technical terms, as he himself acknowledges, were borrowed directly from the French. He was generally quite successful in finding Russian equivalents for them, although his description of the caesura is not so precise as to leave no room for confusion. Trediakovskij apparently considered the caesura a complex phenomenon—primarily a break of the anticadence type with its pitch on the seventh syllable, which is realized in recitation both by the rising intonation and by a pause; in this he was clearly following the French.[47] However, the difficulty in Trediakovskij's formulation is that the caesura seems to be both syllable and a pause at the same time (see Rule III, p. 42, n. 23; p. 153, n. 37; p. 162; and p. 187, n. 11).

Another problem arises from the fact that Trediakovskij did not explain why he chose the trochee rather than the iamb as the most suitable foot. Some explanation of this was provided by Trediakovskij much later in his essay, "On the Ancient, Middle, and New Russian Versification," in which he wrote: "I was led to trochees by the qualities of our language, because our periods end more frequently and more evenly with a trochee; also our rhyme, in the middle versification, as well as that which is now called feminine, is precisely a trochee."[48] Later in the same essay Trediakovskij admitted that another stimulus to his use of the trochee was an example of trochaic verse that he had seen in a "Dalmatian booklet."[49] This made him feel that trochees are well suited to poetry in the Slavic languages.

It is not clear what Trediakovskij meant by "our periods"; and, in general, his references to the "qualities of our language," like those of folk versification, are not specific enough to be of much use in elucidating his theories. The significant part of the above statement is the connection Trediakovskij makes between the feminine rhyme and the trochaic cadence. Considering that the caesura stress fell on an odd (seventh) syllable, the final stress in each hemistich had to fall on an odd syllable. If an even syllable were to be stressed anywhere inside the two hemistichs, the rhythmic cadence of the line would inevitably suffer. As B. Tomaševskij says:

If one is to make the syllable before the caesura stressed, according to the

French habit, then it will turn out that two fixed stresses (on the caesura and on the rhyme) will fall on the first positions of feet or on the odd positions of the hemistichs. In order to maintain regularity of rhythm it is necessary to hold to trochaic feet.[50]

It is important to point out, however, that Trediakovskij allowed the possibility of pyrrhic and iambic substitutions in his trochaic lines, although iambs, in his opinion, detracted considerably from the beauty of the lines.

Finally, it should be mentioned that Trediakovskij did not regard his treatise as a discourse on metrics alone, for in the second part of his treatise he provided a detailed discussion of various genres and types of poetry and even added a list of those ancient and contemporary poets whom he considered most important. The study of versification in Trediakovskij's time had not developed to the point where it could be regarded as a separate discipline, and Trediakovskij did not differentiate between matters of meter, rhyme, stanzaic structure, genre, poetic language, etc. What he aimed at was a general *ars poetica* to guide the aspiring and practicing Russian poets of his day.

The first treatise written at least partly in response to Trediakovskij's "Method" was Lomonosov's "Letter on the Rules of Russian Versification." Mixailo Vasiljevič Lomonosov was born in 1711, the son of a fisherman, in far northern Russia, near the town of Xolmogory, in the vicinity of the White Sea.[51]

In 1730, at the age of nineteen, Lomonosov left home for Moscow where, masquerading as a nobleman's son, he gained admittance to the Slavo-Greco-Latin Academy. He progressed in his studies rapidly and was selected as one of the small group of bright seminary students to be sent in 1736 for further study to the Imperial Academy of Sciences in St. Petersburg.

The desperate need for native Russian scholars and specialists in various fields of technology provided Lomonosov with his next opportunity. In the same year, he was sent to Germany to be trained in chemistry and metallurgy, so that he could participate in a great Siberian expedition planned at that time by the Academy. At first Lomonosov was sent to Marburg with two other Russian students to study mathematics, German, and other languages, and to acquire a general education under the famous scholar and philosopher Christian

Wolf. Later the Russian students went to Freiberg to study mining chemistry under Professor Johann Friedrich Henckel. While in Marburg, Lomonosov distinguished himself both as a capable and diligent student and as a young man of rather rowdy disposition, inclined to drinking, who wasted his scholarship money and ran up debts. He behaved similarly in Freiberg, where he had several violent conflicts with Professor Henckel, one of whose duties was to watch over the general behavior of his Russian charges. Lomonosov, for his part, accused Henckel of being reluctant to initiate his Russian pupils into the secrets of chemistry and mineralogy. Partly as a consequence of these quarrels, Lomonosov left Freiberg in 1740 for a year of wandering around Germany and Western Europe, during which time he visited Frankfurt, Rotterdam, Leipzig, and the Hague; was married, in Marburg, in 1740; and even, according to the none-too-reliable memoirs of Academician Stählin, was recuited into Prussian military service for a short time.[52] He finally returned to Russia in the summer of 1741.

However stormy these years may have been, Lomonosov never lost his passion for knowledge, not only in the natural sciences but also in the humanities. While in Marburg, he became acquainted with the writings of Johann Christoph Gottsched and, more important, with the poetry of Johann Christian Günther, Germany's foremost writer of odes. Under the strong influence of Günther, as well as of Boileau, whose "Ode sur la Prise de Namur" he quotes in his "Letter," Lomonosov wrote his famous "Ode on the Taking of Xotin," celebrating the victory of Russian troops over the Turks in 1739. This he sent to the Academy together with his "Letter on the Rules of Russian Versification."

On January 8, 1742, Lomonosov was appointed adjunct of the St. Petersburg Academy in the department of physics. From the very beginning of his academic career Lomonosov's scientific genius and literary talents gained him prestige and power in the Academy.[53] He soon became the "poet laureate" of the Academy, in charge of translating the congratulatory odes written on various state occasions by the German academicians, notably Stählin; later he composed similar odes of his own.

At the Academy Lomonosov soon became involved in the struggle for power which was continual in the institution, sometimes to the detriment of its scholarly achievements. Lomonosov seems to have identified himself with the cause of Russian science against the foreign academicians, whose power was said to be out of all proportion to their scholarly contributions. And it was true that there were at the Academy many foreigners of little talent, who often impeded the progress of native Russian scientific genius, such as Lomonosov's. Nationalistic feelings in themselves, however, were not the main cause of Lomonosov's struggles with the foreigners at the Academy, for he was on good terms with such talented men of science as the academician Georg Wilhelm Richman.

In the midst of these battles, Lomonosov continued his scientific work. He was appointed professor of chemistry in 1745, wrote a number of scholarly treatises on various problems in the exact sciences, and in 1748 achieved his long-standing aim of having a chemistry laboratory established under his direction. Lomonosov's work in the exact sciences was the first Russian exploration in many fields and won him the praise of such famous scholars as the German mathematician Euler.

About 1750 Lomonosov acquired an important protector in the person of Ivan Šuvalov, the favorite of the Empress Elizabeth. This powerful magnate, who was also something of a man of letters, even took lessons in versification from Lomonosov, while the latter depended on Šuvalov for support within the Academy. Šuvalov himself seems to have believed that his protegé should concern himself with literature and the humanities, whereas Lomonosov was rather inclined to regard these activities as secondary to his scientific work. However, Lomonosov continued his interest in literature, producing a monumental work on rhetoric (two editions, 1744 and 1748), as well as a multitude of odes, poetic prefaces to firework displays, a Russian grammar, and several tragedies in verse, as well as contributing to the development of Russian literary language.[54]

His literary activities involved Lomonosov just as deeply in personal controversies as had his scientific work. This time his enemies were primarily native Russian writers, especially Sumarokov and Trediakovskij. These controversies were partly literary, partly personal. His conflict with Sumarokov was largely a matter of rivalry with a new literary generation. Lomonosov represented the older type of official court poetry, solemn in mood and formal in style, while Sumarokov, who denounced the abstractness, complexity, and exaltedness of Lomonosov's language, aimed at lyricism, directness, and simplicity, at least in his short poems if not in his tragedies. [55]

The controversies with Trediakovskij revolved mainly around grammatical questions, such as the proper endings for the nominative plurals of masculine adjectives, and around the principles of versification. Here, too, the disputes reached the personal level, and Trediakovskij, on the whole, was the loser.

In the heat of all these controversies Lomonosov continued his literary work. His *Russian Grammar*, written in 1755, was published in 1757. He also achieved further successes at the Academy, becoming a member of its Chancellery in 1757—an administrative position which gave Lomonosov power equal to that of his enemy Taubert.

One of Lomonosov's finest achievements, near the end of his life, was his contribution towards the establishment of Moscow University (the first Russian university); he drew up the regulations for that institution and for a gymnasium.[56]

Lomonosov had been tormented by serious, though intermittent, illnesses from 1762 on, and he died on April 4, 1765, in the midst of fierce conflicts with his old enemies at the Academy.

Lomonosov's reaction to Trediakovskij's "Method" of 1735 must be understood in the context of the foreign, specifically German, concepts influencing him in both the theory and practice of versification. When he travelled abroad in 1736, Lomonosov took along a copy of Trediakovskij's "Method,"[57] and therefore he could study and evaluate it in the light of the new ideas he had obtained from his reading of German theoreticians and poets.[58]

Lomonosov's German masters seem to have been Johann Christoph Gottsched, Johann Ludwig Prasch, and Tobias Huebner in theory, and Johann Christian Günther in poetic practice.[59]

Günther's influence is especially important in Lomonosov's choice of a rhetorical, solemn style in his poetry and in his dependence on the ode as the supreme poetic genre. In metrics, Lomonosov also followed Günther's ten-line stanzas of four-foot iambics, and his alternating masculine-feminine rhymes. Nevertheless, Lomonosov's stanza, with the rhyme scheme *ababccdeed*, is exacly the same as that of Boileau's "Ode sur la Prise de Namur," so that Lomonosov cannot be said to have followed Günther alone.

Some critics claimed that Lomonovos's "Ode on the Taking of Xotin" also followed Günther's ode, "Eugen ist fort, ihr Musen nach," very closely in content; a contemporary German academician, Schlötzer, even wrote that Lomonosov had "mer übersetzt als nachgebildet"[60] Günther's ode. This is not true, however. Aside from the metrical and stanzaic structure of the ode, there are some similarities of poetic device, such as the calling forth of the spirits of dead heroes in stanzas 9, 10, 11, and 12, resembling the device used by Günther in his ode, but common to the works of many other poets as well. There are also images, such as the rhetorical demand that the defeated Turks kiss the hand and foot of the Empress, reminiscent of the lines in which Günther tells the enemies to kiss the conqueror's sword. While similarities of that sort can at most point to Günther's work as a poetic model for Lomonosov, they do not amount to plagiarism or even close imitation. In certain other passages of his ode Lomonosov also comes close to the images and poetic devices used by Boileau in his ode on the taking of Namur.[61]

Trediakovskij's "Method" also had some influence on Lomonosov's poetry, at least in the beginning. Attempts to follow Trediakovskij's precepts can be seen in one of Lomonosov's first poems—a translation of Fénelon's ode, "Montagnes de qui l'audace," written in 1738, while Lomonosov was still a student in Marburg. The meter is trochaic rather than iambic. The "poetic license" in the use of words—abbreviations, etc.—corresponds in many instances to Trediakovskij's rules in his "Method" (see p. 48). Also, the very fact that Lomonosov chose an ode by Fénelon may be indicative of the influence of Trediakovskij, who in the "Method" also translated an ode by Fénelon to illustrate this genre.[62]

However, there the resemblance ends, for Trediakovskij's translation is in his 13-syllable heroic meter, with coupled rhymes, while Lomonosov uses four-foot trochees with alternating rhymes, thus giving his version an entirely different rhythmic movement. In this one may perceive the major difference between the two authors: Lomonosov has completely discarded the syllabic tradition and, except for the trochee, has chosen the verse form of the German odes.

The next ode by Lomonosov—the previously mentioned "Ode on the Taking of Xotin"—is composed in iambics. In his own "Letter," he claims that the pure iambic line by its upbeat increases the nobility of the material (see p. 75), thus echoing Hübner's statement: "Die jambischen Versen steigen demnach gleichsam in die Höhe."[63] Lomonosov also differs from Trediakovskij in insisting on pure verse feet, without the pyrrhics that Trediakovskij permitted (see p. 40). However, he soon tacitly discarded this requirement, even in his first odes,[64] for he realized the impossibility of writing Russian binary meters without pyrrhic feet.

Moreover, in his "Letter" Lomonosov rejects Trediakovskij's argument that trisyllabic feet are unsuitable for Russian verse, insisting that "we can introduce into our verse bisyllabic and trisyllabic feet without any strain and thus follows the Greeks, Romans, Germans, and other peoples who proceed correctly in versification" (see p. 73). This passage could very well have been inspired by Gottsched: "So halte ich es für nötig zu zeigen, dass es uns Deutschen auch an anderen Arten der Füsse nicht fehle, die bey den Alten mit so vielem Vortheile gebraucht worden. . . ."[65] As a logical consequence of this Lomonosov also permits the masculine, and the dactylic, as well as the feminine rhyme, again opposing Trediakovskij who would accept only the feminine rhyme.

Thus, having found that "Russian verse can be composed just as beautifully and naturally as German" (p. 76), Lomonosov offers examples of various combinations of verse feet, altogether finding 30 possible variants. This is certainly no mere reform of the existing syllabic verse; it is a lifting of the barriers, an opening of entirely new possibilities for Russian versification. Lomonosov's "Letter" does not present a restrictive versification system, as did Trediakovskij's treatise; it simply proposes that Russian poets freely adopt and assimilate those versification techniques that are suitable to the structure of the Russian language. It must also be added that Lomonosov's success was in no small measure due to the fact that he was a much better poet than Trediakovskij. While Trediakovskij could argue closely and with apparent logic (though often proceeding from the wrong premises) that the 13-syllable line was best and noblest for Russian poetry, he could not write anything that would compel readers or poets to accept his theories. Lomonosov, on the other hand, succeeded in capturing the imagination of his readers by his verse and thus established much more effectively the new approach to Russian versification.

Trediakovskij's "Method" of 1735 also played a prominent role in provoking the first Russian theoretical statement on the syllabic system of versification. Since Russian syllabic poetry was an imitation of the Polish, no syllabic poet had attempted to formulate the theoretical principles of this system. Instead, poets simply followed the practice of Polish and Ukrainian poets and the rules contained in the Polish and Ukrainian textbooks on poetics, written in Latin, which circulated in the ecclesiastical academies of southern Russia and the Ukraine and were later adopted by the Slavo-Greco-Latin Academy in Moscow as well. The appearance of Trediakovskij's treatise, however, provoked a response from certain practitioners of syllabic poetry. The most important reaction, taking the form of a theoretical treatise on Russian syllabic poetry, came from the foremost Russian poet of the day, Prince Antiox Dmitrievič Kantemir.

Kantemir was born in Constantinople on September 10, 1708, the son of Prince Demetrius Kantemir, who, with the title of "hospodar," ruled the then Turkish province of Moldavia as the representative of the Ottoman Empire. According to various sources, the Kantemir family was of Tartar origin, supposedly reaching all the way back to Tamerlane.[66] Kantemir's mother, on the other hand, came from an old Greek family.[67] The home atmosphere was highly cultivated and aristocratic; Demetrius Kantemir possessed a wide and profound knowledge of ancient Greek and Latin as well as of contemporary Western European languages and literatures, especially Italian.[68] The education of young Antiox, however, had to take place in Russia, for as early as 1711 his father was forced to flee Moldavia, in consequence of his secret dealings with Peter I of Russia and the latter's unsuccessful war with the Turks.[69] Kantemir had abundant opportunity to observe life at the Russian court, since his father remained close to Peter I, was lavishly rewarded by him with estates and titles, and even accompanied the tsar on his expedition to Persia in 1722, taking his son with him.

Kantemir's attention was drawn to Russian language and literature by his tutor Ivan Iljinskij, a poet and a graduate of the Slavo-Greco-Latin Academy, who later worked as secretary to Demetrius Kantemir. Iljinskij taught Kantemir to write verse in the manner of another syllabic poet—Simeon Polockij.[70] Like many other well-rounded gentlemen of the eighteenth century, Kantemir did not limit his interests to literature, but also studied history, philosophy, and the exact sciences, especially algebra, in which he maintained an interest throughout his life; he received instruction in these subjects at the newly established Imperial Academy of Sciences in St. Petersburg.[71] His first literary efforts included a translation from the French of an anonymous description of Paris[72] and, following a tradition begun by Meletij Smotrickij, a concordance in verse of the Psalms of David, written in 1727. In 1729 Kantemir wrote his first satire, which was directed against the opponents of learning and education; other satires soon followed. In general, it may be said that his literary talents lay in the direction of "classical" satire, based on imitations of the ancients—Juvenal, Persius, Horace—and of the French pseudo-classicists, in particular Boileau. He went beyond mere imitation by giving his satires a decidedly Russian flavor. In all, at home and abroad, Kantemir wrote nine satires, some touching on various aspects of Russian life, and some, especially the later ones, exhibiting a more general philosophical content.[73]

Kantemir was to spend only a short time in Russia, for a combination of personal and political circumstances soon resulted in his appointment to the post of Russian diplomatic representative in London. On the political scene, two parties of influential nobility had formed after the death of Peter II and upon the ascension to the throne in 1730 of Anna Ioannovna. One was a group of powerful magnates who wanted to limit the absolute rule of the monarch and had drawn up a set of "conditions" to this effect. The other party, actually a more "progressive" one, was paradoxically in favor of autocracy because, in the days of Peter I, reforms were realized by the autocratic ruler against the resistance of the old aristocrats. Among those who believed in continued reforms executed through a central authority were Kantemir and the Novgorod archbishop and poet Feofan Prokopovič, a close associate of the late emperor. This group presented a petition to Anna Ioannovna, asking her to remain an absolute ruler.[74] The new empress graciously agreed. The "conditions" were abolished, and the authors of the petition, including Kantemir, were now to be rewarded for their loyalty. Kantemir's reward may have been the return of his father's estates, which his elder brother Konstantin had seized, taking advantage of the lack of any clear provision in their father's will concerning his successor.[75] Kantemir's brother was eager to have him out of the country to prevent the resumption of his patrimony, and he persuaded the empress to appoint Kantemir to the post of Russian diplomatic representative in London, which she did in 1731.[76]

Russia's international position at this time was rather difficult since the great Western powers—France, Prussia, and England—were following an anti-Russian policy, partly as a reaction to Russia's pressure on Poland and partly because of Russian designs on Constantinople. Kantemir's mission was to try to win England over to the side of Russia. The young diplomat tried very conscientiously to fulfill his responsibilities, but was not very successful. On the personal level, however, his London experience may have been the happiest part of his life. He entered a closely knit circle of lesser diplomatic representatives, mostly from the Italian states, whose lack of political importance was fortunately compensated for Kantemir by their fine humanistic education.[77] In their circle he perfected his knowledge of the Italian language, music, and literature, especially poetry, and he seems to have had many "philosophical" evenings with his friends. He also interested himself in contemporary English culture and read the works of Locke, Hobbes, Steele, and others.[78] According to some reports,[79] Kantemir was impressed by the English form of government and by the belief in personal liberty, which influenced some of his satires.

In 1737, after conducting successful negotiations for the resumption of relations between France and Russia, Kantemir was appointed the new Russian representative to the French government. He arrived at the French court in 1738,[80] but found the atmosphere decidedly less pleasant than that of England. It was a difficult post, since Russia, involved in a war with Turkey, encountered French diplomatic machinations which robbed it of the fruits of its victory over the Turks at Xotin. At times it seemed that the Russian government itself was not too eager to help Kantemir. Count Ostermann, Anna Ioannovna's chief of the Collegium on Foreign Affairs, apparently never trusted him very far, at least partly because of his youth,[81] and the Russian treasury was not willing to supply him with the funds he needed to conduct his affairs with suitable dignity and efficiency.

It is small wonder, therefore, that Kantemir, while fulfilling his obligations very conscientiously and while maintaining relations with

French cultural figures, notably Montesquieu,[82] showed an increasing tendency to withdraw to his private study for scholarly work and meditation. His interest in the formal aspects of Russian versification found expression in the "Letter of Xariton Makentin to His Friend on the Composition of Russian Verse," written toward the end of his life. In general, it seems that Kantemir's major interests in life were scholarly rather than diplomatic.[83] There are even indications that he entertained the thought of becoming the president of the Russian Academy of Sciences.[84]. He seemed to think that this position would afford him an opportunity for intellectual intercourse and a shelter from the noisy affairs of politics and society life. In his biography, Gouasco refers to Kantemir's character as "moins vif que profond" and "plus solide que brilliant," which suggests a temperament perhaps better suited for academic than for political life.[85]

Kantemir's health, always poor, began to fail more and more. He died on March 31, 1744, at the age of thirty, after a stomach illness which had tormented him for a long time.

Kantemir's reaction to Trediakovskij's first treatise (which he probably read between 1738 and 1740) was decidedly negative concerning matters that seemed extremely important to Trediakovskij.[86] From the very beginning of his "Letter" Kantemir seems intent on reducing to insignificance Trediakovskij's claim to have found the one "correct" way to write Russian verse and thus, by implication, to have accomplished a revolution in Russian versification. To Trediakovskij's statement that "Maxim's Prosody" (i.e., quantitative versification) is ridiculous (see p. 38), Kantemir answered that the differences between Greek and Russian "grammar" were not great enough to justify laughing at Smotrickij; to the rule that there must be paired feminine rhymes, he opposed the idea of unrhymed syllabic verse "following the Italians" (see p. 82), although the lines of this verse still had trochaic endings. When he did accept rhymes, he again opposed Trediakovskij by admitting not just one—the feminine—but three types of rhymes, masculine, feminine, and dactylic, or, in Kantemir's terminology, "blunt," "simple," and "gliding," respectively. Moreover, whereas Trediakovskij did not propose to reform the short lines at all, with the exception of dividing them into "regular" (with an odd number of syllables per line) and "irregular" (with even numbers) (see p. 47), Kantemir also elaborated rules for the short lines,. irrespective of whether they had an odd or an even number of syllables per line. It is precisely in these short lines that Kantemir often achieved a rhythmic movement practically indistiguishable from that of the later syllabo-tonic lines. In many ways, the very approach of the two men toward versification as such was different. Whereas Trediakovskij erected a logical structure based on precedents and established norms of ancient versification, organized along strict lines of formal reasoning, Kantemir asserted (p. 94) that it was his instinct for rhythm, his "ear" alone that guided him in the formulation of his rules.[87]

The most important difference between Trediakovskij and Kantemir, however, is that Kantemir rejected the basic unit of verse measurement proposed by Trediakovskij—the verse foot (p. 86). Kantemir agreed that there must be some rhythmic organization of the line, but his point of departure seems directly opposite to that of Trediakovskij. The latter took the old syllabic line and rebuilt it, proceeding from a new basic entity, the foot. Kantemir, on the other hand, kept the line itself as a basic entity and merely tightened its internal organization by postulating two obligatory stresses—one in each hemistich, in certain defined positions (p. 87). In contrast to this, the older syllabic Russian verse had, essentially, only one compulsory stress—on the penultimate syllable.

The positive impact of Trediakovskij's first "Method" on Kantemir is seen precisely in Kantemir's agreement that a better form of rhythmical organization of the line was indeed necessary. Furthermore, Kantemir agreed that the particular instrument of such improved organization was word stress. S. M. Bondi maintains that the attention to stress "as a rhythmical factor in verse"[88] was the only thing Kantemir borrowed from Trediakovskij. That this was indeed a borrowing from the latter's "Method" is also suggested by Kantemir's definition of the "long" syllable in verse, which is the same as Trediakovskij's—that syllable on which the stress falls is considered long (compare p. 40 and p. 86).

Having accepted the stress as the organizing element of a verse line, Kantemir devoted most of his "Letter" to elaborating his ideas on stress distribution. First of all he made it clear that a number of syllables should be left unspecified and be either "short" or "long," depending on the poet's choice (p. 87 and p. 95). This of, course, limits the capacity of stress to produce a regular rhythmic cadence. On the other hand, the syllables for which stress *is* specified are for the 13-syllable line: the fifth or seventh in the first hemistich, and the fifth in the second (p. 87). Consequently, both Kantemir and Trediakovskij defined the positions of obligatory stress in such a way that a trochaic cadence became possible (actually favored in terms of probability) and, in Trediakovskij's case, clearly preferred. As a result certain scholars have concluded that the development of Russian versification can be described as a progression from Polish syllabic verse, with its trochaic cadence receiving support in the feminine rhyme, to Kantemir's strengthening of this trochaic principle, and finally to Trediakovskij's actual advocacy of trochees.[89] The objections to such an argument are, of course, that Kantemir's "Letter," although written at a later date than Trediakovskij's treatise, was actually a refusal to move on to the next stage in this sequence, for he rejected the trochaic (and any other) verse foot.

If Kantemir did not follow Trediakovskij with regard to stress distribution in the line, the question arises whether or not there were any other sources for Kantemir's system. Kantemir himself (see p. 95) fails to mention any and, instead, cites his sense of rhythm as the only source of his ideas. The fact is, however, that in the long lines it is difficult, at least for the present-day reader, to perceive any particular rhythmic cadence. Lines like

Что́/ по́ль/зу/ет/ мно́/же/ство// лю/де́й/ без/рас/су́д/но

or

Ве/ли/ча́/ют,/ спус/ти́/ ча́с// ни́з/ят/ уж/ и ма́/лят

do not strike one as being especially melodious. Yet Kantemir chose these lines as examples of verse in which stress is distributed according to his rules. The pre-caesura stress on the seventh syllable (second example, above) is not an imitation of Trediakovskij's seven-syllable stress, since Kantemir's poetic practice developed quite independently of Trediakovskij, and Kantemir, unlike Trediakovskij, did not regard such a stressed caesura syllable as being also a pause. It has been suggested that Kantemir was influenced by Italian syllabic poetry,[90] and that he borrowed some elements of the heroic line from the Italian alexandrine. It is true that the Italian alexandrine allowed several unstressed syllables before the caesura, often in a dactylic pattern;[91] this might explain why Kantemir provided the alternative of a stress on the fifth syllable in the first example. However, the earlier Russian syllabic verse, which did not observe any compulsory pre-caesura stress, also often placed it on the fifth syllable. There are other resemblances between Kantemir's rules and the stress distribution of Italian poetry in some of the shorter lines (see nn. 32 and 34, pp. 181, 182), but this evidence is limited and inconclusive; it is necessary to wait for more information on this question before the importance of Italian versification in the formulation of Kantemir's theories can be properly assessed.

With respect to the short lines of verse, however, one may more readily agree that Kantemir's ear was his guide. Moreover, it should be added that it was a very good guide indeed, for many of these lines have an astonishingly regular rhythm (see pp. 91–92). In this connection, one may remember that the short lines in the poetry of Feofan Prokopovič were also often quite rhythmical (see p. 6). Kantemir, before he left Russia, was a close friend of Prokopovič, who praised his verse and gave him encouragement.[92] It is very likely that they discussed problems of versification—Prokopovič, who had a lively interest in these matters and even wrote a treatise on versification and poetry entitled *De Arte Poetica*,[93] certainly may have influenced Kantemir in the matter of rhythmic structure in his short verse lines.

Kantemir's refusal to discard the syllabic system bound him to the older tradition of Russian versification—a tradition attacked by Trediakovskij and terminated after Lomonosov. Furthermore, one could argue that his tendency to regularize the meter of short lines thus perfecting their metric structure, placed Kantemir in the continuum of the development of Russian versification, which extended from syllabic verse to present-day poetry and which, although influenced, was never completely destroyed, by the theoretical treatises on versification written in the eighteenth century or later.[94] On the contrary, Trediakovskij's very special form of the 13-syllable "heroic hexameter"[95] never took root in Russian poetry.[96] Trediakovskij did not belong to the continuum, even though he stimulated others to formulate their own theories of versification.

Seventeen years after the appearance of his treatise of 1735, Trediakovskij found it necessary to issue a revised version, which he included in the 1752 edition of his collected works. The new version has every appearance of a definitive, final statement of Trediakovskij's views on versification, and in many ways it is quite different from its predecessor. Trediakovskij claimed that there was no substantial change in his views and that the second treatise merely furnished what was lacking in the first: "True, this whole Method is composed in different words (except for the technical terms) and in different order, but the foundation and basis are still the same, and therefore it itself is the same, only, I repeat, amended and supplemented" (p. 127). However, even a superficial glance at the two treatises reveals differences that clearly go beyond mere supplementation and emendation.

The most obvious change appears in his attitude toward verse feet. In 1735 Trediakovskij completely rejected trisyllabic feet and was most unfavorably disposed toward iambics. This time he not only included iambics among the "feet used most often in our present versification" (p. 103), but even stated that the dactyl and anapest, "far from being antagonistic to our verse, even appear pleasant to those who know their strength" (p. 104). If Trediakovskij's preference for the trochee in his first treatise was primarily a matter of choosing that type of foot which would fit most easily into the old syllabic framework, then the admittance of all the other meters shows that Trediakovskij had thoroughly revised his earlier conceptions of the verse line. What the 1752 treatise actually represents is a formal acceptance of all the basic features of syllabo-tonic versification as it existed in German, and as Lomonosov had adapted it to Russian verse. Mere reform was no longer necessary; Trediakovskij's chief aim now was to provide Russian poetry with a formal code of regulations governing all aspects of Russian versification as it had developed since 1735.

It must be remembered that in his first treatise, despite its essentially deductive, quasi-mathematical method, Trediakovskij also insisted on tradition and experience, and on the example of good poets, Kantemir in particular. It is not altogether surprising, then, that in 1752 he accepted newly acquired experience and sought to integrate it into his original scheme.

Trediakovskij's acceptance of iambic feet may have been caused at least partially by a discussion which he, Sumarokov, and Lomonosov had in 1744 about the comparative merits of iambic and trochaic meters. This resulted in a kind of "public competition," for which the 143rd Psalm was translated by Lomonosov and Sumarokov in iambics, and by Trediakovskij in trochees. At that time Trediakovskij took the position that neither the iamb nor the trochee as such had any special "emotional" value which would make one of them exalted and the other lyrical in mood. He also developed the idea that iambs and trochees are essentially only variations of one and the same rhythmic alternation; the two meters have a "secret affinity," because "a verse consisting of pure iambics, if one were to pronounce its first syllable in a quieter voice than usual, will at the same time be a pure trochee; also, if a verse were constructed of pure trochees, then by a very quiet pronunciation of only its first syllable, it will at the same time consist of pure iambics."[97] Formally speaking, Trediakovskij was right. One may describe a trochaic line as an iambic line with a one-syllable anacrusis.[98] In actuality, however, the characteristic movement of a poem written in iambics is entirely different from that of one written in trochees. Nevertheless, his discovery of an affinity between the two meters may have paved the way for Trediakovskij's acceptance of iambic as a legitimate meter.

Trediakovskij's adoption of trisyllabic meters provided the basis for what was perhaps his greatest achievement in versification—the development of the Russian hexameter. His best examples of this verse form are found in *Argenida* and *Tilemaxida*, where his rich hexameters combined dactyls and trochees in a manner that approached the expressiveness and flexibility of the classical hexameter. In Trediakovskij's lifetime these two works were the subject of many jokes and occasional contemptuous references to the author's poetic talent, but this was due largely to Trediakovskij's unweildy archaic language and syntax. L. V. Pumpjanskij thinks that Trediakovskij deliberately sought to make the reading of "noble" poetry difficult, mostly by means of "Latinized" syntax. Later poets, beginning with Radiščev and afterwards Pushkin, believed that from a metrical point of view Trediakovskij's handling of the Russian hexameter in these epic works had been much underestimated.[99]

Another important difference between Trediakovskij's treatises of 1735 and 1752 was his acceptance in the latter work of the division of short lines into verse feet. Here again it was essentially a matter of recognizing an established fact, for Lomonosov's odes had amply demonstrated how this could be done. However, Trediakovskij preferred to justify his change in attitude by a formal argument. In the preface to the 1752 edition of his works, he explained the matter in the following terms:

After long and deliberate subsequent considerations and thought I was able to assure myself with my own proofs that both long and short lines must necessarily consist of feet because the component parts of a prose syntactic unit cannot be distinguished from verse in any other way except by the fact that the syntactic unit has unsystematic stresses, while the stresses of a verse line are arranged by certain positions every other or every two syllables, which is what constitutes our feet, of which some begin and others end with a stress; that is, the essential difference between verse and prose is precisely the feet, combined in a line in a systematic way.[100]

Another change pertained to rhyme. In 1735 Trediakovskij regarded rhyme in heroic verse as highly desirable if not structurally essential, but in 1752 he condemned it, repeating this condemnation in 1755. In 1735 he stated: "Even though rhyme in our verses is not so essential that without it a verse could not be called verse and be distinguished from prose, it is nevertheless necessary enough so that without it verse loses its best embellishment" (see p. 61). In 1752, on the other hand, rhyme was only a "marginal embellishment" "thought up in barbaric times," not used by either Greeks or Romans, who nevertheless had reached the "very pinnacle" in poetry (see p. 120). In his preface to *Tilemaxida*, Trediakovskij maintained that rhyme disrupted the majestic flow of an epic narrative in verse: "Such [rhymed] verses do not constitute a river flowing from upstream downward, incessantly and uninterruptedly, to its distant goal. They are like tiny rivulets, struggling upward; and when they reach their not too distant summit, they are cut off and rush impetuously downward again, with the result that each verse has its own rapids, so to speak, and sounds forth at that point."[101] Finally, in 1755, Trediakovskij denounced rhyme in rather strong language as a downright fault of epic verse: "In these Greek and Roman verses the hexameters, which form integral units by themselves, are not made to agree with rhyme; this clamor would have been insulting to the ancient noble gold at the line endings."[102]

According to Trediakovskij, rhyme was permitted in poetry with short lines or in other verse forms which were written in stanzas. In these rhymed lines he made another departure from his position of 1735. He now allowed not only the alternation of masculine and feminine rhymes, but also rhyme schemes other than couplets. Apparently he felt that a continued flow of epic narrative was not called for in such verses and that rhyme would therefore not be a hindrance. There are even indications that Trediakovskij attempted to use rhyme in such verses as a device contributing to the metric structure of the stanza.

Trediakovskij's "Method" of 1752, like his first treatise, attempts to discuss questions of genres and types of poetry as part of a system of versification. This time Trediakovskij does not describe genres in detail, but enumerates various types of poetry: epithalamic, bucolic, propemptic, etc. In this, as well as in the introductory discussion on what distinguishes prose from verse, his desire to provide a complete treatment of poetics is evident. It is significant that in the 1752 edition of Trediakovskij's works the treatise on versification follows his translations of Horace's *Ars Poetica* and Boileau's *L'Art Poétique*.

In conclusion, it may be said that Trediakovskij's work in the treatises of 1735 and 1752 demonstrates a scholastic mind, seeking justification for every rule or definition in logic rather than in the realities of the Russian language. However, he was certainly not unaware of the realities. Indeed, the very impetus for the development of a new versification system arose from his desire to take account of linguistic reality, especially of Russian word stress. B. Tomaševskij sees in Trediakovskij's changing attitudes a reflection of the process by which certain requirements, added as marginal correctives to an accepted canon, were later incorporated into the canon, and even became predominant:

The views of Trediakovskij quickly underwent considerable change in connection with the evolution of versification practice. What he had proposed as a corrective to the canonized meter [i.e., the syllabic] itself became meter. The system of stress distribution in verse became canonized and now constituted the very content of scholastic metrics. Iambs and trochees were no longer the marks of a variation, esthetically better or worse; they became law. Trediakovskij accepted the *change* that had taken place and in his second treatise himself decisively changed the structure of the metric system.[103]

It may well be that Trediakovskij, observing the development of Russian syllabo-tonic verse in directions which did not conform to his precepts of 1735, tried to accomplish two things: first, to reformulate the laws of syllabo-tonic versification in such a way that they would encompass the new developments and again establish him as the foremost authority, and, second, to reassert his claim to being the original reformer by establishing a close connection between the two treatises.

II

Trediakovskij's Method of 1735

TREDIAKOVSKIJ first indicated his intention of composing a treatise on Russian versification in his speech on the opening of the Russian Assembly on March 14, 1735; he remarked: "A poetic word arousing enthusiasm in the heart and in the mind could easily emerge based on a solid grammar and gracious rhetoric, except if incorrect means of composing verses were to cause difficulty. But this, too, gentlemen, could be overcome and a proper system devised. We are not without the means for this; some of these means I possess myself" (*Sočinenija Trediakovskogo*, I, 266–67). P. N. Berkov, in *Lomonosov i literaturmajá polemika ego vremeni*, p. 26, expresses the opinion that when Trediakovskij delivered this speech he may already have had his treatise prepared, at least in outline. The first verses written by Trediakovskij in a meter closely resembling that of his heroic line were dedicated to Baron Korff, the president of the Academy, and date from September, 1734. At any rate, the publication of the "New and Brief Method for Composing Russian Verse" followed soon after the speech. According to V. N. Peretc (*Iz istorii razvitija russkoj poezii*, p. 48), the treatise was written at the beginning of 1735, printed by the Academy press, and published on April 20, 1735.

The treatise includes a number of poems written by Trediakovskij and offered as examples of various meters or genres. In the present translation these poems have been omitted; short descriptions of them are provided at those places where they occur in the original.

The text of Trediakovskij's treatise of 1735 used for the present translation is the one published in A. Kunik, ed., *Sbornik materialov dlja Imperatorskoj Akademii Nauk v XVIII veke* (St. Petersburg, 1865), I, 16–74. An identical text has been published in V. K. Trediakovskij, *Izbrannye proizvedenija* (Moscow and Leningrad, 1963), pp. 365–420.

A NEW AND BRIEF METHOD FOR COMPOSING RUSSIAN VERSE

With Definitions of the Essential Terminology

BY VASILIJ TREDIAKOVSKIJ,

*Secretary of the Saint
Petersburg Imperial Academy of Sciences
Printed in Saint Petersburg at the
Imperial Academy of Sciences*

MDCCXXXV

Est Deus in nobis, agitante calescimus illo,
Impetus hic sacrae semina mentis habet.

Ovidius, Lib. 6, Fastorum

That is:

Only God teaches us versification
And, the Holy One, gives birth to a fiery eagerness in us.[1]

To all Most Highly Respected Persons of Superior Rank who are most skillful in Russian versification and enjoy its practice; to my most gracious gentlemen

Most Highly Respected Sirs!

It is not without substantial reason that I most humbly inscribe to you this my new and brief Method for composing Russian Verse. Who should more properly than you, with your great skill, judge the correctness of the rules which I have set down here, by virtue of which I do not call our old verse true verse? And those who enjoy practicing versification may find here examples of verse never yet seen in Russia, and may use them to their advantage should they deem it proper to imitate them.[2]

If my rules are incorrect or inadequate for our versification, I most humbly beg those of you who possess the greater skill both to correct and to supplement them.[3] On the other hand, for those who write verse these rules will provide an occasion to reflect upon versification more carefully and henceforth to present to the Russian public more perfect verse—the fruit of careful thought. I hope my rules will not be useless to either the former or the latter among you, because I will, with the

novelty of my method, at least stimulate you to examine our old verse
and to decide, after due consideration, whether or not it has rightfully
borne the name of verse up to now.

Such is my intention in this new and brief Method for composing
Russian Verse which I dedicate in your honor, since you are the most
worthy. I submit it for your emendation, knowing your wisdom,
knowing your love for truth in all matters; as for this one, I place it in
your care and protection; not so much because I desire to show the
indeed small and not at all genuine spark of my mind as because I
wish to be of service to you and in this manner to pay you the most
profound respects.

Most Highly Respected Gentlemen,
your most humble and obedient servant
V. Trediakovskij

Generally speaking, one should consider two things in poetry:
First, the subject matter or that which the poet undertakes to write;
Second, versification, that is, the method of composing lines of verse.[4]
The subject matter is something common to all the languages[5] of the
world, so that it cannot be regarded as the exclusive property of one,
for the rules of the epic poem do not serve the Greek language in
Homer's *Iliad* and the Latin in Virgil's *Aeneid* any better than the
French language in Voltaire's *Henriade*, the Italian in Tasso's *Jeru-
salem Delivered*, or the English in Milton's poem on the loss of para-
dise. But the method of composition differs according to the differences in the languages. Thus, the author of the Slavonic grammar
which is generally called "The Great" or "Maxim's,"[6] wishing to
make the composition of our verse similar to that of Greek and Latin,
wrote his quantitative prosody in such a ridiculous manner that, however often one picks it up, one can never refrain from being, while
looking at it, ceaselessly the laughing Democritus.[7] If he had realized
then that the nature of our language does not admit of this, he would
never have included such a prosody in his grammar.

Others have heretofore proceeded more correctly in the composition
of our verse by setting down a certain number of syllables per line,
dividing it into two parts and making the final syllables of [each] two
lines of verse identical. But such verse lines appear so insufficient that
it is more suitable to call them prose lines systematically arranged in a

certain way, but lacking the measure or cadence which makes a verse line sing and distinguishes it from prose, that is, from that which is not verse.[8] For this reason it seemed fitting, having first expended much effort on the invention of our true verse lines, to publish this new and brief method for composing Russian verse which will contain the number of syllables suited to the nature of our language as well as a measure by feet with a cadence pleasant to our ear, which is the reason why verse is called verse. If some shortcoming should be found here, wise and knowledgeable persons are humbly asked to inform the Russian Assembly of this, for it will expend every effort either to resolve their doubts concerning verse or to correct the shortcomings existing in these new rules, with all possible gratitude to such persons for their kindness.

And since the composition of Russian verse requires that one know two things, namely, the proper terms used in versification, and the method of composing or writing verse, for this reason the proper terms of versification will be defined, and rules as clear and as brief as possible will be formulated for composing verse.

And so:

DEFINITION I. Every specifically verselike line is a *verse line* (*stix.*) The Romans call it *versus*, and the French *vers*.[9]

DEFINITION II. A *syllable* (*slog*) is the simultaneous and uninterrupted movement of the tongue and lips [in the pronunciation] of two or several consonantal letters [10] combined with some vowel or diphthong, or of one vowel, or one diphthong. The Romans call a syllable *syllaba*, and the French *syllabe*. It is assumed that letters and their components are known to everyone from grammar; a *letter*, however, is called *littera* in Latin and *lettre* in French.

DEFINITION III. A *foot* (*stopa*) is a metrical unit or a part of a verse line, consisting in Russian of two syllables. The Romans call it *pes*, and the French *pied*.[11]

DEFINITION IV. A *hemistich* is one half of a verse line, the first half in the heroic line consisting of seven syllables and the second of six. As derived from the Greek, the Romans call it *hemistichium*, and the French *hemistiche*.[12]

DEFINITION V. A *break* is the division of a verse line into two parts; the first hemistich, if the verse line is to be good, must always end in a long syllable. But a long syllable in Russian versification is understood to be the one on which the prosody (*prosodija*), or, as it is said, the stress (*sila*) falls. Thus, in the word *slagaju*, the long syllable is *ga*, while *sla* and *ju* are short. The Romans call the break a *cesura*, and the French *césure* or *repos*.[13]

COROLLARY 1. Hence it follows that all monosyllabic words can only be long.[14] The Romans call the length and brevity of syllables *quantitas*, and the French *quantité* or *longueur et brièveté des syllabes*.

COROLLARY 2. From this anyone can clearly see that the terms, length, and brevity of syllables, as they are used in this new Russian versification, are not the same as those the Greeks and Romans used. They are *tonic*, that is, consisting of voice stress (*udarenie golosa*) alone. Thus, whereas the Greek and Latin quantity of syllables is recognized with great difficulty, ours can be known to every Great Russian easily, readily, without any difficulty and, finally, from general usage alone; in this lies the whole strength of our versification.[15]

COROLLARY 3. Thus, as it will appear in the rules, the feet which are to compose our new verse line (I accept for this purpose the spondee, which consists of two long syllables, its sign being – –; also the pyrrhic foot,[16] which consists of two short syllables, its sign being ◡ ◡; the choree or trochee, which consists of one long and one short syllable, its sign being – ◡; and finally the iamb, which consists of one short and one long syllable, its sign being ◡ –), must be understood in the sense and meaning established in the second corollary.

DEFINITION VI. *Rhyme* is not number,[17] but the like endings of two verse lines, consisting of the same letters or of different ones which sound alike and which are always better perceived in the penultimate or sometimes in the final syllable of a verse line, For this the Latins had no name, because the endings of their verse lines are not identical, but in French poetry, which is the same as ours except for certain substantial qualifications, it is called *rime*.

DEFINITION VII. *Enjambement* (*perenos*) is a thought which has not been completed in one full line of verse and has been run on into a part of the following line but does not continue to the end of that line. The Latins often used such enjambement; since their verse did not have rhyme, there was no need tor them to make one feel the last syllable of a verse line through equality of measure and identity of sound with the preceding one. But the French called this defect of verse *enjambement*, that is, hopping over.[18]

DEFINITION VIII. *Cadence* is a smooth progression of the line, pleasing to the ear, by means of feet, to the very end. This is accomplished when the first syllable of each foot is long, or at least when there are several such feet, or when one letter is not too often repeated, or again when the feet are connected with each other, which is what prevents the verse line from being prosaic. The Latins, in their poetry, called this *cadentia*, and the French call it *cadence* in theirs.

DEFINITION IX. There is merging (*slitie*) when a word ends with a short *i* (и) thus: *j* (й) and the next word begins with the same letter; then the short *i* is not pronounced and seems to be swallowed, and is blended with that other letter into one. For instance,

> Каждый имеет счинять кто стихов любитель

is pronounced thus:

> Кажды имеет счинять, etc.[19]

The Romans call it *elisio*, and the French *élision*.

SUPPLEMENTARY REMARK. Russian verses must have either a continuous or a mixed rhyme. A rhyme is called continuous when the second verse has an ending similar to that of the first. A rhyme is mixed when the ending which is similar to that of the first line occurs one line or two and occasionally even three lines later, if a stanza does not have an even number of lines. The French call the continuous rhyme *rime suivie*, and the mixed *rime mêlée*.

Having stated the meaning of the terms, I now proceed to set forth what the heroic verse line should be and to discuss everything that concerns the beauty of this line.

RULE I. The Russian heroic verse line consists of thirteen syllables and of six feet; in the first foot it allows a *spondee* – –, a *pyrrhic foot* ◡ ◡, a *choree*, otherwise called a *trochee* – ◡, or an *iamb* ◡ –; similarly, in the second and third foot (after which must be the long syllable of the caesura), and so also for the fourth, fifth, and sixth foot. However, the line perfect in all its components, and the best line, consists only of trochees or contains a large number of them, while the worst line consists only of iambs or of a large number of them. The line which consists of spondees or pyrrhics or has a large number of them is of middling worth.[20] The reason why this line contains thirteen syllables is the usage accepted by all our older poets.[21] We will take as an example the first line[22] of the first satire by Prince Antiox Dmitrievič Kantemir, without doubt the most prominent and skillful Russian poet:

1	2	3	4	5	6	7	8	9	10	11	12	13
ум	толь	сла	бый	плод	тру	дов	крат	ки	я	на	у	ки

COROLLARY. Consequently, our new verse line is composed only of bisyllabic feet beacuse it contains a certain set number of syllables, and it can by no means have trisyllabic feet of the dactylic kind (as happens in Greek and Latin verse, because Greek and Latin verse, having only a set number of feet, does not have a set number of syllables, so that, upon comparison, some lines have more and others fewer syllables).

RULE II. A heroic verse line should be divided into two hemistichs, of which the first should consist of seven syllables, and the second of six. This is because the verse has thirteen syllables, and hence, one of the hemistichs must have seven syllables. But reason itself tells us that it is more fitting for the first to consist of seven syllables because in the beginning the reader has more and stronger breath and toward the end his breath weakens. As an example I take the verse quoted above:

1	2	3	4	5	6	7	1	2	3	4	5	6
ум	толь	сла	бый	плод	тру	дов	крат	ки	я	на	у	ки

RULE III. The heroic verse line should have the caesura at the seventh syllable which must complete a word and be long. The reason for this is that the measure of human breath demands it because, if one were to read the whole line in one breath, the rhyme at the end would not sound sufficiently strong and also the whole line would have to be read in a monotone, rendering it unpleasant, as anyone can easily discover through practice. But when a verse line is read in two parts then it seems quite pleasing, and there is enough breath to enunciate each syllable clearly. The reason why the seventh syllable should complete a word and why it should be long is this: since one should pause for a moment on the seventh syllable, it is clear that it would be bad to do so on an unfinished word; and the syllable must be long because it has a slightly higher pitch, while the second hemistich is begun at a somewhat lower pitch.[23] The French are very skillful in the reading of verse, but it is said that the Persians, Arabians, and Turks are no less skilled. Oh, if only it might become a habit among us! Then we would recognize the true sweetness of verse. To demonstrate correct caesura I again quote the same verse:

ум толь слабый плод трудо́в/ краткия науки

And since one should pause at the caesura, the meaning of the word on which the caesura is placed should not be grammatically related to the word which begins the second hemistich. Below I will cite examples which are not to be followed of these defective caesurae united with the first word of the following hemistich.

Preposition before its case:
Не зовем пииту чрез/ рифму доброгласну.

Subject before predicate:
Стихотворчеству нас Бог/ научает токмо.

But this line would be good as follows:
Стихотворчеству нас Бог/ токмо научает.

Predicate before subject:
Стихотворчеством нашли/ многи славу в людях.

But the line would be well-written thus:
Стихотворчеством нашли/ в людях славу многи.

Verb before its direct object:
Ныне уж я не люблю/ стихотворства стара.

But a good line would be as follows:

Стара уж я не дюблю/ ныне стихотворства.

The same is true when the verb is in the infinitive:

Невозможно и дюбить/ стихотворства стара.

The line would be perfect when written thus:

Стихотворства и любить/ невозможно стара.

Adjective before noun:

Пресечением худый/ стих быть может худший.

But if written as follows, it would be quite good:

Пресечением худый/ быть стих может худший.

Noun before adjective:

О приятен много стих/ гладкий слуху нежну.

But the line would be quite good when written thus:

Слуху нежну много стих/ о приятен гладкий.

Here it should be noted that the noun may be separated from its adjective by the caesura if that adjective is followed by a second or third one, which also completes the verse; in the same way, an adjective may properly be separated from its noun when a second or third adjective follows that noun and when it also completes the verse. I give an example of each.[24]

Noun separated from adjective:

Больше стóит слов пример/ ясный и способный.

Adjective separated from noun:

Выше мудрость, неж драгий/ адамант и злато.

Moreover, the thought which continues after the caesura must not end before the end of the verse line, for this would obviously make two caesurae and consequently, three hemistichs, which would completely deprive the heroic verse of meaning and turn it into a loathsome freak. For example:

Добрый человек во всём/ добрым есть всё; а злой
тщится пребывати в зле/ всегда; бес есть такой.

SUPPLEMENTARY REMARK. The particle *čto* may not be the syllable of the caesura, either in its own function as conjunction or when

substituting for the relative pronouns *kotoryj, kotoraja kotoroe.* For
example:

In its own function:
Мо́жно ль уповать нам, что/ты всем будешь верен.

The verse would be good as follows:
Можно ль уповать, что ты/ всем нам будешь верен.

When substituting for relative pronouns:
Я двором владею, что/ всех у нас был общий.

But the line would be all right as follows:
Двор, что всем нам общий был,/ тем один владею.

RULE IV. The Heroic verse line must not run an unfinished thought
into only part of the following line, because then the rhyme, which
makes for the greatest beauty of our verses, is not clearly perceived,
and the verse cadence is uneven. For example:

Суетная чести стень! для тебя бывает
Многое здесь; но увы! всё смерть отнимает.

However, if the thought is continued to the end of the following line
and is completed with it, then the enjambement will not be defective.
For example:

Суетная чести стень! для тебя бывает
Многое, что на земли смерть нам отнимает.

RULE V. If a heroic verse must have elisions, there should not be more
than two, for they make the verse sound coarse and unpleasant.[25]
For instance:

Преподобный и святый/ избранный и верный.

RULE VI. When frequent repetition of one letter or one syllable occurs
in a line of heroic verse, a sound results that is neither pleasant nor
sweet. Therefore one should be quite wary of this, For instance:

Мне всегда тогда туда/ идти мзда беда худа.

RULE VII. The rhyming of the caesura syllable with the end syllable of a heroic verse line is clumsy and uncalled for, because this produces not one but two lines of verse. For instance:

Тварей Бог есть всех отец:/ тот бо всех есть творец.

RULE VIII. It is altogether unfitting for a line of heroic verse to have the rhyming word and the one immediately preceding it sound alike. For instance:

Мудрым человеку быть/ хоть не скоро, споро

RULE IX. Heroic verse will lack beauty and be quite prosaic unless it has a sweet, pleasant, and light cadence. Such cadence is produced when each foot or at least a majority of the feet have a long first syllable, and when one letter and one syllable are not often repeated; and finally, when each foot or the majority of feet are connected with each other; then, as I have mentioned in the eighth definition, the verse line is saved from being prosaic. As an example I quote the line of Prince Antiox Dmitrievič Kantemir which I have already quoted many times, because this line of verse has a very pleasant cadence in all its feet:

Ӯм то̄ль сла̄ бы̄й пло̄д трў до̄в / кра̄т кй я̆ нӑ ӯ кй.[26]

For this purpose lines of heroic verse must be measured in feet and not in syllables, as many of our poets up to now have been doing incorrectly, especially the cheerful bandura players and the shaggy band of songsters,[27] because if measured in syllables the verse will become quite prosaic and uninviting, except, perhaps, when it may turn out well by blind chance.

And measuring by feet must be done in this way:

1 2	3 4	5 6	7 8 9	10 11	12 13
Ум толь	сла бый	плод тру	дóв / крат ки	я на	у ки
1 2	3 4	5 6	7 1 2	3 4	5 6

Or, as in the following example of a couplet of my own:[28]

1 2	3 4	5 6	7 8 9	10 11	12 13
Вы ше	зла то	се реб	pá / зла та ж	доб ро	де тель,
Доб ро	де те	ли, нич	тó: / выс ша	сам со	де тель.
1 2	3 4	5 6	7 1 2	3 4	5 6

Through this schema one can see that our heroic verse line is a hexameter, that is, a six-unit line, not counting the long syllable of the caesura. Due to the latter it can be called a hypercatalectic line, that is, a line having an extra syllable over the required number of feet. What has been said about our heroic verse line must also be understood to apply to our verse line of eleven syllables, except that the latter has the fifth syllable as the caesura, and consequently, its second hemistich consists of six syllables. But because it is scanned in five feet, it can be called pentameter, or a five-unit line. And since the syllable of the caesura is also long and stands outside the number of feet, it must also be called a hypercatalectic line.

This can be seen sufficiently in one of my Sapphic stanzas quoted below. Its first three verses, which are pentameters, read as follows:

1	2		3	4		5	6	7		8	9		10	11	
Си	лы		в се	реб		ре́ /	всяк	ску		пой	не		зна	ет,	
Срам	но		то ког	га́		да́ /	в зем	лю		за	ры		ва	ет;	
Тра	тящ		глуп	и		мо́т; /	тем	то		в нуж	де		вер	но	
1	2		3	4		5	1	2		3	4		5	6	

1	2	3	4	5
кто	в нем	чив	мер	но;

Our regular verse lines which consist of nine, seven, and five syllables, and also the irregular lines consisting of eight, six, and four syllables, do not contain anything characteristic of the verse line aside from syllables and rhyme as can be seen above in our five-syllable line, which is generally called an Adonic in the Sapphic stanza; therefore I propose to say nothing more about them here.[29]

It is a matter of conscience for me to admit to the whole Russian public that in both the hexameter and pentameter I myself have sinned much against the rules I have set forth; I did so because of the way I had been taught. But having seen that our verse was all prosaic and did not resemble verse, I applied myself with unrelenting zeal and constant concern to the goal that our verse not be called verse in vain; and I flatter myself that I have found its strength. And so I dare hope that the most exalted, most glorious, the greatest, most flourishing Russia will find me worthy to be forgiven for my previous errors considering that I was the first, as it seems to me, to arrange our verse properly, and am also the first who promises to correct all my verse, since the greater part has not yet been published.

On Poetic License in Versification

By poetic license [*vol'nost'*] in verse, which the Latins call *licentia* and the French *licence*, I understand certain words which may be used only in verse but not in prose. Even though Russian verse contains few instances of poetic license, it is none the less necessary to declare which are the more important.

I. Verbs in second person singular may end in -*ši* instead of -*š'*, and the infinitive may end in -*ti* instead of -*t'*. For example, *pišeši* instead of *pišeš'* and *pisati* instead of *pisat'*.

II. Pronouns *mja*, *tja* instead of *menja*, *tebja;* also *mi*, *ti* instead of *mne*, *tebe*. Not infrequently *ti* is used instead of *tvoj*.

III. Words *bud'*, *bol'š*, *il'*, *než*, *mež*, *odnak*, *xot'* instead of *bude*, *bol'še*, *ili*, *neželi*, *meždu*, *odnako*, *xotja*.

IV. The masculine singular adjectives which end in short *i* (и) thus: *j* (й) may, if need be, leave out the short *i*. Thus instead of *dovol'nyj* [satisfied] one may write at the end of a line *dovol'ny*. However, one must see to it that some other word preceding it makes it clear from the context that this is the singular of an adjective.[30] Moreover, one must take great care to exercise this poetic license as rarely as possible, because it does go rather far.

V. The nouns and adjectives which in the instrumental singular end in -*ju* after some vowel may in verse end with short *i* instead. Thus, instead of *soveršennoju pravdoju* one may write *soveršennoj pravdoj*. The nouns which end in -*ie* may in the prepositional have only *i*, without the *ï*. Thus, instead of *o vosklicanïi* one may write *o vosklicani*.

VI. All nouns which end in -*ie* may change the *ï* in verse to a soft sign, depending on the needs of the meter. Thus *sčastïe* may be written *sčast'e*.

VII. Many words which have the prefixes *so*, *voz*, *vos*, and also *iz* and *ob*, before *o* may, if necessary in verse, omit the letter *o*. Thus *sočinjaju* may be written *sčinjaju*, *vodružaju: vdružaju*, *vozobnovil: vzobnovil*, *vospoju: vspoju*, *izožgu: izžgu*, *obošlju: obšlju*.

VIII. Many vocatives, which in our language resemble the nominatives (except for the most blessed and most exalted names, *Bože*,

Gospodi, Iisuse, Xriste, Syne, Slove, that is, the word which became flesh) may sometimes in verse end in the Slavonic manner. Thus instead of *Filot* [the Greek poet] one may write *Filote!* as I have done in one of my satires.

IX. the words *rycar', ratoborec, rat', vitjaz', vsadnik, bogatyr',* which are not used in prose now, may remain in use in verse.[31]

X. If the subject matter is facetious rather than lofty, then it is not improper to use the adjectives and their nouns which are used in poetry (but measured by length and brevity or syllables throughout) peculiar to our simple people, for instance: *tugoj luk, bel šater* and a multitude of other, similar ones.[32]

XI. In addition, words which can be stressed on any syllable and words whose proper stress is uncertain may be used in verse in two ways, for instance, *cvéty* and *cvetý*. However, in this case it is more proper to follow common usage. Incidentally, there is no need, it seems, to mention the short adjectives, which, since they are often used in prose as well, can be used in verse if the need arises, and even more frequently.

XII. In verse, if the need arises, some words may change their vowels for others, but in a way for which there should be at least some foundation in general usage, and in which the word should retain its meaning; in the same way, when two identical or different consonants occur in a word, one can be thrown out if necessary. Thus instead of *kamera, kamora;* instead of *million, milion;* instead of *prelestnyj, prelesnyj.* However, this is rarely necessary.

XIII. The well-founded rule which always changes the accusative case governed by a verb in a positive statement into the genitive case if the phrase is negative may, in extreme need, not cause the accusative case to change. Thus, one may write in verse as follows:

Во́ды пламень не гасят ваши тем сердечный;

instead of:

Во́ды пламеня не гасят ваши тем сердечного;

and

Внутренний покой никак мне сыскать не можно;

instead of:

Внутреннего покоя никак мне сыскать не можно.

But this amounts to taking a very great poetic license, and therefore it should be done only occasionally and, if possible, not at all.[33]

XIV. Supplementary Remark. Poetic license in general must be such that the word on which it is exercised can be readily recognized as a true Russian word, and also as a word which is to some extent in current general usage. For instance: *bregu* may be written instead of *beregu*, *brežno* instead of *berežno*, and *stregu* instead of *steregu*; but *ostrožno* cannot be written instead of *ostorožno*. And so it seems to me that those poets who write, for instance, *iz glubiny duši* as *z glubiny duši*[34] and *meju sposob* instead of *imeju sposob*, although they may deserve praise in other respects, exercise a poetic license which is very great indeed and also contrary to our language.

On Rhyme, That Is, on the Likeness of Final Syllables in Verse

There should be no need to refer to the agreement of the final syllables, for all our poets know that it is better if it starts with the penultimate syllable, that is, with the syllable which immediately precedes the last; although sometimes, but only in comical and satirical verse (and the less often, the better), the likeness of sound occurs between the ultimate, that is, the very last syllables. However, some say, with subtle sophistry, that an agreement of final syllables harmonizes poorly if it is between adjectives, participles, infinitives, etc., and they give as their reason that plenty of such agreements can be found in a short time; but why these gentlemen forbid also the agreement of reflexive verbs ending in -*sja*, not only I, but, I suppose, they themselves do not know. In order to refute this I submit that the whole strength of this agreement, as our sense of hearing tells us, consists only in the similarity of sound and not in any similarity of syllables or letters, and therefore there is no reason to choose a particular part of speech; it is only necessary to select a sound which would not be disagreeable to the ear and which would sound like the ending of the preceding line, regardless of the part of speech. That there are enough such similar sounds in certain parts of speech not only should not be considered a defect, but, in my opinion, one should be happy that such consonances are readily available.

True, one should not always end with the same word, or repeat the same sound very frequently; but in any case, those who observe this unnecessary subtlety in rhyme seek in vain for midday when the sun is already setting. From this it can be seen that these gentlemen are talking only in order to talk and not in order to say anything substantial.[35]

Conclusion: On the Alternation [*sočetanie*] of Verse Lines

The French, and also some other European languages which have feminine and masculine lines, alternate them. The French call verse alternation *mariage des vers*. An if the ancient Latins had had to alternate their verses, they could not have chosen a better name than *connubium versuum*.

The masculine verse line in French poetry consists of twelve syllables in the heroic line, or, as the French generally call it, the alexandrine, in their hexameter; in the pentameter it consists of ten syllables; the rhyme stress in both is on the ultimate, that is, on the last syllable. They call that verse line feminine which has thirteen syllables in the hexameter and eleven in the pentameter with the rhyme stress on the penultimate, that is, on the syllable before the last. The masculine verse has one syllable less than the feminine, and the feminine verse always has one syllable more than the masculine.

The whole effect [*sila*] of the French alternation of verse lines is that in lines with contiguous rhyme they place two feminine lines after two masculine, or two masculine after two feminine, and so everything proceeds in consecutive fashion to the end of the poem. In lines with mixed rhymes, which almost always consist of quatrains, if a masculine line is placed first, then the next rhyme is feminine, then again there is a masculine rhyme, corresponding to the first, and then a feminine rhyme which has an ending identical with that of the previous feminine line. And if a feminine line is placed first in a stanza, then a masculine follows, and so on consecutively. It often happens also that after a masculine line the French will place two contiguous feminine lines with contiguous rhyme, and then a masculine, rhyming with the first or, if a feminine line is placed first, two masculine lines with masculine rhymes follow, and then a feminine, rhyming with the first feminine line.

The reason why this alternation of lines cannot be introduced into our versification is, *first of all*, because our hexameter can have neither more nor less than thirteen syllables. If our hexameter were alternated, then either our masculine line would have to have thirteen and our feminine fourteen syllables, or else the feminine would have to consist of thirteen and the masculine of twelve syllables. We would have to do the same with our pentameter, according to its measure. And that is as opposed to our ancient but very well-founded usage as fire is to water and slander to truth.[36] The *second* reason is that the nature of our verse line always demands a stress on the rhyme, that is, it brings the penultimate syllables into harmony with each other, which is well-nigh the main sweetness of verse, whereas if the rhyme in more trivial or facetious verse is placed on the final syllable, that is done only in case of need, and should be done only rarely.[37] And if our lines were alternated, then our feminine line would inevitably have the stress of its rhyme fall on the penultimate syllable, and the masculine, on the final syllable. Such an alternation of lines would be as loathsome and odious for us as though we saw someone give in marriage the most adorable, sweetest European beauty, shining in the very flower of youth, to a decrepit ninety-year-old blackamoor. This will be clear to him who has applied himself fully to our versification. Consequently, an alternation of verse lines of the kind that the French have, or of any similar kind, cannot and must not be introduced into our versification.

Some have suggested to me with very little, or rather, without any, justification, only with a shrewd mockery, raising their eyebrows and smiling, that, if the alternation of lines were not introduced into my new versification, then the new versification would not be quite similar to the French. Those gentlemen most certainly thought that I had borrowed my new versification from the French, but this is as far from the truth as French versification is different from mine. That I am right here, I call to witness all those who know French versification; they can testify that French versification does not resemble mine in anything except caesura and rhyme.

From now on, let those who think otherwise cease to think so, for, indeed, I have taken the whole strength of this new versification from the very innards of the qualities suitable to our verse;[38] and, were anyone desirous to know this, I must declare that I was led by the poetry of our simple people. It is no matter that its composition lacks beauty because of the poets' lack of skill,[39] the sweetest, most pleasant, and most regular cadence of its various feet, sometimes surpassing that of Greek and Latin [verse], has given me unerring guidance for the introduction into my new hexameter and pentameter of the bisyllabic tonic feet described above.[40]

It is true, I borrowed almost all the poetic terms from French versification, but the substance itself I took from our most ancient native poetry that of the plain folk. And so everyone will agree that in this case a better comparison could not be made than to say that I owe French versification the purse and ancient Russian poetry the whole thousand rubles. Thus, I am indebted to France for the words, but as a Russian I most sincerely thank Russia for the substance itself.

It must not be concluded from the aforesaid that inasmuch as our versification cannot have alternation of lines, it may not have mixed rhymes either.[41] No matter what the rhyme or what the line, a rhyme consists only in the harmony of sound, which may bind similarities to the first line one or two verse lines later. The Poles, whose versification resembles ours in everything except cadence and feet, frequently use mixed rhymes in their verse with beautiful effects, as I, too, have already done in my "Ode on the Taking of Danzig" and in my other poetry.[42]

In songs we, too, sometimes cannot avoid the alternation of verses but only in such songs as are composed to French or German tunes, because these tunes are arranged by the musicians according to the versification patterns of their poets. As an example of this I present here the first stanzas of two songs of mine, of the kind that the French call *couplets* (which I have composed to French tunes and in which, according to the melody, alternation of verse lines has been used).

A stanza of the first song

> Худо тому жити,
> Кто хулит любовь:
> Век ему тужити,
> Утирая бровь.

A stanza of the second song

> Сколь долго, Климена,
> Тебе не любить?
> Времен бо премена
> Не знает годить.

Ныне что есть можно,
Драгая моя,
То ж утре есть ложно,
И власть не своя.

But in other songs and in our other verses intended only to be read, this alternation must not be used.[43]

Enough, however, of my explaining merely in words my method for the composition of our new verses; it is time to demonstrate by deed and example.

[There follows a translation of Fénelon's poem "La sagesse humaine, ou le portrait d'un honnête homme" in the 13-syllable heroic hexameter of Trediakovskij.]

Here I intend to present, also as an example of our heroic verse, a sonnet translated from the French of the late Mr. Barreaux. This sonnet is so excellently composed in French that it would be hard to find others like it. Indeed, this sonnet may be called that very Phoenix for which Mr. Boileau-Despréaux hoped in his teaching on verse, when speaking about sonnets.[44] Its style is as beautiful and elevated as its material is dignified and devout. Some French authors, in presenting their rules of rhetoric, cite this poem as an example of the best-written piece from the point of view of rhetoric. Even though my translation cannot equal the original, for even my betters would find it difficult to accomplish this, I have tried to write it in the best Russian heroic verse that I could compose.

Incidentally, the sonnet had its beginnings in Italy and is derived from the French and Italian madrigal and the Latin epigram. It always consists of fourteen verse lines, that is, of two quatrains with two rhymes that are mixed and of one six-line stanza always having in the last line some idea that is either pithy, exalted, or noble; this the Latins call *acumen*, and the French, *chute*. The order of verse lines is always like that presented here (except that in the quatrain the rhymes are sometimes differently mixed).

[There follows the sonnet, arranged in the following rhyme scheme: *a b a b a b a b   c c d e d e*.]

The following rondeau, of my composition, which is also presented as an example of our heroic verse, was written at the request of a certain court personage as a most humble salutation to the Most

Gracious Sovereign, our Empress Anna Ioannovna, the all-Russian Autocrat, on Her exalted birthday, which falls on the 28th of January and is celebrated every year with great and general jubilation. The rondeau is also a kind of epigram and invariably consists of thirteen lines, always having only two rhymes, sometimes contiguous, sometimes mixed. Its first phrase, or sometimes two or three, but never more than that, must be repeated twice, but in such a way that it will make sense, and one repetition will have an entirely different meaning from the other as will be seen in my rondeau below. It is called a rondeau because of its roundness, since, as the ends meet in a circle or a wheel, so in the rondeau the first phrase meets the last. No one was more successful in composing rondeaus in French than Voiture.[45]

[There follows a rondeau arranged in three stanzas of five, three and five lines, with the following rhyme scheme: *a a b b a   a a b   a a b b a*. The word *prosto* (simply) is placed at the end of each stanza.]

I think that, if I am not mistaken, no one before me has written epistles in Russian verse; therefore I present one here as an example both of the new hexameter and of this verse form.

Epistle is a Greek word which derives from ἐπιστολή and means *message* [*poslanie*], *writ* [*pisanie*], or simply *letter*, because the Greek verb ἐπιστέλλω means *I send, I write*. An epistle is a conversation in writing between two persons not in each other's presence, of the kind that occurs orally between two persons if both are present. In the epistle, since it is a conversation in writing, one must carefully see to it that its style is brief, forceful, neither high nor low, presenting the matter in a straightforward manner, without including any extraneous matters. All that is contrary to this will lead the reader into boredom and draw blame on the writer who has sent the epistle. There are many kinds of epistles, as for instance: advisory, congratulatory, condolatory, mercantile, and amorous. They are not discussed here for lack of space.

In epistles one must also consider the following: who writes, to whom, where, why, and about what, since different epistles can be written according to different circumstances.

In friendly epistles one must be careful not to introduce among pleasant matters mean things unworthy of being heard. If this must be done, then it is proper to describe them in such circumspect but honest words that they can only be surmised because failure to do so shows a man to be ill-bred and will cause the sender to be held in great contempt. In satirical epistles a man should be denounced in such a way that none but his bad aspects would be exposed, and then not without circumlocutions and sidestepping, concealing as much as possible the proper name and everything that would allow anyone to guess that one is writing exactly about this person and not about some other; his honor, however, should not be touched in the least, and all this should be done in such a way that later there will be no cause for regret, for, as the saying goes, what has been written with a pen can never be cut out even with an axe. In epistles about important matters, especially about science, one should be moderate in the use of the apollonian style, because anything exalted is out of place in an epistle; and he who *projicit ampullas et sesquipedalia verba*, as Horace says,[46] that is, throws out blown-up words of a foot and a half each, is always called an idle babbler. The style in epistles should be smooth, sweet, and ingenious, especially in dedications, since a dedication is as delicate and artful in prose as the sonnet is subtle and intricate in poetry. But in order not to exceed further the limits of my task in discoursing about epistles in general, I come to epistles in verse, since my intention was to discourse about these.

The poetic epistle is all but the same as a simple one. This anyone can see in the works of Ovid, in the Heroides epistles. Epistles of many kinds are found in the works of Horace, However, present-day poets compose mostly panegyrical ones, which I have considered proper to do also in my epistle below, as the reader will kindly note. In France Mr. Boileau-Despréaux has written such excellent versified epistles that, it seems, nothing better could be written. It is only in style that the poetic epistle differs from the prose epistle, since in the poetic epistle the style, too, must be poetic, apollonian, and not much different from the parnassian. I have called this kind of poetry an *epistle* [*epistola*] and not a message, missive, or letter in order to differentiate the poetic missive from the *messages of the holy Apostle Paul* and from simple letters.[47] The Latins similarly call poetic and spiritual epistles *Epistolae*, and simple ones more often *Litterae*. The French call simple ones *Lettres* and poetic ones, as well as those of St. Paul, *Épitres*.

My epistle is written by Versification, or Russian Poetry, to Apollo, a fictional God of Versification (poetry). But lest someone should be led into temptation by this name, I declare that Apollo here must be understood as the heartfelt desire which I possess that the science of versification, which has led many peoples to great glory, should also have a beginning in Russia. And in any case, whatever is written in this epistle is written as poetry, which initiated people know well enough, and therefore Christians who would vie with us in pious zeal have no occasion for temptation here.[48]

[There follows the "Epistle to Apollo from Russian Poetry," composed by Trediakovskij in his 13-syllable verse.]

The following two elegies, composed in our hexameter, are also presented here as examples of our verse of this kind.

The word *elegy* comes from the Greek ἐλεγεία and means a tearful and sad verse, according to the testimony of the glorious Roman poet Ovid, who in one of his elegies bemoans the untimely death of a friend, the sweet elegiac poet Albius Tibullus, in the following way:

> Flebiis indignos Elegeia solve, capillos,
> ah! nimis ex vero nunc tibi nomen erit,

that is:

> Tearful elegy! let down your disarrayed hair
> ah! you now all too truly derive your name from weeping.

Indeed, even though the exalted or the amorous is found in the elegy, these qualities are always expressed in tearful and mournful language. Any interested Russian can convince himself of this from the Greek elegies of Philetas; from the excellent Latin elegies of Ovid and those of Tibullus, which are equally good, also from those of Propertius and Cornellius Gallus; and in French from the very touching and tender elegies of the late Countess de la Suze.[49]

I am publishing my two elegies without apprehension as to their being mournful; as for their being amorous, following the example of many ancient and present-day poets, I ask the virtuous Russian readers' forgiveness and explain to them that I describe in these two elegies not a sinful love, but a lawful one, that is, such as is praised between spouses blessedly loving each other.[50]

In the first of my elegies, a fictitious husband is weeping because he has been separated from his beloved wife Ilidara, also fictitious, and because he can no longer hope to see her due to the distance between them; and in the second elegy he grieves inconsolably after learning the truth about the death of his Ilidara, and yet loves her and cannot cease loving her even after death. The word *Cupidon*, used in my second elegy, must not give cause for temptation to a Christian of stern virtue, since here it is not to be taken as the name of the fictional pagan son of Venus, but as that of a sincere feeling, which in lawful love, fiery as it may be, has never yet deserved blame anywhere.

Although my clear conscience fully exonerates me in this, I have little hope of escaping some possible morose person's denouncing me in every way, because we do not lack such people who, sometimes without Christian love and oftentimes without reason, will talk less about their fellow man only in February and this only because there are fewer days in that month, even in a leap year. Therefore I can find no means to offer them of avoiding harm to their moral uprightness except to suggest that they should not read my verses, and I have a fair reason to hope that those who understand these matters will take a different view and will do me justice in this. In truth I could never have been tempted to issue to the public these two elegies of mine if some of my friends had not found in them something of the spirit of Ovid's elegies. This excessive and affectionate kindness of theirs did encourage me, even if only because of a certain amount of vanity that all of us possess by nature; but, knowing full well my limited reason and art, and the weakness of my powers in versification, I admit that I am even further removed from the beauty of style, subtlety of thought, and smooth flow of Ovid's verses than Ovid himself is removed from me by the antiquity of the time in which he wrote his elegies.

My elegies resemble nothing so much as that coarse and dark metal which, resulting from the melting together of pure, valuable, and bright metals during the great fire of Corinth, appeared to the Corinthians to be new.[51]

And even though there is nothing in them [the elegies] that would deserve even small praise, may they nevertheless, because of the novelty of the verse, and their very newness, plead for some favor with readers.

[There follow the two elegies, in 13-syllable lines.]

I have considered it necessary to include here two odes of my composition, one as an example of our pentameter, and the other as a demonstration of the verse which we do not measure in feet but in syllables, having nine syllables per line; however, I will not explain anything about odes here, since I have appended a sufficient general discussion of them to my "Ode on the Taking of Danzig," which has been printed. Therefore, those who wish to know about odes are hereby referred to that work, and the following odes I insert here only as an example of verse.[52]

[There follow an "Ode in the Praise of the Flower Rose," composed by Trediakovskij in his new pentameter, and an "Ode Composed to the Glory of Truth Conquering Lies and Always Triumphing Over Them," in nine-syllable verse of the syllabic type.]

PROOF that our verse consisting of nine, eight, seven, six, five, and also of four syllables should have only rhyme, fall in syllables rather than in feet, and must have no caesura.

I had stated in my rules that both the regular verse lines, those consisting of nine, seven, and five syllables, and the irregular, consisting of eight, six, and four syllables, have nothing characteristic of verse, that is, neither feet nor caesura, except for the rhyme, and I did not wish to say anything more of them.[53] However, some were curious to know why they should not have feet and caesura, and they have made it necessary for me to present a circumstantial proof of this.

I apologize to my readers who love order in all things and proper arrangement of materials for the fact that this proof has not been inserted in the proper place, the reason being that the pages in which this proof should have been inserted were already printed when the curious induced me to write this. Nevertheless, I have considered it not unfitting to introduce this proof here, in connection with the "Ode to the Glory of Truth," presented above, each line of which possesses only the rhyme, is measured in nine syllables but not in feet, and has no caesura.

PROPOSITION

These lines need not fall in feet, but only in syllables because they need not have a caesura; the reason for this is the very brevity of these lines, which do not use completely even the shortest human breath. Since,

FIRST, A caesura is the division of a verse line into two parts, terminating the first part with a single syllable. The purpose of this division is to avoid depriving the human breath of its strength, with the voice ringing weak at the end of the line, as would happen if one were to read the whole line without a pause.

But the lines presently under discussion do not completely exhaust even the shortest human breath, as everyone is capable of finding out for himself.

Consequently, there is no need to divide them into two parts or to fear that the human breath might be weakened and that thus one might be forced to finish the line in a weak-sounding voice.

Moreover, the caesura must consist of one syllable and must not be counted as one of the feet. But some of these verses have an even number of syllables, and thus cannot have a syllable of the caesura which would not be one of the feet in the line. Consequently, this too is a reason why some of these lines cannot have a caesura. Therefore none of these lines must have a caesura.

SECOND, All these lines of ours should be scanned not in feet but only in syllables.

BECAUSE, our foot is a combination of two syllables (either the first tonically long and the second short, and this foot is the best; or the first short and the other long, and this foot is the worst; or, finally, two long and two short, and these in our verse are of middling merit) invented and introduced in our hexameter and pentameter in order to mark more clearly the caesura consisting of one syllable and thereby, some rest being taken on it, to separate the first hemistich from the second. But in order to mark the caesura better, it is necessary to separate [or differentiate] the syllable of the caesura from the other syllables. This separation can be made in no other way than by having each foot consist in two syllables, because if trisyllabic feet were to be introduced into our verse, then, aside from their unseemly galloping over the verses, our hexameters, which have a fixed number of syllables, could not have six measures and the pentameters could not have five; this is self-evident.[54] Consequently, our foot can consist of only two syllables. Since the caesura consists of one syllable and the feet of two, our bisyllabic feet will clearly mark the monosyllabic caesura and thus will separate the first hemistich from the second, after a rest on that syllable.

But inasmuch as the lines here considered should not, as has been demonstrated, have a caesura, there is no need to mark that which they do not have, and if there is nothing to mark, then there is no need for that which serves for marking.

Therefore all these lines of ours should be measured not in feet but only in syllables.

Moreover, the feet were introduced into hexameters and pentameters only for the purpose of saving these, our longest lines, from being prosaic, for the verse line is sung by means of feet, as every reader cannot fail to recognize. And if those long lines did not have tonic feet, as our old lines do not, then they would in all respects resemble metrical prose more than melodic verse. But the above-mentioned verse lines, concerning which this demonstration is being made, have a verse-like cadence and sound [sing] smoothly and sweetly enough even without feet, *by reason of their brevity.* Of this everyone can convince himself through his own efforts, if he will read such verse correctly.

And since, according to the irrefutable philosophical axiom, or rule, *sine necessitate Entia non sunt multiplicanda,* that is, *things should not be multiplied without necessity,* feet would be introduced into these verse lines without any need at all, because the syllables alone adequately perform their task in such lines.

Therefore, as a general conclusion, these lines should not fall in feet because they may not have the caesura; and the reason for all this is the brevity of the lines, which does not fully engage even the shortest human breath. Which is what was to be proved.

Would anyone be curious enough to ask why the rhyme was left in these verse lines when everything else that characterizes verse has been excluded? To him I reply that they are also Russian verse lines, even if they have no feet or caesura. And if one should take away the rhyme, then this would not be Russian verse, but Italian verse of a sort, because the Italian verse is sometimes not rhymed.

Even though rhyme in our verse is not so essential that without it verse could not be called verse and be distinguished from prose, it is nevertheless necessary enough that without it the verse loses its best embellishment. Our people are so inclined to rhyming that even in simple proverbs, not composed as verse, our ear likes and enjoys rhymes because of a certain[55] attractive pleasantness inherent in them. For example, this proverb, *ja čelovek prostoj, em prjaniki ne pisanye, xot' by glatki, tol'ko by slatki,* and a multitude of others. The rhyme has been left in these lines only because its exclusion would deprive the Russian reader of something he likes and enjoys even in plain speech.[56]

Some of these verse lines, concerning which the proof has been made, I have called regular and others irregular.

I have called regular those verse lines which consist of nine, seven, and five syllables, that is, which have an odd number of syllables. They are called regular because, being hypercatelectic, they resemble the most regular and most important of our lines, that is, the hexameter and pentameter, and also because, if they had to have feet, then a caesura consisting of one syllable could also be found in them. For instance, in the nine-syllable verse line the fifth syllable could be the caesura, and each hemistich would consist of two feet. In the seven-syllable line, the third syllable would be the caesura, and the first hemistich would consist of one foot, and the second of two. In the five-syllable verse, the third syllable would also be the caesura, and each hemistich would consist of one foot.[57]

From this it follows that, by reason of being hypercatalectic, even the trisyllabic verse could be called regular if it were not so very short. However, children's rhymes can be written in this verse line, too, and it is better that the rhyme always be on the last syllable; or else this verse line could be combined with a longer line, but then the rhyme should be on the penultimate syllable.

Those verse lines are termed irregular which consist of eight, six, and four syllables, i.e., of an even number of syllables. They are called irregular because they do not possess a hypercatalectic element; two hemistichs can be arranged in feet, but the syllable of the caesura is nowhere to be found. If the brevity of these lines did not protect them, they would be entirely excluded from the category of verse lines.

From this it is clear that lines composed in twelve and ten syllables by those who do not know where the strength of verse lies not only cannot be called verse lines, *because of their considerable length and of their not being hypercatalectic,* but they cannot even be termed irregular verse lines, because they are just loathsome monstrosities in versification.

In my rules I stated that the first hemistich of our heroic verse line consists of seven syllables because the reader has more breath at the beginning of the line than at the end. This is true of the heroic verse line, which is the longest we have. But here I will give another reason for it, a reason that applies to our pentameter as well as our hexameter.

Both of these verse lines consist of an odd number of syllables, one having thirteen, and the other eleven; consequently, one or the other hemistich must have more syllables.

But inasmuch as the syllable of the caesura must always be placed after the first and immediately before the second hemistich, it is clear that in heroic verse the seventh syllable must be the syllable of the caesura and both hemistichs must consist of three feet each, for this is demanded by proportion.

The reason why in the pentameter the fifth and not the seventh syllable becomes the syllable of the caesura and why the first hemistich consists of two feet and the second of three is this: if in the pentameter the caesura were the seventh syllable, then the second hemistich would necessarily consist of four syllables. But this composition of the verse line would be quite disproportionate because the first hemistich would be three syllables longer than the second. However, the proportion is proper if the second hemistich is only one syllable longer than the first.

Perhaps someone might present the following objection: in a heroic verse line the seventh syllable is the caesura because the reader has more breath at the beginning; then, for the same reason, the first hemistich should have more syllables in the pentameter, too.

This I solve in the following manner:

The hexameter has the seventh syllable as the caesura for the good reason that the reader has more breath at the very beginning, and this is why it should not be cut in half at the fifth syllable. But by having the caesura on the seventh syllable it also leaves even hemistichs, and in this consists the proportion of its division.

The pentameter cannot be divided at the seventh syllable because proportion does not allow it, as shown above. But if no consideration is shown here for the human breath, it is because none is called for; since the pentameter is not as long as the hexameter, there will be enough breath for both hemistichs.

For this reason our hexameter must regularly have a break at the seventh syllable, and the pentameter at the sixth.

From the "Ode to the Glory of Truth" given above, one can see how our nine-syllable verses are composed; and from the following song anyone can easily see how one composes all simple verses containing a smaller number of syllables.

I have already stated in my discussion accompanying the ode composed on the surrender of the city of Danzig that the following song
and similar ones which the French call *stances* have their place, with
respect to style, between the odes and the simple songs, and that they
borrow more from the loftiness of odes than from the lowness of songs.
For this reason I merely present this song here, that is, without any
interpretation of its style, and only as an example of our short, simple
verses.

[There follows the "Song Composed to a Melody and Sung Before
the Empress Anna Ioannovna." It consists of fifteen six-line stanzas,
seven syllables to a line, with the following rhyme scheme: *a a b b c c*.]

In speaking previously of the sonnet, I said that it derives from the
Italian and French madrigal and the Latin epigram; for this reason I will
now state the differences between these last genres of the short poem.

Over a long period of time I often sought to discover differences
between the epigram and the madrigal, but I found nothing but the
following. The madrigal is a short poem, like the epigram; like the
epigram it has a pithy thought at the end; but its subject matter is
always noble, important, and exalted; consequently, its concluding
pithy statement must be equally dignified, noble, and exalted. In
addition, it is more often written in imparisyllabic lines than the
epigram. The latter is also a short poem, like the madrigal, but its
subject matter is always either popular, light, or low, or ironic, or,
finally, satirical. Consequently, its concluding pithy statement must
also be either popular, light, or low, or ironic, or, finally, satirical. As
an example I include here a madrigal which I composed in praise of
the grand Audience Hall built on orders of Her Imperial Majesty here
in St. Petersburg, as well as several epigrams on various topics. From
these it will be easier to see the difference between madrigals and
epigrams than from explanations.

[There follows a madrigal, written in syllabic verse, mostly in
11-syllable lines, although three lines are of six syllables. After the
madrigal follow four epigrams.][58]

If I were to discuss the whole science of poetry instead of versification alone, I would mention the rules of the epic, which is the noblest
and greatest of all narrative poems, and also of all lyric, dramatic and
bucolic poetry. I would speak more extensively about elegiac and

epistolary poetry, as well as about satirical and, finally, epigrammatic verse. However, I announce here to interested Russians the most famous authors who should be imitated in all these above-mentioned kinds of poetry.

IN EPIC POETRY
In the Greek language: Homer is famed.
In Latin: Virgil.
In French: Voltaire.
In Italian: Tasso.
In English: Milton.

I do not expect that any language has more sharp-witted, marvelous epic works written in prose than the French, works which sometimes surpass even Homer and Virgil; the French call these works romances. However, all such romances put together hardly equal in excellence Barclay's *Argenis*, which is masterfully written in Latin.

IN LYRIC POETRY
In Greek: Pindar and Anacreon.
In Latin: Horace.
In French: Malherbe and Mr. De la Grange, the imitator of Anacreon.[59]

IN DRAMATIC POETRY
In Greek: Euripides and Sophocles, tragedians.
            Aristophanes and Menander, comedians.
In Latin: Seneca, tragedian.
            Terentius and Plautus, comedians.
In French: The two Corneilles,[60] Racine and Voltaire, tragedians.
            Molière, comedian.

IN BUCOLIC POETRY
In Greek: Theocritus.
In Latin: Virgil.
In French: Fontenelle,[61] the corrector of the eclogue.

IN ELEGIAC POETRY
In Greek: Philetas.
In Latin: Ovid, Tibullus, Propertius, and Cornelius Gallus.
In French: Countess de la Suze.

IN EPISTOLARY POETRY
In Latin: Horace and Ovid.

In French: Boileau-Despréaux.

In Latin: Juvenal, Persius, and Horace.

In French: Boileau-Despréaux, and Regnier.[62]

In Russian. Prince Antiox Dmitrievič Kantemir, whose first line from his first satire was often quoted in these rules as an example of our hexameter. However, I have changed this line somewhat, but without changing its meaning in the least and keeping almost the original words, for the original reads as follows:

Уме слабый, плод трудов не долгой науки!

And the changed line:

Ум толь слабый, плод трудов краткия науки!

For this boldness I humbly ask forgiveness of the brilliant author, whom I have always profoundly respected. What caused me to do it was the following: I intended to quote the first line of this our foremost and outstanding satirist from his first satire, "To My Mind," as an example of my new hexameter. And if I had quoted the original line, it would contain, according to my rules, two instances of poetic license; there would also be two according to the old custom of writing. According to my rules, the vocative case *ume* [mind] is poetic license, as is the genitive *ne dolgija* [not long] instead of *ne dolgoj;* whereas, according to the old custom of writing, the vocative case *plod* [fruit] should be written *plode*, and the genetive *ne dolgoj, ne dolgija.*[63]

But since each example and model must be presented in perfect form so that others can copy it, and by copying will not learn to imitate shortcomings, I have made bold, therefore, to eliminate both the two new and the two old types of poetic license and to present it in all measures in a somewhat more perfect form.

There was still another consideration which caused me to do this, namely, that this noble author, who will never die in the memory of our present and future poets, would see how easy it is and how little change it requires to make new verse from our old verse, if it should please him to amuse himself again by composing verse as a pastime and if his high and important business and occupations will allow him to do so (business which at the present time is entrusted to his perspicacity and vigilant solicitude as the plenipotentiary minister at the court of Great Britain).[64]

IN EPIGRAMMATIC POETRY
  In Greek: Philetas.
  In Latin: Martial and Owen.
  In French: many authors, in particular Rousseau and Boursault.[65]
  Finally, I deemed it proper to close this my "New and Brief Method for Composing Russian Verse" with what Mr. Boileau-Despréaux, the best poet and famous satirist, wrote in his speech composed in verse to his sovereign Louis XIV, the king of France, in anger against the versemakers of his nation who did not know the first thing about versification and who thought (for example, at the end of a line writing the word *lavku* and joyfully ending the next with *bulavku*) that they were writing verse:

> Mais je ne puis souffrir, qu'un esprit de travers,
> qui pour rimer des mots, pense faire des vers,[66]

that is:

> I cannot stand it when someone,
> Having clumsily rhymed some lines, thinks he has written verse.

III

Lomonosov's Letter on Russian Versification

THE "Letter on the Rules of Russian Versification," together with his "Ode on the Taking of Xotin," was sent by Lomonosov from Germany to the Academy. There is some difference of opinion concerning when and where these two works were written. The older view, based mainly on the memoirs of Academician Stählin, held that the ode was written while Lomonosov was still in Marburg and was sent from there to the Academy in 1739. Stählin had said that the ode was "printed by the Academy of Sciences, presented to Empress Anna and distributed at court, where everybody read it and was astonished by the new verse meter" (see *Sočinenija Lomonosova*, I, *Primečanija*, 34). However, Suxomlinov, in his edition of Lomonosov's works, noted that no trace of this supposed first printing was ever found, and, except for the testimony of Stählin, no contemporary reference to the ode exists. Suxomlinov himself (*ibid.*, p. 35) came to the conclusion that "the ode on the taking of Xotin was sent from Freiberg and not from Marburg, and that it was not printed either in 1739 or 1740, or later, until 1751," when Lomonosov himself issued a collection of his works, including the ode but not the letter on versification.

Suxomlinov's view is supported by the chronological sequence of events. Russian armies took Xotin on August 29, 1739, and news of this victory appeared in Russian and German newspapers early in September, 1739. The group of Russian students, according to a written report by Raiser, one of the students sent abroad with Lomonosov, left Marburg on July 20, 1739 (Kunik, ed., *Sbornik*

68

materialov, p. 156). Consequently, Lomonosov could have written the ode and the treatise in Freiberg, either in 1739 or at the beginning of 1740. This is corroborated by Trediakovskij in a letter to the Academy in which he asked for the return of his communication to Lomonosov defending his own "New and Brief Method for Composing Russian Verse," where he wrote: "In 1740, being in Freiberg, the student Mixailo Vasil'evič Lomonosov, who is now an adjunct at the Academy, sent a letter to the Academy of Sciences in which he disputed the rules established by me and proposed his own rules instead" (*Sočinenija Lomonosova*, III, *Primečanija*, 5). In *M. V. Lomonosov, polnoe sobranie sočinenij* (Moscow, U.S.S.R. Academy of Sciences, 1952), VII, 782, the supposition is made that Lomonosov wrote the treatise in Freiberg in September, 1739. See also V. L. Čenakal, ed., *Letopis' žizni i tvorčestva M. V. Lomonosova* (Moscow, 1961), p. 49, where it is stated that Lomonosov completed the "Letter" in November of 1739.

The available evidence also indicates that the ode and the "Letter" were sent not to Baron Korff, the president of the Academy at that time, as Stählin had said, but to the Russian Assembly, of which Trediakovskij was a very active member. In fact, Trediakovskij seems to have understood that the letter, especially, was intended for him personally, as he said in the introduction to his *Argenida* in 1751. This provoked a correction from Lomonosov (*ibid.*, p. 3): "In the introduction written by Professor Trediakovskij to Barclay's *Argenida* it is stated that supposedly Professor Lomonosov wrote to him, Trediakovskij, from Freiberg about iambic verse, but professor Lomonosov has announced orally to the Chancellery that this letter was not written to him, Trediakovskij, alone, but to the whole Assembly." It was, of course, natural for Lomonosov to address himself to the Assembly, since its declared purpose was "the purification of the Russian language," which at that time included such matters as a theory of versification.

Both the "Letter" and the "Ode on the Taking of Xotin" were probably conveyed to Russia by Academician Junker, who visited Lomonosov in 1739 (Kunik, ed., p. xxxviii). The "Letter" itself was not published until 1778, that is, after Lomonosov's death. B. Tomaševskij, in *Stilistika i stixosloženie*, p. 329, points out that the original manuscript, which was in Trediakovskij's possession, burned during a fire in his house and that the printed text now available is

taken from a handwritten copy of this original manuscript. The most
that Suxomlinov is able to state about this matter is the following:
"Lomonosov's Freiberg letter appeared in print for the first time in
1778, in the edition of Damaskin, with the following title: 'A Letter on
the rules of Russian Versification,' and with the following note of the
publisher: 'From certain passages in this letter it can be seen that
the author wrote it soon after having composed the ode on the victory
over the Turks and Tartars, that is, in 1739. It has never been printed
before. It has been conveyed to me from St. Petersburg for inclusion
among his works'" (*Pokoinago Mixaily Vasil'eviča Lomonosova
Sobranie raznyx sočinenij v stixax i v proze*, II, 3–16). (See *Sočinenija
Lomonosova*, III, *primečanija*, p. 5.) Consequently, it is not clear what
copy Damaskin used or how authentic its contents were.

The following translation of Lomonosov's "Letter" is from
Sočinenija Lomonosova, III (1895), 1–11.

LETTER ON THE RULES OF RUSSIAN VERSIFICATION[1]

Most respected gentlemen!

The ode which I now have the high honor of presenting for your
consideration is no more than the fruit of the great joy aroused in my
faithful and zealous heart by our most invincible monarch's most
glorious victory over her enemies. My extreme boldness in troubling
you with my unskilled pen proceeds only from sincere love for the
fatherland and its language. In truth, I should have better remained
silent, because of the inadequacy of my strength for this enterprise.
However, I do not doubt that in your dedicated zeal for the propagation
and improvement of the Russian language you will forgive both my
lack of skill and my insufficient ability in Russian versification, and
will give me credit for my good intentions; I have therefore dared to
lay before your learning this most insignificant work of mine together
with the following *discussion of our versification in general*. It was not
any urge to set down rules for those who have more skill that incited
me to do this; but rather I was compelled to do it by my sincere
eagerness to learn from you whether these opinions are correct which
I hold concerning our versification and which I have up to now
followed in composing verses. And so, in presenting this matter to you,

my dear sirs, I begin first of all by explaining briefly on what grounds I base them.

The first and most important thing, it seems to me, is this: Russian verse should be composed according to the inherent nature of our language, and that which is entirely alien to it should not be brought in from other languages.[2]

Second, that which the Russian language possesses in abundance and which is suitable and proper to it for versification should not be taken away because of the poverty of some other language or the negligence of the poets writing it, but should be used as something that is natural and that belongs to us.[3]

Third, since our versification is only just beginning, it is necessary to be careful about whom it is better to follow and in what, so that we should not introduce anything unsuitable or abandon anything good.

On these three foundations I have established the following rules: FIRST, in Russian only those syllables are long on which the stress falls, and all others are short.[4] This is very easily demonstrated to us by our natural pronunciation itself. This is why Smotrickij proceeded quite badly and against the nature of the Slavic language, which is not very different from ours, when he counted *e* and *o* as short, *a, i v*, [either long or short] and *i, ě* and *w*, as well as some diphthongs and all vowels that stand in front of two or more consonants, as long. As can be seen from the first paragraph of his prosody, he was deceived by the Sarmatian Chronology of Matvej Strikovskij,[5] or else he was perhaps basing his writing on the following verses of Ovid (*De Ponto*, lib. IV, Eleg. 13):

A! pudet, et Getico scripsi sermone libellum,
Structaque sunt nostris barbara verba modis,
Et placui, gratare mihi, coepique poetae
Inter inhumanos nomen habere Getas!

If Ovid, while in exile in Tomi,[6] wrote verses in the ancient Slavonic or Bulgarian or Sarmatian language according to the Latin system, then I do not see where the author of the Slavonic Grammar got the idea of adopting in its entirety the Greek and not the Latin length and brevity of syllables. And even though Ovid did use feet in his verse, according to the custom of the Latin poets, and, as far as one can conclude from his hexameter, *Materium quaeris? Laudes de*

Caesare dixi (*ibidem*), those feet were bisyllabic and trisyllabic in his heroic poem, I do not, nevertheless, suppose that a poet of such intelligence would have made such a blunder as to introduce the length and brevity of syllables inherent in the Latin or Greek languages into the verse which he was writing in a foreign and quite special tongue. And if that ancient language was not very different from our present one, then this sagacious poet used in his verse as long syllables none other than those on which the stress falls, and as short all the others. Consequently, using trochees instead of spondees because of the small number of the latter, he wrote hexameters in the same way in which the following Russian hexameters are composed:

Счáстлива, крáсна бы́ла веснá// всё лéто прия́тно.
Тóлько мути́лся песóк,// лишь бéлая пéна кипéла.

And pentameters:

Кáк обличáешь смотри́// больше свой на делá
Хóдишь с кéм всегдá// бойся тогó подопнуть[7]

And not like the author of the Slavonic Grammar:

Сарматски новорастныя музы стопу перву
Тщащуюся Парнас в обитель вечну заяти,
Христе Царю приими, и благоволис тебе с отцем, etc.[8]

Everyone who understands the Slavonic language will see how contrary these lines are to its nature. However, I cannot show a preference for those lines in which all monosyllabic words are counted as long. The reason is known to every Russian. Who will drag out monosyllabic conjunctions or, often, many of the prepositions? The nouns, pronouns, and adverbs themselves, standing next to other words, lose their stress. For instance, *za sto let, pod most upal, revet kak lev, čto ty znaeš'*.[9] According to one Corollary, in which this rule is happily presented, the verses composed there purporting to be hexameters are in fact true and proper pentameters, consisting of anapests and iambics, for instance:

Не возмóжно сéрдцу, áх! не имéть печáли

In my opinion, some of our monosyllabic words are always long, such as *Bog, Xram, svjat;* others are short, for instance, the conjunctions *že, da, i*; and others are sometimes short and sometimes long, for instance, *ná more, pó godu, na vól'ju, po goré*.[10]

SECOND, in all regular Russian verse lines, long and short, one must use
the verse feet which are natural to our language, arranging them in
definite number and order. The nature of words found in our language teaches us what these feet must be like. Benevolent nature has
given Russia a sufficient abundance of these, as of everything else. In
the treasure of our language we have an inexhaustible richness of long
and short words, so that we can introduce into our verse bisyllabic and
trisyllabic feet without any strain and thus follow the Greeks, Romans,
Germans, and other people who proceed correctly in versification.[11] I
do not know why except to imitate the rhymed French and Polish
lines, we should, on the one hand, so imprison our hexameters and all
other verses that they should have no more and no less than a set
number of syllables and, on the other, allow such license that one
could freely use an iamb, a pyrrhic foot, or a spondee instead of a
trocheee, and consequently give the name of verse to any kind of
prose.[12]

This unfounded usage, which has been brought to the Moscow
schools from Poland, cannot give any law or rule to our versification.
How is one to follow such verses, when their authors themselves take
no care to observe proper regularity in them? The French, who always
seek to act naturally, but almost always proceed contrary to their intentions, cannot be an example for us in matters concerning verse feet,
because putting trust in their imagination rather than in rules, they
put together words in their verse in such a haphazard manner that
it can be called neither verse nor prose. And although they, like the
Germans, could use verse feet, which is what nature itself sometimes
put in their mouths, as can be seen in the first stanza of the ode which
Boileau-Despréaux composed on the surrender of Namur,

> Quelle docte et sainte yvresse,
> Aujourdhui me fait la loi?
> Chastes Nymphes du Permesse, etc.[13]

these sensitive gentlemen, disregarding this, satisfy themselves mainly
with rhymes alone. Someone depicted French poetry with a very
suitable symbol when he represented it on the stage as a woman who,
stooping and bandy-legged, danced to the music of a fiddling satyr. I
cannot exaggerate my joy over the fact that our Russian language is
not inferior to Greek, Latin, and German in its verve and heroic

sound, and that it can, moreover, have a versification system which is both similar to theirs and yet natural and unique to itself. In order that this pleasure, long neglected, should not become entirely forgotten, I have conceived the idea of composing our regular verse lines in certain regular feet and of giving them names, as is usually done in the three languages mentioned above.

The first type of verse line, which consists only of iambs, I call *iambic:*

Белеет, будто снег лицом

the second, in which only anapests are found, I call *anapestic:*

Начертан многократно в бегущих волнах

The third, in which these feet can be placed according to need or choice in any manner, I call *mixed iambic and anapestic:*

Во пишу себе червей хватать

The fourth—*trochaic*, containing only trochees:

Свет мой знаю, что пылает
Мне моя не служит доля

The fifth—*dactylic*, consisting only of dactyls:

Вьётся кругами змий по траве обновившись в расселине

The sixth—*mixed dactylic and trochaic*, in which either the one or the other foot can be used, according to need or choice:

Ежель бойться, кто не стал бы силён безмерно[14]

Having in this manner arranged our regular lines, I find six kinds of *hexameters*, the same number of *pentameters, tetrameters, trimeters,* and *dimeters,* and consequently, thirty kinds of verse lines altogether.

I call free and irregular verse lines in which one may use a pyrrhic foot instead of an iamb or a trochee. Such lines I use only in songs, where the number of syllables must always be the same. For instance, in this verse line a pyrrhic foot has been substituted for an iamb:

Цветы румянец умножайте

and here, for a trochee:

Солнцева сестра забыла

In free verse I very seldom use a trochee instead of an iamb or an iamb instead of a trochee, and I do it only because of pressing need or great haste, the reason being that they are quite opposed to each other. As far as the *caesura* is concerned, it seems to me that it can be used and placed in the middle of our regular verses. Whether it has to be in our hexameter only in order to catch one's breath, anyone can decide according to his strength. Whoever cannot read thirteen syllables in one breath may always maintain it in his verse.[15] I consider the lines which consist of anapests and trochees[16] to be the best, most beautiful, and easiest to compose and the most capable of expressing in all instances both speed and slowness of action and the intensity of any passion.

Pure iambic verse, however, even though rather difficult to compose, by its discreet upbeat increases the nobility of the content, its magnificence and exaltation. Nowhere can it be used better than in solemn odes; this is how I have composed my present ode.[17] The falling verse, or verse which consists of trochees and dactyls, seems also to be very well suited for the expression of both strong and weak efforts and of swift and quiet action.

An example of rapid and fierce action:

Брéвна катáйте на вéрх, кáменя и гóры валúте,
Лéс бросáйте, живýчей Дýх задавúте

Other types of verse, according to their content and the importance of the subject matter, can also be used very suitably, but I refrain from treating this in detail for lack of time.

THIRD, Russian verse lines may end beautifully and naturally with *masculine or feminine rhymes,* or *with rhymes having three vowels,* similar to those in Italian. However, until now only feminine rhymes have been used in Russian verse, while masculine rhymes and those beginning with the third syllable from the end were forbidden. Such a ban is no more just in our versification, no more natural and fitting to it, than if someone had ordered a man with two healthy legs always to hop about on one foot. This rule evidently originated in Poland, whence it has come to Moscow and there firmly taken root. This unfounded custom can no more be followed than can the Polish rhymes themselves, which can only be feminine, since all Polish words, except for some monosyllabic ones, have the stress on the penultimate syllable. In our language words that are stressed on the last syllable and on the third syllable from the end are just as abundant as those that are stressed on the penultimate syllable; why then should we ignore these riches, suffer self-imposed poverty without any reason, and jabber along with feminine rhymes alone, abandoning the verve and force of the masculine rhymes and the surge and loftiness of the trisyllabic rhyme?[18] I see no reason why masculine rhymes should be so ludicrous and vile that they can be used only in comic and satirical verse, and even then only rarely.[19]

And why should the feminine rhymes *krasovuljax* and *xoduljax*[20] be any holier than the masculine *vostok* and *vysok?* In my opinion, the baseness of rhymes does not depend on their having more or fewer syllables, but on whether or not the words mean something base or undistinguished.

FOURTH, Russian verse can be composed just as beautifully and naturally as German verse.[21] Since we can have *masculine, feminine,* and *three-vowel* rhymes, then variety, which always pleases human feelings, demands a proper mixing of these, which is what I have done in almost all of my verse. It is true that all those using feminine rhyme alone will think the alternation and mixing of rhymes strange, but if they would only apply themselves to it, they would see that it is just as pleasant and beautiful as in other European languages. The masculine rhyme would never appear before the feminine as a decrepit ninety-year-old blackamoor before a most adorable, sweet European beauty, shining in the very flower of youth.[22]

Here I submit several stanzas from my own verse as examples of verse feet and alternations.[23] Tetrameters composed of anapests and iambs:

На восто́ке со́лнце как задри́тся
Вылета́ет вспы́лчиво хи́щный Восто́к,
Глаза́ крова́вы, са́м верти́тся;
Уда́ра не сно́сит се́вер в бо́к,
Госпо́дство дае́т своему́ победи́телю
Преси́льному во́д морски́х возбуди́телю
Свой тот зыби на пре́жни возводит,
Явля́ет по́лность си́лы свое́й,
Что ю́жной страно́й владе́ет все́й,
Инди́йски бы́стро остро́ва прохо́дит.

Free rising tetrameters:

> Однá с Нарцѝсом мнé судьбѝна.
> Однáко с нѝм любóвь моя́
> Хоть я́ не сáм тоѝ причѝна,
> Люблю́ Миртѝллу, как себя́

Free falling tetrameters:

> Нѝмфы óкол нáс кругáми
> Танцовáли поючѝ
> Всплéскиваючи рукáми
> Нáшей ѝскренной любвѝ
> Веселя́ся привечáли,
> И цветáми нáс венчáли.

Iambic trimeters:

> Веснá теплó ведéт,
> Прия́тной Зáпад вéет,
> Всю зéмлю сóлнце грéет;
> В моéм лишь сéрдце лéд,
> Грýсть прóчь забáвы бьéт.

But, my dear sirs, fearing to bore you for long with my unimportant letter, I conclude with an humble plea to your magnanimity to forgive me if the *opinions concerning Russian versification* presented here are not proper and suited to our language. I have made bold to write this letter with no other intention than to obtain from you sympathetic emendations or disinterested approval for the sake of greater encouragement to poetry, and hoping for this with assurance, I remain, most respected sirs,

Your humble servant
Mixailo Lomonosov

IV

Kantemir's Letter on Russian Versification

THE PRECISE date of the "Letter of Xariton Makentin" has not been established with certainty. According to documentary evidence in the archives of the Russian Academy of Sciences, Prince Nikita Jurjevič Trubeckoj transmitted the manuscript of the treatise to Sergej Volčkov, the secretary of the Academy, on February 16, 1743. The decision to print it was then made; Trediakovskij was put in charge of reading the proofs. However, the treatise was published only in the middle of 1744, that is, posthumously, as an appendix to Kantemir's translation of the ten epistles of Horace, which he had sent to the Academy in 1740. (See Antiox Kantemir, *Sobranie stixotvorenij*, pp. 521–22, notes.)

There is, on the other hand, no exact information as to how long Kantemir had known Trediakovskij's "Method" before the composition of his own "Letter," which is in large part a commentary on, and criticism of, Trediakovskij's work. The first paragraph of the "Letter" seems to indicate that he received a copy of Trediakovskij's "Method" only a week before he wrote his own treatise. Considering that in one of the examples of verse given in the body of the treatise (38, p. 189) Kantemir refers to a collection of satires and other works prepared by him at the end of 1742 as having been completed "recently," one might conclude that the treatise was written after that date. The following interpretation of available data may be quoted (*ibid.*, p. 522): "If we keep in mind that: 1) On February 16, 1743, the 'Letter' was already transmitted by Trubeckoj to the Academy of Sciences, 2) that the introductory lines of the 'Letter' mention books sent 'last year, which had reached the author 'this week,' then one must conclude that the 'Letter' was written by Kantemir at the very beginning of 1743 and not in 1742, as A. A. Kunik, P. A. Efremov, V. Ja. Stojunina and a number of other scholars have thought."

On the other hand, it is difficult to believe that Kantemir could have produced his rather complex work, showing careful consideration of the ideas expressed by Trediakovskij, in such an extremely brief period of time. It seems that Kantemir must have known Trediakovskij's treatise much longer than the one week suggested in the introduction to his "Letter." S. M. Bondi ("Trediakovskij, Lomonosov, Sumarokov," in Trediakovskij, *Stixotvorenija*, p. 101) is even inclined to doubt that Kantemir's introductory statement was meant seriously: "One would have to assume that he had this theory ready for a long time and that the acquaintance with Trediakovskij's 'Method' provided only the occasion for putting it in writing and publishing it' But, apparently, this statement about having received the book 'only this week' (let us remember that Trediakovskij's 'Method' was published in 1735 and the 'Letter of Xariton Makentin' was published in 1744), as well as the form of a letter to a friend, and this 'friend. himself are, like 'Xariton Makentin,' only parts of a literary frame, of a device."

The anagram "Xariton Makentin" (Antiox Kantemir) is, of course, a device, but there seems to be no reason to think that the "friend" was also fictional—it could have been Prince Trubeckoj, to whom, after all, the "Letter" was sent. But Bondi's contention that Kantemir had been acquainted with Trediakovskij's theories for a longer time receives support from the biography of Kantemir written by Gouasco in his *Satyres du Prince Cantemir*, pp. lv–lvij: "M. Trediacofski avoit aussi voulu hasarder des vers hexamètres & pentamètres, & composa sur ce genre de versification une prosodie Russienne: mais ces vers ne réussirent pas & le prince Cantemir a fait plusieurs remarques sur cette prosodie, qui restent en manuscrit, ou il n'approve pas les régles données par cet auteur."

Whether this "manuscript" was a preliminary or a final version of the "Letter," Gouasco's statement implies that Trediakovskij's "Method" had been in Kantemir's hands earlier than the introductory statement of the "Letter" would suggest; the words "restent en manuscrit" obviously suggest a certain lapse of time rather than the reading of Trediakovskij's "Method" and the consequent writing of the "Letter" all in one week. Pumpjanskij ("Kantemir," *Istorija russkoj literatury*, pp. 186–87) surmises that Kantemir had read Trediakovskij's treatise while still in London and that, due to the influence of his Italian friends and of Italian versification, he was not favorably disposed toward Trediakovskij's syllabo-tonic system. Z. I. Gerškovič (*Antiox Kantemir*, p. 523) believes that the "Letter" was composed in a relatively short time, but he also thinks that Kantemir knew Trediakovskij's treatise before the beginning of 1743; considering the prominent place given by Trediakovskij to Kantemir, as well as the fact that the treatise was dedicated to members of the high nobility most skillful in versification, this scholar surmises that Trediakovskij must have done his best to get a copy of his opus into the hands of Kantemir before 1743 or even 1742.

In his "Letter" Kantemir sets forth certain rules reforming syllabic versification. Of special interest are those pertaining to the caesura in the thirteen-syllable line; it was to fall on the seventh syllable if stressed; if not stressed, the accent was to fall on the fifth syllable, the rest of the syllables then being unstressed; in other words, the first hemistich was to end in either an iambic of a dactylic foot. It is significant that Kantemir followed these rules beginning in 1737 or early in 1738 when writing his later satires and revising his earlier ones. Kantemir, consequently, not only established, but actually applied, the rules concerning the caesura and certain others well before formulating them in his "Letter."

An authoritative handwritten copy of Kantemir's works made at the Academy in 1755 and found by Academician A. Kunik in 1862, contains two titles of the "Letter"; the one given in the present translation (*Pis'mo Xaritona Makentina k prijatelju o složenii stixov russkix*), and *Pis'mo Xaritona Makentina soderžaščee pravila rossijskogo stixosloženija* (Letter of Xariton Makentin containing the rules of Russian versification). The manuscript copy has an inscription on its title page: "Work of Prince Antiox Kantemir," written in another hand (*ibid.*, pp. 432–33 and 522).

The translation of the "Letter" that follows has been made from Antiox Kantemir, *Sobranie stixotvorenij*, Z. I. Gerškovič, ed. (Leningrad, 1956), pp. 407–28).

LETTER OF XARITON MAKENTIN TO A FRIEND
ON THE COMPOSITION OF RUSSIAN VERSE

My dear Sir!

I do not know for what reason the books sent by you last year have reached me only this week; but this, you will kindly realize, is the reason why I delayed in carrying out your wish with respect to the booklet entitled "A New and Brief Method for Composing Russian Verse."

The labor expended by its sagacious author is all the more commendable because until now our nation has indeed been lacking any kind of guide in the progress of versification, and many have strayed from the true path. And he is especially to be praised for submitting his essay, with a modesty unusual among poets, for trial and emendation by those among us who possess some skill in writing of verse.

Taking advantage of the permission given by him and, more important still, wishing to assist him in his zealous efforts, I made bold to put together a few remarks which may serve the same end, that is, *the establishment of rules of Russian versification*, by which I will also show my obedience to your orders.

Chapter I. On Kinds of Verse Lines

MEASURED VERSE

1. I divide Russian verse lines into *three kinds*. Verse lines of the first kind are composed like those of Greek and Latin, in feet without rhyme, such as the following:

Христе любви пламень един еси вышнего сыне[1]

2. It is true that no one among our poets has practiced this kind of verse; but notwithstanding, I do not see why such lines should not have their place in Russian versification. The differences between the Russian and Greek languages in grammatical constitution are not so great as to provide sufficient excuse for laughing at Maxim's quantitative prosody.[2]

3. To those curious to test their powers in this type of verse I recommend it, and I would not advise despising anything simply

because it has not hitherto been put to use. Once it is put to use, perhaps it will prove agreeable.

FREE VERSE

4. The *second kind* of verse lines consists of a set number of syllables, preserving also a definite regularity of voice stress. This type, taking my example from the Italians, I would call *free verse*, such as the following:

> Долго думай, что о ком и кому имеешь
> Сказать. Любопытного беги: говорлив он;
> Бесперечь отверстые уши не умеют
> Вверенное сохранять; а слово, однажды
> Выпущенное из уст, летит невозвратно.

5. As I do not believe that Russian versification is *the same as the French*, I cannot agree that such *unrhymed verses are not beautiful in the Russian language* merely because they are not in habitual use among the French. The French language (1) does not have a poetic idiom; it must use the same locutions in verse and in ordinary composition. Moreover (2), it must put the pronoun before the noun, the noun before the verb, the verb before the adverb, and finally, the word governed by the verb, in its proper position; that is, the French language does not allow the *transposition* of parts of speech, and without those two aids it is necessary to embellish verse with rhyme; otherwise it would be ordinary speech.[4]

Our language, on the contrary, liberally borrows elevated words from the Slavonic in order to depart, in composing verse, from ordinary plain language and thereby to strengthen the verse; it also possesses full freedom of transposition, which embellishes not only verse but also simple speech.[5] The Italians, the Spanish, the English, and perhaps still others whose languages I do not know, having means similar to ours, were very successful in *free verse*. Why then should we not accept the judgment of so many peoples?

VERSE LINES WITH IDENTICAL ENDINGS

6. The *third kind* of verse is exactly the same as the preceding kind, except that at least each pair of lines must end in a rhyme; such are the following:[6]

Ездок, что в чужой земле, ему неизвестной,
Видит на пути своем лес вкруг себя тесной,
Реки, болоты, горы и страшны стремнины
И, оставя битый путь, ищет пути ины,
Бедный, блудит, многие, где меньше он чает,
Трудности, и наконец погибель встречает
Так в течение житья, где предлежат многи
Бедства и страх, гинет тот, конечно, кто ноги
Сведет с пути, где свои расставлиа вехи
Добродетель, сгладив все опасны помехи.

7. We shall proceed to discuss these two latter verse types, but, before taking up their rules, we should not omit, it seems to me, a few remarks about rhymes.

Chapter II. On the Choice of Rhymes

DEFINITION OF RHYME

8. Rhyme is properly defined as *the like ending of the final syllables of two words*, but I am of the opinion that one must also note that some polysyllabic Russian words are stressed on the last syllable, as *ruká zvezdá, toloknó;* others are stressed on the penultimate syllable, as *sáža, sočevćca, okóško;* while some are stressed on the third syllable from the end, as *stenánie, izrjádnee, ljubímica* (not to mention others in which the stress is still further removed, as in the word *vsjáčeskaja*, but these do not serve our purpose).

THE KINDS OF RHYME

9. Consequently, rhymes can be *monosyllabic, bisyllabic,* and *trisyllabic*. The first are called *blunt*; the second, *simple*; the third, *gliding* rhymes.[7]

THE RULES OF BLUNT RHYMES

10. *Blunt rhymes* ending in vowels must have at least one identical letter preceding that vowel; but the more the better; thus *snoxá* and *vexá* make a better rhyme than *krupá* and *sová;* and better still are *tesló* and *vesló, bloxá* and *soxá*.

11. In rhymes ending in a consonant, not only the preceding vowel, but also the following conjunct vowel, must without exception be

identical, as in these words: *poklon"*, *zvon"*, *trud"*, *prud"*; in *zvon"* and *von'*, *jad"*, and *jad'*, merely the difference of ъ (") and ь (') does not make a rhyme.[8]

RULES OF SIMPLE RHYMES

12. Simple rhymes must have two identical syllables, so that at least beginning with the vowel in the penultimate syllable, on which the stress lies, all letters to the end, not excluding the conjunct vowels ъ (") and ь ('), would be identical, as in the following words:

> *priméta, otveta,   kníga, vjazíga*
> *rubáška, Iváška*
> *igrájut", stupájut"*.

13. And it is still better if one or two of the letters preceding this vowel are also identical, as in these words: *obez'jána* and *iz'jána*, *letáju* and *vstretáju*.

RULES OF GLIDING RHYMES

14. Gliding rhymes demand that, beginning with the vowel in the syllable preceding the penultimate, the one on which the stress falls, all the following letters be identical, not excluding the reduced vowels, as in the following words:

> *letánie, zvánie*
> *skólzajut, pólzajut*.

Chapter III. On License with Respect to Rhyme

15. Although the precise adherence to these rules in making rhymes seems necessary to me in shorter compositions, such as epigrams and others not exceeding one hundred lines, one must, however, allow some degree of freedom. For instance:

(1) One may consider as identical the consonants *d* and *t*; *b* and *p*; *z* and *s*; *g* and *x* when they are followed by a consonant, so that the following words make up an excellent rhyme:

> *vódka, glótka; útka, dúdka; udóbnyj, stópnyj; núžnyj, vozdúšnyj; dróglyj, issóxlyj*.[9]

(2) The vowels *a, e, i* in the penultimate syllable may be considered identical with the diphthongs *ja, e, y*,[10] so that an excellent rhyme will be:

> *výti, vopíti; sýto, vlíto; vjálju, sálju; sijáju, vnimáju; skorotéčnyj, věčnyj; sijánie, blistánie; unlýlye, xvílye; xměl'nye, cel'nye*.

(3) The conjunct vowels ъ and ь may be considered identical when they occur between two consonants, so that an excellent rhyme will be: *polnyj, vol'nyj.*[11]

These three kinds of poetic license have no place in *blunt* rhymes; they are tolerable in *simple* rhymes and fully excusable in *gliding* rhymes, considering the small number of such rhymes.

(4) One may omit a consonant if it occurs between two vowels [sic],[12] so that an excellent rhyme will be:

izvéstnyj, tésnyj; slástnyj, krásnyj.

(5) One may make rhymes from words with different meanings, such as:

luk [onion]—vegetable, *luk* [bow]—weapon

carjú—vocative of Tsar, *carjú*—I rule, etc.

(6) One may add the letter *i* to infinitives, so as to have for example:

pisáti instead of *pisát'*

péti instead of *pet'*

píti instead of *pit'*[13]

(7) One may disregard the [final] *j* in adjectives, so that an excellent rhyme will be:

prjány, p'jányj

vólny, pólnyj

(8) The words *próstyj* and *óstryj* can sometimes form a rhyme because of the great similarities of sound in the pronunciation of these two words. I do not know if another two as similar can be found.

16. But with respect to all these kinds of poetic license, one should remember that the less they are used, the better, and that it is very bad to use two kinds together, for instance in this rhyme, *prjány-zványj*, where the *ja* is treated as similar to the letter *a* and the short *i* [j] is disregarded in the word *zvanyj*.

17. Most of all I recommend leaving to the vulgar versifiers the rhyme of infinitives in *–ati*, because it is quite unpleasant to the ear except perhaps when one of the words is a noun, and another a verb, as, for instance:

máti, spáti; tetráti, pisáti, and others.[14]

18. I am not at all in favor of the shifting of stress from one syllable to another, so that instead of *glavá* one would write *gláva*, instead of *zakón, zákon*, etc.[15]

Chapter IV. On the Measure of Verse Lines

THE KINDS OF LINES

19. A Russian verse line may comprise from thirteen to four syllables.[16]

CONSIDERATION OF FEET IS NOT NECESSARY

20. In my opinion it is superfluous to take feet into consideration in composing all these lines of verse. But it is necessary to observe that in each line two particular syllables should be stressed.[17]

WHAT ARE LONG AND SHORT SYLLABLES?

21. Such [stressed] syllables I call *long*, but all others are *short*. For instance, in the word *izrjádnaja*, the syllable *rja* is long, and the syllables *iz*, *dna*, and *ja* are short.[18]

ENJAMBEMENT IS ALLOWED

22. I do not see why one should proscribe enjambement when the signification of speech cannot be completed in one line. The Greeks, the Latins, the Italians, the Spaniards, and the English not only do not consider this a flaw, but even regard it as embellishment of verse. Enjambement does not prevent a good reader from feeling the stress of the rhyme, and it is very much needed in satires, comedies, tragedies, and fables, in order to bring the language closer to ordinary conversation. Moreover, without such enjambement, a lengthy rhymed work becomes tedious, the frequent repetition of rhymes causing a rather unpleasant monotony, of which the French themselves accuse their poets.[19]

ELISION IS NOT REJECTED[20]

23. Elisions (the letter short *i* [j] is understood) do not appear harmful in the least. On the contrary, I feel that the more elisions in a line of verse, the more it pleases the ear, for they cause a certain ease in the flow of voice which the sensitive ear distinguishes with delight.

24. But the frequent repetition of like consonants in a line, expecially when so prominent as in the following corrected line,

Ум так слабый, плод трудов краткия науки

is very irritating to the ear and must therefore be avoided.[21]

RULES FOR THE THIRTEEN-SYLLABLE LINE

25. The *thirteen-syllable* line, fittingly called heroic, because it corresponds best to Greek and Latin hexameter, should consist of two hemistichs.

26. The word ending the first hemistich must be connected with the preceding [ones] and not with those that follow in the second [hemistich], so that no conjunctions, prepositions, or pronouns become the syllable of the caesura. This rule is generally valid for the caesurae of other types of verse.[22]

27. The first hemistich has seven syllables, the second, six.

тот/ лишь/ в жиз/ни/сей/ бла/жен// кто/ ма/лым/ до/во/лен[23]
1   2   3 4 5 6 7   1   2 3 4 5 6

28. The first four syllables of the first hemistich may be either long or short, however they occur; but it is absolutely necessary that either the *seventh* or the *fifth* be long, and in the latter instance, that the *sixth* and the *seventh* be short.

29. The penultimate syllable of the second hemistich must always be long; so that if one writes rhymed verse, that rhyme would always be bisyllabic, for I think that blunt rhymes in such lines are altogether unbearable to the ear.[24]

Example

Что/ поль/зу/ет/ мно/же/ство//лю/дей/ без/рас/суд/но
1   2   3 4 5 6 7   1 2 3 4 5 6
Привесть в удивление, когда в оном трудно.

Час/ о/ни/ мо/гут/ сто/ять//и/что/ те/перь/ хва/лдт,
1 2 3 4 5 6 7 1 2 3 4   5 6
Величают, спустя час низят уж и малят,
Когда честный, мудрый муж, сколь часто случится
Ему на нас вскинуть глаз, от дел наших рдится.

30. But if someone desires to end this line with a blunt rhyme, he must set up the last hemistich in such a way that the *third* and the *sixth* syllable are always long, and the *fourth* and *fifth* short.

Example

Что/ поль/зу/ет/ мно/же/ство// без/рас/суд/но/ лю/дей.
1   2   3 4 5 6 7   1 2 3 4 5 6

RULES FOR THE TWELVE-SYLLABLE LINE

31. The *twelve-syllable* line of verse is divided into two six-syllable hemistichs, of which the latter must always have the *fifth* syllable long, and the *sixth* short. The first hemistich may either 1) be exactly like the second one, or, 2) may have, and this is much better, the *sixth* syllable long, or 3) the *fourth* long and the *fifth* and *sixth* always short.

Example

Лег/ко/ не/воз/дер/жный// я/зык/ в бе/ду/ вво/дит.
1   2   3   4   5   6   1 2   3   4   5 6

Дой/дет/ тот/ да/ле/е// кто/ и/дет/ не/ спеш/но.
1   2   3   4 5 6 1   2   3   4   5   6

Не/воз/врат/но/ бе/жит// кры/ла/то/е/ вре/мя.
1   2   3   4   5   6   1   2   3 4   5   6

32. Therefore this verse line invariably demands a simple rhyme.

RULES FOR THE ELEVEN-SYLLABLE LINE

33. The *eleven-syllable* line also consists of two hemistichs, of which the first has five syllables, and the second six.

Example

Мед/ны/я/всхо/дят// в ру/ках/ на/ших/ сте/ны.
1   2 3 4   5   1   2   3   4   5   6

34. The second hemistich follows the rules prescribed for the second hemistich of the heroic and twelve-syllable line.

35. And the first, five-syllable hemistich must have a stress on the *fourth* syllable.[21]

Example

Вла/сте/лин/ ми/ра// нуж/ду/ тво/ю/ зна/ет,
1   2   3   4 5   1   2   3   4   5   6
Не лишит пищи, не лишит одежды
Кто того волю, смирен, исполняет,
Не отщетится в нем своей надежды.

36. It is self-evident that this line also does not tolerate any but bisyllabic rhyme.

37. But if one wishes the line to end in a blunt rhyme, then the first hemistich must contain six syllables and the second five; and in

the first hemistich the *fifth* syllable must be long, while in the second, the *second* and *fifth* must be long and the *third and fourth*, always short.

Example

В нем/ не/от/ще/тит/ся// на/деж/ды/ сво/ей.
1   2   3   4 5 6   1   2   3   4 5

RULES FOR CATULLIAN ENDECASYLLABIC

38. If one is inclined to imitate the *endecasyllabics* of Catullus, he must: 1) divide the eleven-syllable verse in such a way that the first hemistich has six, and the second five syllables; and 2) always keep the *fourth* syllable long in the first hemistich, the *fifth* and *sixth* being short, and in the second hemistich, the *fourth* syllable long.[28]

Example

Ко/му/ дам/ но/ву/ю// книж/ку/ ис/прав/но
Многим очищену трудом недавно?
Книжку забавную тебе дам, другу,
Никито, ты мои стишки с досугу
Охотно преж сего чел, признавая,
Что в шутках кроется польза какая.[29]

RULES FOR THE TEN-SYLLABLE LINE

39. The *ten-syllable* line must consistof two five-syllable hemistichs or (and this is much better) of one four-syllable hemistich, and one six-syllable hemistich.[30]

40. When a line consists of two five-syllable hemistichs, then the second one must always have the *fourth* syllable long. In the first hemistich, the stress must lie either on the *third* syllable (and then the fourth and fifth must always be short), or on the *fourth*, or on the *fifth*; but in this latter instance, the *second* syllable, too, must always be long.[31]

Example

К кон/цу/ бли/жим/ся// мы/ по/вся/час/но,
1   2   3   4   5   1   2   3   4 5

Те/бе/ мы/ слу/жим,// силь/но/му/ Бо/гу.
1   2   3   4   5   1   2   3   4 5

Те/бе/ мы/ по/ем,// тва/ри/ вла/ды/ке.

41. I feel that a blending of these three types of ten-syllable verse lines would not lack in beauty.

42. And when a line consists of four-syllable and six-syllable hemistichs, then the four-syllable hemistich must always be the first, and the six-syllable, the second.

43. The four-syllable hemistich may have the stress either on the *third* syllable,

Ви/дим/ страш/нў// на/ле/та/ти/ бӯ/рю̆

or on the *fourth*, which is much better:

Те/бе/ по/е̄м,// выс/ше/му/ вла/ды̄/кӗ.

44. The *fifth* syllable of the second hemistich must always be long.

45. From all this it is clear that this line requires a bisyllabic rhyme.

46. But it is also possible to compose *ten-syllable* lines in a different manner, without a caesura, and these may end pleasantly in blunt rhyme.

Example

Сла̄/бо/е/ здра̄/ви/е/ лю̄/бйт/ по̆/ко̄й,

   Стужа скучна тому, скучен и зной,

Всего ж вреднее бывает печаль,

   Что сердце грызет та, как ржа грызет сталь.

Lines of this type must necessarily have the *seventh* and *tenth* syllable long, and the *eighth* and *ninth*, short; but the verses will be more sonorous if the *first* syllable is long, too.[32]

RULES FOR THE NINE-SYLLABLE LINE

47. The *nine-syllable* line has a caesura, and therefore two hemistichs. The first has four, and the second, five syllables.

48. In the first and the second hemistich, the *fourth* syllable must always be long, and therefore the rhyme will be bisyllabic.

Example

Пер/вый/ о/те̄ц// на/ше/го/ ро̄/дӑ

1   2   3 4   1 2 3 4 5

Вкусом плода// рая лишился.

49. If the hemistichs were reversed, such a line would properly end with a blunt rhyme.

Example

На/ше/го ро̄/дӑ// пе̄р/вы̆й/ о̆/те̄ц
1 2 3 4 5 1 2 3 4
Рая лишился// вкусом плода.

But then one must add to the above that the *first* syllable of the second hemistich (which now has four syllables) should be long; and the *second* and *third*, always short.[33]

50. There is also another way of composing *nine-syllable* lines without caesura, but it is difficult because it always requires a *gliding* rhyme and also that the *first*, *fourth*, and *seventh* syllables always be long, and the *eighth* and *ninth*, invariably short.[34]

Example

Лӣш/ня̆/ го̆/ря̄ч/ность/ к поз/на̄/нй/ю̆
Зла и добра была гибелью
Нашего рода начальнику.

RULES FOR THE EIGHT-SYLLABLE LINE

51. The *eight-syllable* line has no caesura, but one must see to it that the *third* and the *seventh* syllables are long.[35]

Example

Сколь/ко̆/ бе̄д/ный/ сў/е/тӣт/ся̆
1 2 3 4 5 6 7 8
Человек за малу славу.

Ночь не спит, и день томится,

Чтоб не сел сосед по праву,

Чтоб народ ему дивился

И с хвостом всегда тащился;

Знатно бедный забывает,

Что по смерти прах бывает.

52. Such a line will be even more beautiful if the *first*, *fourth*, and *seventh* syllables are kept long, and the remaining one short.[36]

Example

Тва̄/рй/ вла̄/ды̆/ко̄/ всӗ/мо̄ч/ны̆й,
1   2   3   4   5   6   7   8
Если мой глас тебе внятен,
Нуждам доход моим точный,
Кратку хоть жизнь, но без пятен,
В здравом дай теле мысль здраву,
В страшный день дай стать по праву.

53. It is self-evident that such verse demands simple rhyme.

54. But if one wishes to conclude with a blunt rhyme, it is necessary that the *fifth* and *eighth* syllables be long, and the *sixth* and *seventh*, always short; and it is even better if the *second* syllable is long.

Example

Не/ до̄л/го/чис/ло̄/ нӑ/шйх/ дне̄й,
1   2   3   4   5   6   7   8
За днем другой бегло летит.

55. Those who know how to compose thirteen-, twelve-, eleven-, and ten-syllable lines can easily compose seven-, six-, five-, and four-syllable lines, because the latter are the hemistichs of the former and do not require a caesura.

RULES FOR THE SEVEN-SYLLABLE LINE

56. Following the rules already outlined, the *seven-syllable* line must have a stress either on the *seventh* syllable or on the *fifth*, and in the latter case the *sixth* and the *seventh* must invariably be short.

Example

Тот,/ кто/ до̄/бро/дӗ/те̄/лӗй
1   2   3   4   5   6   7
Идет путем, дерзностно
Ждет себе свидетелей,
Зная, что те мерзостно
Де/ло/ об/ли/чить/ е/му
Не могут, и тишину
Совести он предпочтет
Богатству, славе, чину
Высокому и всему
Тому, что бессудно чтет,
В сластях погруженное,
Сердце изнуренное.

57. It follows that either the blunt or the gliding rhyme is suitable for this verse.

58. The *twelve-syllable* line broken into its two hemistichs produces two six-syllable lines.[37]

Example

Лег/ко́/ не/воз/де́р/жный
1   2   3   4   5   6
язык в беду вводит.

До́й/дет/ тот/ да́/ле́/е,
1   2   3   4 5 6
кто идет неспешно.

Не/воз/врат/но/ бе/жи́т
1   2   3   4   5   6
крылатое время

59. It follows that in this verse one may use the blunt, simple, or gliding rhyme.

60. The *five-syllable* line may have a stress either 1) on the *third* syllable, and in this case the *fourth* and *fifth* mustal ways be short, or 2) on the *fourth*, or 3) on the *fifth*. Consequently, one can use any of the three types of rhyme in such verse.

Example

Ес/ли/ зо́/ло/та́
1   2   3   4   5

Ку/ча/ мог/ла́/ бы́
1   2   3   4   5
Жизнь продлить нашу,
Я бы охотно

Сби/рал/ и/ ко/пи́л
1   2   3   4   5
Сильно богатство.

RULES FOR THE FOUR-SYLLABLE LINE

61. The *four-syllable* line may have the *third* syllable long, and the *fourth*, short, and therefore it may end in a simple rhyme.[38]

Example

Чи/сты/ нра̅/вы̆
1   2   3   4
Суть приятны
Царю славы.
Из уст чистых
Ему внятны
Мольбы. Истых
Он слуг знает,
Проницает
Человека.
Его века
Утаиться,
Сколь ни тщится
Сердце злобно,
Неудобно.

62. It may also, contrariwise, have the *fourth* syllable long, and the *third*, short, and therefore require a blunt rhyme.

Example

Те/бе/ по/ю̅,
1   2   3   4
Те/бе/сво/ю
жизнь предаю,
Небес царю.

63. From all the rules presented above one may note: 1) that long lines of verse (which I term those containing thirteen to nine syllables, inclusive) end more beautifully in simple rhyme than in any other; 2) that in certain lines the gliding rhyme is not unpleasant, but the syllables demand a special arrangement; 3) that if we wish to end them with blunt rhymes, it is always necessary that two short syllables precede the rhyme, thus preparing the ear for such an ending; and 4) that in those lines of verse containing two hemistichs of unequal length it is necessary, when desiring to end them with a simple rhyme, to make the first hemistich longer than the second. For instance, in the

eleven-syllable line the first hemistich should have six syllables, and the second, five. If one were to ask my reasons for all this, I could give none; however, my ear advises me to exert care in these matters.[39]

64. It will not be amiss to explain once and for all that whenever these rules do not maintain that syllables should be long or short, then such syllables may either be long or short, as they occur.

65. In order to see more conveniently and quickly all the measures of the various verse lines mentioned above, I am appending the following table, in which numerals indicate the number of syllables; the sign — means long syllable, the sign ⌣ means short syllable, and the sign // means caesura.[40]

Table of Russian Verse Lines

Types of verse lines	The measure of verse lines													Suitable rhymes

Thirteen-syllable

1	2	3	4	5	6	7 ‖	1	2	3	4	5	6	Suitable rhymes
·	·	·	·	—	⌣	⌣	·	·	·	·	—	⌣	simple
·	·	·	·	·	·	—	·	·	·	·	—	⌣	
·	·	·	·	—	⌣	⌣	·	·	—	⌣	⌣	—	blunt

Twelve-syllable

1	2	3	4	5	6 ‖	1	2	3	4	5	6	Suitable rhymes
·	·	·	·	—	⌣	·	·	·	·	—	⌣	
·	·	·	—	⌣	⌣	·	·	·	·	—	⌣	simple
·	·	·	·	·	—	·	·	·	·	—	⌣	

Eleven-syllable

1	2	3	4	5 ‖	1	2	3	4	5	6	Suitable rhymes
·	·	·	—	⌣	·	·	·	·	—	⌣	simple
1	2	3	4	5	6 ‖ ·	2	3	4	5		
·	·	·	·	—	⌣	1 —	⌣	⌣	—		blunt

Catullian endecasyllabic

1	2	3	4	5	6 ‖	1	2	3	4	5	Suitable rhymes
·	·	·	—	⌣	⌣	·	·	·	—	⌣	simple

Ten-syllable verse of equal hemistichs

1	2	3	4	5 ‖	1	2	3	4	5	Suitable rhymes
·	·	—	⌣	⌣	·	·	·	—	⌣	
·	·	·	—	⌣	·	·	·	—	⌣	simple
·	·	·	·	—	·	·	·	—	⌣	

Ten-syllable verse of different hemistichs

1	2	3	4 ‖	1	2	3	4	5	6	Suitable rhymes
·	·	—	⌣	·	·	·	·	—	⌣	
·	·	·	—	·	·	·	·	—	⌣	simple

Table of Russian Verse Lines, continued.

Types of verse lines	The measure of verse lines										Suitable rhymes
Ten-syllable verse without caesura	1 −	2 .	3 .	4 −	5 .	6 .	7 −	8 ˘	9 ˘	10 −	blunt
Nine-syllable with caesura	1 . 1 .	2 . 2 .	3 . 3 .	4 − 4 −	1 . 5 ˘	2 . 1 −	3 . 2 ˘	4 − 3 ˘	5 ˘ 4 −		simple blunt
Nine-syllable without caesura	1 −	2 .	3 .	4 −	5 .	6 .	7 −	8 ˘	9 ˘		gliding
Eight-syllable	1 . − .	2 . ˘ −	3 − ˘ .	4 . − .	5 . ˘ −	6 . ˘ ˘	7 − − ˘	8 ˘ ˘ −	}		simple blunt
Seven-syllable	1 . .	2 . .	3 . .	4 . .	5 − .	6 ˘ .	7 ˘ −				gliding blunt
Six-syllable	1 . . .	2 . . .	3 . . .	4 − . .	5 ˘ − .	6 ˘ ˘ −					gliding simple blunt
Five-syllable	1 . . .	2 . . .	3 − . .	4 ˘ − .	5 ˘ ˘ −						gliding simple blunt
Four-syllable	1 . .	2 . .	3 − .	4 ˘ −							simple blunt

Chapter V. On Poetic License in the Measure of Verse Lines
WHAT IS THE REASON FOR POETIC LICENSE?

66. One who has not yet ventured to compose verse may think that it is not a difficult task to fit several syllables into a line. And truly,

those who think that verse lines consist of that alone can easily, standing on one foot, scribble a great many of these, but it is a different matter when one undertakes to compose proper verse, according to rules, and pleasing to both the ear and the mind. Then one meets with a good many difficulties in the blending of good sense and rhyme as well as in the arrangement of syllables. That is why poets are sometimes forced to deviate from the rules, but in such a way that the deviation is unimportant and temporary, and not a complete break with the rules; such deviations are called *poetic license*.

67. I have already presented above the license which may be exercised in the selection of rhymes; now I will mention the excusable deviations in the measure of the verse lines.

68. The nature of our language has assigned stress to all one-syllable words, such as *vse, ty, drug, stol, lob*, and others. Consequently (according to #21) all such words are long. Nevertheless, when necessary they may be properly counted as short—a poetic license which our ear itself forgives. Thus, in the following line, the pronoun *moj* is a short syllable:[41]

если мой глас тебе внятен.

THE CONTRACTION OF A WORD IS POETIC LICENSE PROPERLY EXERCISED

69. All the abbreviations of words made lawful by the Slavonic language may, when required, be freely accepted in Russian verse. Thus, for example, it is proper to use *vek, čelovek, čist, sladok*, instead of *vekov, čelovekov, čistyj, sladkij*. Least of all, however, do I advise the frequent use of *mja, tja, mi, ti*, instead of *menja, tebja, mne, tebe*.[42]

SLAVONIC ENDINGS IN ADJECTIVES ARE PERMITTED

70. No less freely should one use all the Slavonic adjectival endings instead of Russian endings; thus it is proper to write *sladkij* instead of *sladkoj, izrjadnyj* instead of *izrjadnoj*. But this poetic license pertains more to rhyme than to the measure of verse.

ABBREVIATION OF CERTAIN PARTICULAR ADVERBS AND CONJUNCTIONS

71. Instead of *bude, bol'še, eželi, ili, koli, meždu, xotja, pozadi*, and similar words one may write *bud', bolš', ežli, il', kol', nežel', odnak, mež pozad', xot'*.

ABBREVIATIONS OF ADJECTIVES ENDING IN *-ami* AND *-oju*

72. Instead of using the instrumental case endings, *-ami* or *-oju*, one may properly abbreviate them to *-y*, *-i and -oj*. Thus one may write *rogi*[43] instead of *rogami*, *sovety* instead of *sovetami*, *rukoj* instead of *rukoju*.

But with respect to this license, it must be noted that if two adjectives or an adjective and a noun occur together, then both must take the same kind of ending. For instance, instead of *čistoju rukoju* one may write *čistoj rukoj*, but *čistoju rukoj* is very repulsive to the ear.

ABBREVIATION OF SOME PRONOUNS

73. I do not know whether one is free to admit *tvojmu* or *tvomu* instead of *tvoemu; svojmu* instead of *svoemu; mojmu* or *momu* instead of *moemu; svogo* instead of *svoego*.

CHANGE OF SYLLABLE *-ie* TO *-'e*

74. One may freely write all nouns having the ending *-ie* with-*'e*, for instance, *sčast'e* instead of *sčastie*, *znan'e* instead of *znanie*.

s INSTEAD OF *iz* ALLOWED BY USAGE[44]

75. *S* instead of *iz* has been consecrated by the common usage of everyday speech. Who does not know that every day we say *s ust, ego, s zolota* instead of *iz ust, iz zolota*.

THE ADDITION OF THE LETTER *o* AFTER THE PREPOSITION *iz*

76. It must be remembered that one may put in the vowel *o* after the preposition *iz* when the following word begins with a vowel: *izo ust* instead of *iz ust*.

Vo, so, ž, b INSTEAD OF *v, s, že*, AND *by*

77. Thus one may properly write *vo, so,* instead of *v, s,* and, contrariwise, *ž* and *b*, following a vowel, instead of *že* and *by*.

THE CHANGE OF THE SECOND PERSON IN VERBS TO *-š'* INSTEAD OF *-ši* AND OF INFINITIVES TO *-t'* INSTEAD OF *-ti*

78. The second person singular of verbs may end with *-ši* instead of *-š'* and the infinitives with *-ti* instead of *-t'*; for instance, *pišeši* instead of *pišeš' čitati* instead of *čitat'*. But it is my strong desire to avoid lines

of verse ending with such words, because rhymes of that type are very repulsive to the ear.

THE CHANGE OF ADVERBIAL ENDINGS TO -*ej* INSTEAD OF -*ee*

79. Adverbs which end in -*ee* can be written as -*ej*; thus one may write, for instance, *umnej, čestnej*, instead of *umnee, čestnee*, etc.[45]

80. There is no doubt that other kinds of poetic license can be found which are equally well justified, but I have not encountered any. They will be found and, with time, rendered normal by our skilled poets. These discoveries are necessary because, to tell the truth, the composition of our verse seems to me to be very difficult and confined within a narrow framework.

81. Moreover, a poet will be helped a great deal by assimilating the poetic speech models of Greek and Latin. Having enriched his language by means of these models, he will find himself capable of expressing one thing in many different ways and then of selecting that expression which will best suit his verse measure.

82. One other thing remains to be said: when we have to compose a song to a given tune, we may completely free ourselves from the rules presented above as far as measure is concerned, if they do not agree with the character of the melody, because, in songs it is necessary that the word stress correspond to the length or brevity of the notes, the number of syllables to the number of notes, and the caesurae, to the phrasing of the song.

83. And thus, I think, my dear sir, that I have to a certain extent fulfilled orders with the contents of my letter, which I conclude signing sincerely,

my dear sir,

Your obedient servant X.M.

V

Trediakovskij's Second Treatise on Versification, 1752

THE SECOND treatise originally appeared in Volume I of Trediakovskij's collected works, published in 1752. In the preface to this edition ("K čitatelju," *Sočinenija Trediakovskogo*, I, xx.) Trediakosvskij explains the composition of the second treatise as follows: "You have already been informed, kind reader, that after Boileau's teaching [Trediakovskij means his translation of *L'Art Poétique*, included in this edition] you will see here Horace's epistle [*Ars Poetica*], translated in prose. After this I have placed a Method for the composition of our verse lines. It is a correction and emendation of the one which I published in 1735. I decided that, while conversing with Horace and Boileau about various kinds of poetry, one should also talk a little about the composition of verse lines, since from ancient times poetry has for the most part been written in verse lines."

In preparing the 1752 edition of his works, to be published at his own expense, Trediakovskij asked that Lomonosov should not be one of the readers appointed by the Academy to comment on the collection before its publication (it was a standard procedure at the Academy to appoint two or more of its members to read and comment upon each work by one of their colleagues intended for publication). It so happened that two of Lomonosov's bitterest enemies—Taubert and Miller—were appointed to read this edition, and they approved it with only minor criticisms (see Pekarskij, pp. 164–65).

In his second treatise Trediakovskij again quoted large segments of his own poetry, but only one complete work, his translation of Ausonius' poem on the Muses. The quotations are taken from various

100

works—translations of Psalms, odes, etc., and their purpose is mostly to illustrate stanzaic structure. The translation is from *Sočinenija Trediakovskogo*, ed. A. Smirdin (St. Peterburg, 1849), I, 121–78.

A METHOD FOR THE COMPOSITION OF RUSSIAN VERSE
Amending and Supplementing the One Published in the Year of 1735

Chapter I. Introduction

1. Speech is of two kinds: one is free speech, or prose, which belongs in particular to rhetoricians and historians, and the other is bound [*zaključennaja*] speech, or verse, which for the most part is used by poets.

2. Nothing that verse has in common with prose distinguishes it from the latter. And because letters, syllables, and the accent or stress, which is placed only once on each word and on only one syllable, as well as words themselves, and also clauses forming periods, and periods themselves, are common to prose and verse, none of these can serve to make the distinction [between prose and verse].[1]

3. The set number of syllables of the old verse, not ours, but Polish verse, and introduced among us for no good reason, does not distinguish it from prose, for the clauses of the so-called rhetorical *isocolon** are also measured in almost equal numbers, and yet these clauses are not verses.[2]

4. The division of the long and medium-length Polish verse lines, or, rather, lines of prose, into two halves also does not distinguish it from prose, for all the other old lines, the short ones, are not divided into parts; and, in addition to this, clauses of prose periods are similarly divided by punctuation, and sometimes exactly in two halves.

5. Rhyme, of which more will be said below, also does not distinguish verse from prose, for rhyme cannot be rhyme without relating one line of verse to another; which is to say that there can be no rhyme unless there are two verse lines: but each line must be a line independently; it must be a verse line by itself.

---

* A figure which assumes that all clauses in a period are even and have an almost equal number of syllables. Literally translated this term means "even-membered."

6. All the above taken together, that is, the set number of syllables, the division into two parts, and the rhyme, can in no way distinguish verse from prose; for what several parts do not have, the total cannot have either, because the components have nowhere from which to obtain it. Moreover, all the above elements make up only part of a period, and if one makes them [the parts] agree by rhyme, they will still produce only two parts of a period, or else one misshapen period with a figure called *homoeoteleuton*.*

7. The elevation of style, the boldness of descriptions, the liveliness of figures of speech, surging movement, sudden breaks from orderly progression, and the like, do not distinguish verse from prose, for all these are sometimes used by rhetoricians and historians as well. And even if they never did use them, nevertheless all these characteristics belong specifically to the properties of poetry and not to the composition and the essence of verse.

8. But since one kind of speech is free and the other bound, it follows that there must certainly be an essential difference between them.

9. This difference can be no more essential with us than when in the whole sentence there are multiple repetitions of *tone*, which is called *prosody*, *stress*, and *accent*, and when these repetitions occur at certain regular intervals; everyone can immediately recognize this from his own experience.[3]

10. These intervals occur either after the tone or before it. We can never have more than two syllables in such an interval, or less than one.

11. A tone together with the interval between it and the next similar tone is called a *foot*.[4] If the interval occurs after the tone and contains only one syllable, then this foot is a trochee, and its usual notation is as follows: – ◡; a word composed of a trochee is, for instance, *nébo*, because its first syllable is accented by stress, and its second syllable is unstressed. When, on the other hand, the interval occurs before the tone and consists also of one syllable, then the foot is called an iamb, the notation for which is the opposite of the former ◡ –, and an instance would be the word *gremít*, because its second syllable is accented, while the first remains unstressed. But if two unstressed syllables should occur after the tone, or else before the tone,

---

* This figure ends all members of a period identically, with an identical sound. The literal meaning: "ending alike."

then in the first instance the foot becomes a *dactyl*, the notation for which is: – ◡ ◡, exemplified by the word, *mólnija;* in the second instance the foot will be an *anapest*; its notation is the opposite of dactyl, namely, ◡ ◡ –, and it is exemplified by the word, *porazít.*

12. In every word the syllable accented or heightened by stress* is called *long*, while all the others, whatever their number, are called *short*.

13. There is not a single word which can be pronounced without being stressed once, on one syllable; that is, there is not a single word which does not have one long syllable.

14. And since there is a multitude of monosyllabic words, it follows that they, too, cannot be pronounced without tone.

15. Therefore, all monosyllabic words are by their nature long. However, even though this is indisputable, the usage of our poets in making up a foot counts them all as common, that is, as both long and short, depending on need. This license is so necessary that without it one would hardly be able to compose a single line of verse without exceedingly great difficulties.[5]

16. It is precisely this length and brevity of syllables in our versification, called quantity of syllables, which is most certainly tonic,† That is, it raises and lowers the voice in our pronunciation; it differs in its whole nature from the quantity of syllables in Greek and Latin versification, where it is measured by *time* in the tonal accentuation of syllables, that is, by shortening or lengthening the sound.

17. Thus, the Greek and Roman quantity of syllables lengthens and shortens syllables, whereas ours heightens and lowers them.

18. The feet used most often in our present versification are trochees and iambs. Instead of using either of these feet in every

---

* Until the present time only general usage has provided the rules for our stress, which occurs sometimes on the sixth syllable from the end, or further. According to this general usage, the syllables are often accented in some words in two ways, for instance, *žestóko* and *žéstoko*. Such double stress abounds; in such an instance the writer must always designate stress on that syllable which he is accenting; in verse this is absolutely necessary.

† This quantity is inherent in our syllables, and is not termed thus only to follow Greek and Latin examples. This is irrefutably proved thus: "Where there is tension of the voice upwards, there the voice is higher. But *tone* is the tension of the voice upwards. Consequently, where there is tone, there the voice is higher. Between it and the lower pitch of voice there is a distance; that distance is a magnitude; and it is indeed the truest *quantity*." Q.E.D.

position, except for certain positions in certain lines, of which more will be said, the *pyrrhic* foot, consisting of two short syllables, is admitted, since without it one cannot compose a single line of verse.

19. Dactylic and anapestic feet, according to the example of Greek versification, far from being antagonistic to our verse, even appear pleasant to those who know their strength. Our language, unlike some of the European languages, is just as capable of having its accents on various syllables as is Greek and Latin. A sufficient example of this is given in Barclay's *Argenis*, translated into our language.[6]

20. The tonic quantity of our verse is its first and main foundation, its life and soul, as it were. It was introduced into our versification in 1735.[7]

Chapter II. On the Verse Line

1. A verse line is speech composed of a number of words and arranged from beginning to end into a set number of feet.

2. Our verse lines are named differently according to the number of feet they contain. Thus one verse line is a hexameter, that is, it has six units; another is pentameter, having five; another is tetrameter, four; a trimeter, three; a dimeter, two; and finally a monometer, which consists of one foot only.

3. The monometer cannot be properly called a verse line, since each line must have more than one foot, as can be seen from the definition, or description, of verse lines in #1 of this chapter.[8]

4. Our hexameter, which is called great, and heroic, and epic, can be trochaic-pyrrhic and iambic-pyrrhic with rhymes; it also can be dactylic-trochaic-pyrrhic and anapestic-iambic-pyrrhic without rhymes.[9]

5. The pyrrhic foot is added to all the categories because it is admitted in the trochaic verse instead of a trochee, in the iambic instead of an iamb, and also in the dactylo-trochaic instead of the trochee and in the anapesto-iambic instead of an iamb. This poetic license is necessary because of our multisyllabic words. Without it it would be well-nigh impossible to compose a single line; this was referred to in #18 of the first chapter.

SECTION 1. ON THE TROCHAIC HEXAMETER

6. The trochaic hexameter is divided into two parts, each of which is called a hemistich.

7. The middle point, where both hemistichs join in such a way that the end of one is the beginning of the other, is called the caesura. It is always in the first hemistich; it represents the end of a word as well as of the first hemistich.

8. The end of the second hemistich is called rhyme. It consists, both in the trochaic and the iambic hexameter, sometimes of two syllables, sometimes of one. But only in the trochaic tetrameter, trimeter, and dimeter, used especially in ten-line stanzas, of which more will be said, and if it is at the very middle of the stanza, is it also proper that it have three syllables.

9. When it consists of two syllables, then it is pure trochee and is termed feminine, and so the verse line which has such rhyme is also called feminine. But that line which has a one-syllable rhyme, termed masculine, is accordingly called masculine. Such rhyme is the end of an iamb or the beginning of a trochee. And if a rhyme should consist of three syllables, then this rhyme and this verse line should, it seems, be called common, because it is at the same time masculine and feminine, or, more correctly, neither one nor the other; but its foot is a true dactyl.[10]

10. The first hemistich of a trochaic feminine hexameter must consist of three feet and of a long syllable which is the caesura. The second hemistich, having a two-syllable rhyme, must consist of only three feet, of which the last is the rhyme.

Example

```
  1      2      3        1      2     3
Де́лом/ бы́ од/ни́м сти/хи́// не́ бы/ли на/ ди́во
Зна́йтесь/ с дру́жны/ми людь/ми́// живу/чи́й прав/ди́во
  1      2       3          4      5      6
```

On the contrary, the first hemistich of the trochaic masculine verse line must likewise have only three feet and must finish the word with the third foot serving as the caesura; and the second, having a monosyllabic rhyme, must have three feet and a long syllable, which will make the rhyme.

Example

```
  1      2        3       1      2       3
Мно́ги/ми тво/ре́ньми// му́дрость/ изоб/раже/на́
Та сти/ха́ми/ сме́ртным// в по́льзу/ предвоз/веще/на́
  1     2     3          4        5        6
```

This is the reason why the trochaic hexameter, both feminine and masculine, is hypercatalectic, that is, it has six feet plus another syllable.[11]

11. Verse lines of various types may be so mixed together that sometimes after two feminine lines two masculine will follow, and vice versa, which will make continuous rhyme; sometimes after one feminine or masculine line two masculine or feminine will follow, and this will produce mixed rhyme.

12. The first manner of mixing feminine and masculine verse lines, that is, when after two feminine or masculine lines two masculine or feminine follow, occurs especially in hexameters and pentameters. All the other ways of mixing rhyme belong to stanza construction, and it must be done in such a way that, in the ten-line stanza of trochees only, two verse lines with common rhyme can be placed after the first quatrain. Such stanzas are usually written in tetrameters, trimeters, and dimeters, of which more later. It must be added that mixing of rhymes is generally called combining of verse lines.[12]

13. One must be careful not to begin the second hemistich of masculine trochaic line with a monosyllabic word, However, the following are exceptions: 1) all monosyllabic prepositions; 2) the particles *i, ne, ni;* 3) *kto, čto, tot, ta, to, sej, koj, kak, tak, kol', tol';* 4) *no, a;* 5) *da, čtob,* and similar words which do not complete a thought. The reason why one must not begin the second hemistich with a monosyllabic word is that such a word may combine in meaning with the first hemistich, and thus become the caesura, which would produce a first hemistich like that of a feminine [verse line]; this must be avoided. The exempted particles, however, do not complete a thought and therefore may be used to begin the second hemistich, since they cannot make the first hemistich feminine by being counted as a caesura.[13]

14. In our old Polish verse lines [lines in the Polish manner] or rather prose lines, there is a defect which, incidentally, is an adornment in Greek and Latin; namely, when an unfinished thought is carried from the first verse line to the beginning of the following one. In the latter it is an adornment because their lines, due to the inequality of feet, are imparisyllabic and also have no rhymes. Consequently, one line does not look lame next to the other, nor does it, because of unevenness, arouse anticipation earlier than the ear

demands it through an identity of final sounds. Therefore one line is connected with the other even more firmly. But the opposite is true with respect to parisyllabic verse as well as our old prosaic lines; hence, this is quite awkward and repulsive to the sensitive ear, Therefore, because our present hexameter is parisyllabic and rhymed, it is altogether improper to use this *enjambement* from one line to the next one. However, this defect is tolerated in contemporary verse which has a solid foundation whenever a thought runs on to the next line in such a way that it reaches and includes either the caesura, or the end of the line itself. For the first hemistich is a full trimeter verse, and therefore this defect is not noticeable, and also, the rhyme does not cause anticipation because at the caesura there is always a certain small, and as it were, secret pause.[14]

SECTION 2. ON IAMBIC HEXAMETER

15. The iambic hexameter, both masculine and feminine, is divided into two hemistichs: the first consists of three feet; however, the second hemistich in the feminine, but not in the masculine, line contains three feet and one short syllable.

Example of masculine

```
    1        2         3       1      2      3
Повóль/нѣй бы́л/ бы трýд//  коль вáс/ нито/ропя́т
И спѣш/ности/ от вáс//безýм/ныя/ не зря́т
    1     2     3     4     5      6
```

Example of feminine

```
    1       2       3     1     2       3
Испрá/вивши/ ужé//  ещé/ потóм/ их прáв/те
Придáй/те и/ногдá//  но чá/ще то/ убáвь/те
    1     2     3     4     5      6
```

Clearly, the masculine iambic hexameter is *acatalectic*, that is, complete and perfect in all its feet, but the feminine is *hypercatalectic*, that is, it has one syllable more than a full six-foot measure.

16. One must take great care to avoid ending the first hemistich of an iambic hexameter with a pyrrhic foot instead of an iamb; the nature of the line does not tolerate such a fault. It must be known that in iambic verse the acatalectic element, that is full measure, always belongs to the masculine line. And since this hexameter consists of

two full trimeters, and each individual trimeter naturally ends in an
iamb, who would not understand that the first hemistich, being one of
the two trimeters, must end in an iamb. Consequently, those who
oppose this in practice violate the natural composition obligatory to
the iambic hexameter. One should also know that iambic verse was
introduced among us according to the example of German verse, in
which there is always an iambic caesura, this being the command of
common sense.[15]

SECTION 3. ON THE DACTYLIC-TROCHAIC HEXAMETER[16]

17. This verse is an imitation of the Greek and Roman. Our language is also suited for it. Competent people find that it can also be
given a place among our verse and admire it even more than our
ordinary trochees and iambs. Undoubtedly, those used to the rhythm
of the Latin verse enjoy it, but others cannot enjoy it as much or in
the same way, because its movement is so rapid and there is no rhyme.
It does not matter that we will have many kinds of verse. The French,
who have only one kind of hexameter, lament their poverty. These
laments are expressed by Rollin[17] in his ancient history and by Dacier[18]
in his remarks on translations from the ancients.

18. The dactylic-trochaic hexameter consists of six feet so arranged
that in the first two positions there is a dactyl or a trochee, or a
pyrrhic foot in place of the trochee; but in the third position there must
necessarily be a dactyl or a trochee, the long syllable of the dactyl or
the trochee being the end of a word. In the fourth position one may
have a dactyl, a trochee, or a pyrrhic foot instead of the trochee. But
in the fifth position there must necessarily be a dactyl and in the
sixth, a trochee. All the monosyllabic words must be considered as
common.[19]

19. The Latins and Greeks have assigned many kinds of caesura to
this verse line. But we must observe only one unfailingly, namely, the
so-called penthemimeric, occurring after two feet and at the beginning
of the third, which starts with the long syllable of a dactyl or a trochee
and, moreover, must end the word there. The other caesurae will
come by themselves from the composition of the line.

Example

1	2	3	4	5	6

Вы́ше уж/ звёзд как взне/слй// на/ ста́влены/ го́ры Ти/фо́на

Anyone can see that this line is acatalectic, that is, complete and not exceeding the required number of feet.

20. With the Latins and Greeks this line sometimes takes a spondaic foot in the fifth position, when either the *solemnity* of a certain thing, or *grandeur*, or *excessive grief* or *woe*, or something *powerful* and *extreme* presents itself. We can also obtain this effect by following their example, that is, we can place a trochee in the fifth position, or, instead of the regular dactyl, place a pyrrhic foot, but only under these same circumstances.[20]

Example

1	2	3	4	5	6

Стáл, и о/чáми пол/кúй// фри/гúйскии/ осмо/трéл вкрýг

21. And since this type of line is unequal when one line is compared with another, because one may consist of dactyls in four positions; and another partly of dactyls and partly of trochees; and another of trochees alone until the fifth position, in which we always have a dactyl, except under the circumstances mentioned in # 20, it follows that one line does not have to harmonize with another by rhyme;[21] and also that enjambement can be used from one line to the next, following the practice of the ancients.

SECTION 4. ON THE ANAPESTIC-IAMBIC HEXAMETER

22. This verse is newly invented, and is an imitation of the dactylo-trochaic. As the dactylo-trochaic verse resembles the trochaic, so this anapestic-iambic resembles the iambic. It is no less stately than the dactylo-trochaic, as any informed person interested in these matters can feel.

23. This verse consists of six feet and of a short syllable at the end; thus in the first position there may be an anapest, an iamb, or a pyrrhic foot; in the third either an anapest or an iamb is required, but not a pyrrhic foot; and the end of the word must coincide with the caesura, In the fourth and fifth position, an anapest, an iamb, or a pyrrhic foot. but in the sixth always an anapest and a short syllable after it.[22]

Example

1	2	3	4	5	6

Отидú/ премéр/ска мольбá// приношé/ние прóч/ нечестú/во

This verse line is hypercatalectic, that is, having one syllable over the required number of feet.

24. This line can, in the sixth position, in some solemn description, take an iambic foot instead of an anapest, but never a pyrrhic foot.

Example

1	2	3	4	5	6

Бессме́р/тных любе́з/нейший ро́д// превели́/кое Зе́в/са пле́/мя

25. Because of its unevenness [when compared with the next line] and also because it does not rhyme with the following line, this verse line also may carry an expression on to the next line.

26. There is more beauty both in the dactylo-trochaic and in the anapestic-iambic hexameter when not every word constitutes a foot but when a part of the word continues into the next foot. In this way the feet are joined together in a pleasant manner, and the measures are accented according to their stress (scansion). This should be observed mainly in both the trochaic and iambic hexameter, in a word, in all other trochaic and iambic verse, of which more later.

Chapter III. On the Pentameter
SECTION 1. ON TROCHAIC PENTAMETER

1. Feminine trochaic pentameter is divided into two hemistichs. The first contains two feet and a long syllable, which is the caesura, and the second, exactly three feet.

Example

1	2		1	2	3

Зла́т же/де́зна/ ко́ль// е́сть кру/щец дра/жа́йший
О́трас/лей сво/и́х// ке́др коль/ вели/ча́йший

1	2	3	4	5

But masculine pentameter places three feet in the first hemistich, of which the last is the caesura, and two in the second hemistich, followed by a long syllable.[23]

Example

1	2	3	1	2

То́ль ты/ превос/хо́дишь// цвето/но́сный/ ро́д
И цве/ ту́щий/ в тва́ри// вся́кий/ ра́зный/ пло́д

1	2	3	4	5

2. It is clear that masculine and feminine trochaic pentameter are hypercatalectic, that is, they have one syllable more than the required measure.

3. What has been said about the trochaic hexameter in the second chapter, in ≠12, 13, and 14, must be kept in mind with regard to this pentameter as well, and adhered to in composing it.

4. There is also a trochaic pentameter without a caesura, but its composition is a poetic license. It should not be employed, except when urgency requires it; and then only in a short work, such as an epigram. Even though I have composed twenty lines in this free pentameter, and not unpleasant ones, I do not ask anyone to follow me in this.

SECTION 2. ON IAMBIC PENTAMETER

5. Iambic pentameter contains two hemistichs, that is, it is divided by a caesura. It has two feet in the first hemistich of the masculine verse line and the end of the second foot is the caesura. In the second hemistich, it has exactly three feet.[24]

Example

```
1      2      1      2      3
Но ва́м/ узре́ть,// пото́м/ки в гра́/де се́м,
Смотря́/щих всё,// дивя/ щихся/ о всём
```

But feminine iambic pentameter, even though it also has two feet in the first hemistich, and the end of the second foot coincides with the caesura, in the second hemistich has three feet plus a short syllable.

Example

```
1      2      1      2      3
Из всех/ тех мест// слета́/ющих/ся гу́с/то
Глася́/щих се́// рай стал/ где бы́/ло пу́с/то
1      2      3      4      5
```

Thus the masculine iambic pentameter is acatalectic and the feminine, hypercatalectic.

6. In ≠16 of the second chapter an observation was made, and the reason given, concerning the first hemistich of iambic hexameter and its caesura, namely, that this hexameter must never be divided by a pyrrhic foot but always and under all circumstances must be divided

by an iamb. This observation is equally valid for this iambic pentameter. It will be added that even though there is an iambic pentameter without caesura, it is composed, like the trochaic, only as a great
poetic license and in the smallest compositions. I do not advise imitating this in an important work.

SECTION 3. ON DACTYLIC-TROCHAIC PENTAMETER

7. According to the Greek and Latin example, the dactylic-trochaic
pentameter must never stand alone, but must always accompany a
hexameter of the same kind. The ancients have called the combination
of the two measures of verse *heroelegiac*.

8. Even though the ancients also composed it without rhyme, we can
properly give it a rhyme, but, since it must always stand together with
a hexameter, it is most important that this hexameter have a feminine
rhyme, and the pentameter, masculine.

9. In the first position it takes a dactylic or a trochaic foot, or a
pyrrhic foot instead of the trochee; in the second a dactyl or a trochee,
or again a pyrrhic foot, and then a long syllable which is the caesura
and which terminates a word. The following two feet must always contain a dactyl as well as a long syllable which, taken together with the
syllable of the caesura, makes up the fifth foot.

Example

Вы ска/жи́те бре/га́// погра/ни́чны всхо/дя́щего/ Фе́ба
   1   2   1   2

Ко́ль из/ ва́ших/ во́д// Бо́г сей пре/кра́сен вста/е́т
   1   2 $\frac{1}{2}$ 3   4 $\frac{1}{2}$

When these heroelegiac lines are without rhymes, they are written
in couplets, but with rhyme their group must consist of four verse
lines, because of the two feminine rhymes in the two hexameters and
the two masculine rhymes in the two pentameters.[25]

[There is no #10 in the treatise. Evidently Trediakovskij, or his
publisher, inadvertently misnumbered the sections following #9.]

11. Quintilian (Book 6, chapter 4) scans this verse differently,
namely, he describes it as I have in #9 in the two first positions, but
in the third he has a spondee (consisting of two long syllables), so that
his first [long] syllable would be the end of a word and his second the
beginning of another word; two anapests follow.

Example

  1   2   3   4   5

  Та́кже ба/ра́шком вол/на́ вьёт/ся и бли́з/ берего́в

It does not matter which way one measures this pentameter. However, the former way of measuring is more generally taught.[26]

SECTION 4. ON ANAPESTIC-IAMBIC PENTAMETER

12. This pentameter is newly found. It is an imitation of the dactylic-trochaic pentameter. And since the anapestic-iambic hexameter has also newly appeared, it became necessary to devise a similar pentameter.

13. It seems that we should also let this verse combine with its hexameter, but then also add rhyme, so that it would be feminine in the hexameter and masculine in the pentameter.

14. It is constituted as follows. At first, two feet, either two iambs or two anapests, or an iamb with an anapest, or again an anapest with an iamb. They are arranged in such a way that the end of the last foot also terminates a word, and comprises the caesura. Then three anapests must always follow.

Example

 Беззако́н/ники про́ч/ от сего́/ удаля́й/тесь хра́/ма свяще́/на

 У ко́/их сердца́// преиспо́л/нены скве́р/нейших зо́л,

 1 2   3   4   5

 Или у́/тробу// грызе́т/ чью за́/висть всегда́/ умраче́/на

 Ненасы́т/но ль кто́// разграбля́/ет бесси́ль/нейших до́л

 1 2   3   4   5

Chapter IV. On Tetrameter, Trimeter, and Dimeter

SECTION 1. ON TROCHAIC TETRAMETER

1. This verse line does not have a caesura and it consists of only four feet. It is both feminine and masculine.

Examples of feminine

 1 2 3 4

 Что́ тво/е́ я// и́мя/ зна́ю

 Избав/ле́ни//я тем/ ча́ю

Example of masculine

 1 2 3 4

 Испо/ве́м те/бя́ во/ ве́к

 Тва́рь тво/я́ и/ чело/ве́к

2. Anyone can see that the feminine trochaic tetrameter is acatalectic, that is, it has the full requisite number of feet; and the masculine is catalectic; it lacks one syllable of the full measure.

3. The trochaic trimeters and dimeters are composed like the tetrameters of both kinds of feet, except that the number of feet decrease accordingly, and the feminine trochaic lines are acatalectic, while the masculine are catalectic.

SECTION 2. ON IAMBIC TETRAMETER

4. Iambic tetrameter does not have a caesura, and consists of four feet. It is masculine and feminine.

Example of masculine

   1   2   3   4
Свойм/ Бог прáв/ду со/творѝт
И стá/явших/ не у/морѝт

Example of feminine

   1   2   3   4
И у/молён/ об нѝх он бу́/дет
В конéц/ рабóв/ сам не/забу́/дет

5. It can be seen that the masculine iambic tetrameter is acatalectic, that is, full, and the feminine, hypercatalectic, having a syllable more than the required number of feet.

6. Iambic trimeter and dimeter are composed like the tetrameter, with a corresponding decrease in the number of feet; all these masculine iambics are acatalectic, and the feminine, hypercatalectic.

Chapter V. On the Stanza

1. The stanza is a combination of a number of verse lines containing a complete thought.

2. Our stanza does not have less than four lines nor more than ten.

3. Stanzas which have an even number of lines are called *regular*, and those which do not, *irregular*.

4. The stanzas we use more frequently than others consist of tetrameters, but they may also be composed of trimeters and dimeters and sometimes, but only very rarely, of pentameters.

5. Even though it is not unpleasant to use *continuous* rhyme in the

stanzas *mixed* rhyme is used more commonly. Incidentally, one must always see to it that he does not begin a stanza with the same kind of rhyme as that ending the preceding stanza, for this is considered a great and clumsy fault and evidence of the poet's scanty knowledge.

6. Stanzas in which all the lines are of the same kind and measure are called *even;* stanzas which do not have the same kind of lines or the same measure are called *uneven.*

SECTION I. REPRESENTING TROCHAIC STANZAS

7. *Four-line stanza*

> Пра́ведных стези́ весть Бо́г,
> Й всегда́ их са́м защи́тит;
> Пу́ть же злы́х, хотя́ и мног,
> Гро́зна ги́бель ве́сь похи́тит

8. *Five-line stanza*

> О́чи с пла́ча помути́лись;
> О́т враго́в весь сокрушён:
> Па́губно в себе́ озли́лись,
> К не́нависти уклони́лись;
> Я́ наде́жды уж лишён.

9. *Six-line stanza*

> Де́нь всегда́ плыве́т за днём;
> Но́щь мне но́щи пременя́ет;
> Во́лю бла́гу чин явля́ет,
> И строе́ние о все́м;
> Не́т сомне́ния ни ма́ло:
> То́ от тве́рди тве́рдо ста́ло

10. *Seven-line stanza*

> Вни́ду к Твоему́ Престо́лу,
> И в Олта́рь свяще́нный твой,
> Проявле́н в горе́ свято́й;
> В не́м паду́ пред те́м ниц до́лу:
> Ты́ жела́ниям коне́ц,
> Исполне́ние изво́лу,
> И любви́ мое́й вене́ц.

11. *Eight-line stanza*
Сé Язы́ки ворвали́сь,
Бо́же, во твоé наслéдство;
Й, свято́му хра́му в бéдство,
С осквернéнием внесли́сь:
Гра́д, и всé егó простра́нство,
Обрати́ли без следо́в
Во храни́лище пло́дов,
Всé расхи́тивши убра́нство.

12. *Nine-line stanza*
В сéрдце и́х всегда́шня лéсть,
То́кмо ту́ и помышля́ют;
Неизвéстно, что́ за в мéсть
Бра́ни вся́к дéнь ополча́ют:
Вéсь язы́х их изощрéн
На злорéчие как бри́тва;
В их рука́х сéть и лови́тва;
Слéд к дну́ зло́бы приведéн;
Я́д из у́ст течéт, и би́тва.

13. *Ten-line stanza*
На защи́ту мне смирéнну
Ру́ку са́м простри́ с высо́т,
От враго́в же то́ль презрéнну
По вели́кости щедро́т,
Да́руй спо́соб, и изба́влюсь;
Вознеси́ ро́г, и просла́влюсь:
Ро́д чужи́х, как бу́йн во́д шу́м,
Бы́стро с во́плем набега́ет,
Нéмощь о́н мою руга́ет,
И приéмлет в ба́снь и глу́м.

14. *Ten-line stanza with two dactylic endings*
Про́чь, боя́знь, про́чь! Бо́дрсвуй, Дéва:
Бытиé то не мечта́;
Ни судéб, ни хи́трость гнéва;
Ни жела́ний суета́:
Всé, что зри́шь éсть достовéрное:
Торжество́ нелицемéрное!
Стра́х и трéпет тво́й исчéз;
С ни́ми го́ресть и печа́ли:
Ликовство́ предобруча́ли
О́ны времена́ и слéз.

15. *Uneven stanza*

Щáстлив! Бóга ктó бойтся:
Зáповедей вся́ко не престýпит он тогó;
Рóд егó благословится;
Сильно бýдет сéмя на землé, и свéрх всегó,
Слáвен и богáт весь дóм,
Прáвда вéчна в нéм самóм.

16. The uneven stanza may have from four to ten verses and may use uneven measures freely.

SECTION 2. REPRESENTING THE IAMBIC STANZA

17. *Four-line stanza*

Простéр десницу; пожралá
Земля́ в свой протѝвных нéдра;
И укрепила прáвда бéдра,
И всéх людéй тобóй спаслá.

18. *Five-line stanza*

Их из Содóма виногрáд,
И от Гомóрры всé их рóзги;
Их грóзд éсть тóкмо жéлчь и смрáд,
Их я́года горькá стократ;
Сóк отравля́ет шýмны мóзги.

19. *Six-line stanza*

Затéм премýдр, чтоб не хвалился
Отню́дь в премýдрости своéй;
Ни сильный тáкже в силе всéй;
Богáт в богáтстве б не гордился:
Но всéм бы Бóга знáть и чтить,
И в прáвде сýд земны́м творить.

20. *Seven-line stanza*

Пред ним предъѝдет в слóве смéрть,
Изъѝдет на поля́ понóсно;
Падéт под нóги та некóснó,
Как предприймет óну стéрть:
Он стáл, и вся́ земля́ трясéтся;
Подвѝглась и высóка твéрдь;
Язы́ки тáют, вéсть несéтся.

21. *Eight-line stanza*

О! Гóсподи, и Бóже нáш:
Мы мнóго от чужи́х терпéли;
Едвá в госпóсд не возъимéли.
Но мóлим, Ты́ нам бу́ди стрáж;
Твоя́ над нáми влáсть и вóля:
Кроме Тебя́ мы никогó,
Не знаéм рáвно ничегó;
В Твоéм нам и́мени есть дóля.

22. *Nine-line stanza*

Вся высотá по мнé прешлá;
Вся глубинá меня́ прия́ла;
Вся и широ́кость обошлá;
Отвéрста мрáков бéздна стáла;
Всегó покры́ли гóры вóд.
Шу́м тóков оглуши́л ужáсный;
Всему́ яви́лся ви́д зол влáсный,
И влáжный прóпастей испóд.
О! Кóль тогдá я бы́л злочáсный.

23. *Ten-line stanza*

Явля́ющии лю́то злáя,
О! Гóсподи, твои́м рабáм,
Да постыдя́тся здéсь, гонзáя
В поги́бель сáми по судьбáм:
Да вся́кая б своя́ их си́ла,
И крéпость слóмлена срами́ла:
Да знáют, что еди́н Ты Бóг
Что по вселéной всéй Ты слáвен,
И тóкмо Ты́ еди́н держáвен;
С тобóй несмéнен вся́к прилóг.

24. *Uneven stanza*

Он сáм истóргнуть нáс от Áда днéсь суди́л;
   Он спáс от сáмыя нас смéрти;
От пéщаго огня́ соблю́сть благоговéл:
   И злы́м не попусти́л нас стéрти;
Он блáг, к нему́ все воззовéм,
Да в благости́не пожевéм.
Егó поéм мы человéки,
И слáвно величаéм ввéки.

25. What was said in Section 1, #16, of this chapter about the uneven trochaic stanzas must be understood to pertain to these iambic ones as well

SECTION 3. PRESENTING THE SAPPHIC AND HORATIAN STANZAS

26. The Sapphic stanza has been named after its inventor, Sappho of Greece.

27. It usually has four lines of verse. Of these the first three are Sapphic and the fourth Adonic.

28. Our masculine Sapphic stanza may consist of a trochee or a pyrrhic foot in the first as well as in the second position. In the third position it may begin with the first long syllable of a dactyl which terminates the word and also forms the caesura. The dactyl is then completed by the first two syllables of the following word. In the fourth position there may be a trochee or a pyrrhic foot, and in the fifth, a long syllable which also forms the masculine rhyme. These lines are paired. The feminine is composed in the first four positions like the masculine; however, in the fifth position it always has a trochaic foot. There must be only one such verse line in the stanza, the third, and it must be rhymed with the fourth two-foot Adonic line which, according to our quantity of syllables, must always consist of a dactyl and a trochee.

Example

```
    1        2        3      4      5
Со́весть/ кто́ в се/бе́// непо/ро́чну/ ве́сть
Нра́вов/ чисто/та́// завсег/да́ в ком/ е́сть
Небо/и́тся/ то́т// охуж/де́н про/па́сти
```

```
                              1       2
                        Бо́др и в на/па́сти²⁷
```

29. The Sapphic stanza may consist of five Sapphic lines and one Adonic, of seven Sapphic and one Adonic, and, finally, of nine Sapphic and one Adonic. However, it seems best if it is always made up of four or six lines. Incidentally, Seneca the tragedian, in the chorus of Thyestes, third act, has added one Adonic line to 125 Sapphic lines.

30. The Horatian stanza consists always and under all circumstances of four tetrameters of the mixed kind. It is called Horatian because Horace used it often in his odes.

31. Our composition of this stanza is as follows. The first and the second verse have in both the first and second positions a trochee or

a pyrrhic foot; then follows a long syllable which is the caesura and is not counted in the number of feet. In the third and fourth positions there are dactyls, of which the last is the common [dactylic] rhyme. The third verse line consists of feminine iambic tetrameter, but the fourth has in the first two positions a dactyl and in the third a trochee or a pyrrhic foot. In the fourth position it always has a trochaic foot.

Example

```
    1      2       3        4
Кéдры/ не всег/дá// вúхрем ло/мáются
Листá/ не в весь/ гóд// рóщи ли/шáются
      1      2      3       4
    И вéд/ро по/сле тýч/ бывá/ет
      1      2       3       4
    В вéсну и/ дéрево/ процве/тáет
```

32. An example of why our Horatian stanza must have such a composition is given in the preface to Barclay's *Argenis*, 22.[28]

Chapter VI. On Rhyme and Poetic License in the Use of Words
SECTION 1. ON RHYME

1. Rhyme is mutual consonance of sounds at the end of two lines of verse.

2. When in the second line this mutual consonance consists of the same letters as in the preceding line, then such a rhyme is called rich but if it only has similar sounds, and does not consist of the same letters, it is called semi-rich.

3. In feminine verse lines the rhyme is always bisyllabic, and it forms a perfect trochee, but in the masculine it is monosyllabic and constitutes either the beginning of a trochee or the end of an iamb. In the old verse only the feminine rhyme was used because the Polish language always stresses all words, except monosyllabic ones, on the penultimate syllable.[29]

4. It may be added that rhyme is not essential to verse, and is only a marginal embellishment, used to sweeten its sound. It was invented in barbaric times and introduced into poetry. Neither the ancient Greeks nor the Romans have ever used it in their poetry; they did not know it, although these nations had reached the very pinnacle of eloquence and versification.[30]

5. In Polish versification, which we have previously also employed, rhyme is called "cadence," but quite incorrectly. Cadence is the smoothness of a verse line, spreading out through the whole line, from beginning to the end. This comes first of all from the alignment of feet, also from a felicitous choice of vowels and consonants which do not clash among themselves nor produce an awkward hiatus, and from skillful composition. The hexameter of Horace is dignified but not smooth, that of Ovid both tender and smooth, but that of Virgil is smooth, tender, and dignified.

6. In general one should always subordinate the use of rhyme to meaning, that is, in composing verse one should care more for clarity of thought than for rich rhyme; and if it is impossible to have both at the same time, then solid meaning must never, under any circumstances, be neglected for the sake of a rich rhyme.

SECTION 2. ON POETIC LICENSE IN THE USE OF WORDS
Poetic license is a slight change in words which have been established by usage.

7. Poets are usally bolder and freer in the selection of syllables, and sometimes, for the sake of measure, use in verse such words as would never be tolerated in prose. This right is confirmed by many centuries, but nevertheless, poets, too, must be moderate in exercising it.

8. We have also exercised poetic license on numerous occasions. Those who are interested can see the use of poetic license in published verse.[31]

9. Poetic license, in general, must be used so that a word thus freely used can be readily recognized as a true word, and also, in such a way that this word can be found in general usage, rather than being something clumsy, strange, and barbaric.

Chapter VII. On Different Poetic Works Composed in Verse[32]
1. *Epic poetry*, otherwise called epopoeic and heroic, is the highest genre of poetry. Indeed, no other kind of poetry can, as yet, bring so much glory to writers. It alone, if it is properly composed, suffices to bring great fame forever to the poet and to the whole nation to which the poet belongs. It presents with verisimilitude well-known deeds of famous men who have undertaken to carry out something in order to

arouse love of virtue. Its examples are: Homer's *Iliad* and *Odyssey* and Virgil's *Aeneid*.

2. *Lyrical*. This, too, is a high genre of poetic art, but not so difficult as to prevent some from climbing this Helicon Hill. Many have experimented in this genre and have won laurels. It seems to have its beginnings in the inventions of the priesthood for the honor and glory of the Supreme Being, and it also seems that shepherds' songs may have originated it. Another name for it is the ode, consisting of stanzas and singing of the highest, most virtuous, and also sometimes tender matters.

3. *Dramatic*. This includes tragedy and comedy. In these the ancient Greeks, who subsequently achieved true perfection, reached their summit. The Romans were successful in comedy, but less so in tragedy. Among the nations of today, the French have greatly distinguished themselves in tragedy and comedy. Drama in general is described as follows: it is poetry which presents in the theatre, through words and actions in imitation of nature itself, and for the improvement of mores, some deed of famous men, undertaken and carried out at one time and in one place, arousing fear and pity (and this is tragedy), and sometimes of simple people (and this is comedy), causing laughter and entertainment among the spectators.

4. *Bucolic*. It represents various conversations of shepherds and country dwellers. It seems to be the oldest genre of poetry.[33] Its personages are: shepherds, harvesters, hay mowers, gardeners, vegetable growers, fishermen, and gatherers of grapes, fruit, and similar things. The subject matter: the affairs of these people, their misfortunes, complaints, labors, sorrows, arguments, songs, conversations, praises, and condemnations. The objects are: forests, sheep, cattle, beasts, fruit, the beauty of open fields, shades under shrubbery, grottoes, the flowing of rivers, springs, and rivulets, and love; also sun, moon, and stars, and everything that is best known to these people and that surrounds them. Bucolic poetry is represented by Virgil in his eclogues and by Theocritus in his idylls.

5. *Elegiac*. It is often maintained that through the tenderness and sweetness of this kind of poetry many will record their names in eternity, and many have done so already. An excellent example of such poetry is the work of Tibullus, Propertius, and Ovid. It describes in particular matters causing tears and lovers' complaints.

The elegy is divided into the threnodic and the erotic. The threnodic describes sorrow and misfortune, and the erotic, love and all that follows from love. Its form should not be similar to that of the eclogue: it raises its voice, albeit without audacity, but somewhat higher.

6. *Epigrammatic*. This form is just as difficult as it is pleasant and beautiful, and so, some are bold enough to assert that in this genre even the most excellent poets only very rarely did not meet with difficulties because of its brevity and nobility and pithy ending, for it is a short poem producing a subtle and sharp-witted conclusion from a brief proposition. It deals with the same matters as does poetry as a whole. Everything that is grasped by the external senses and inner thought can be considered the substance of epigrams. Martial among the ancients became famous for epigrams, and was called by one of the Caesars a Virgil of his own kind. To this genre belong all inscriptions, epitaphs, French madrigals, and sonnets.

7. *Didactic*. It sets forth certain precepts and prescribes rules having to do with natural, moral, and artistic matters. In this form Empedocles described Pythagorean physics; Lucretius wrote about the nature of things from the Epicurean point of view; Virgil wrote four books, called heroic, about agriculture; Horace, his teaching on poetry, and after him, in French, Boileau-Despréaux, whose work I have now translated into our language, also in verse.

8. *Satirical*. Satire corrects human failings in a pleasing and mocking manner. Its subjects are naught but fools, idlers, rogues, spendthrifts, mischief makers, and other such. Satire must be hot, biting, and prickly. Boileau says that the desire to show oneself and not the desire for false vituperation invented satire. It was first put into use among the Romans by Lucilius. Horace, Persius, and Juvenal are famous for it in Latin, and Boileau-Despréaux, in French.

9. *Epistolary*. The epistle expresses in verse and in a poetic spirit and manner everything that is written in missives in prose by those not present to others not present. There are didactic epistles, love epistles, and epistles morally elevating and panegyrical. To this genre belong both hexameters and poetry written in stanzas. As an example one may take Horace and Ovid in Latin and Boileau in French.

10. *Genethliac*. It is a poem greeting the birth of some person, or someone's birthday. The subject matter of this kind of verse is joy at

the birth, praise of the family, the circumstances of time and place, and the signs that preceded and followed the birth. It is concluded with a wish or with a well-turned remark, or with greetings to the parents. Examples: Virgil, eclogue 4; Propertius, 3, elegy 10; Statius, *Silvae*, 2, 7. It may be composed in hexameters and in stanzas.

11. *Epithalamic*. It is a congratulatory poem on a marriage. The subject matter of such poems is the circumstances of the wedding, ancient and new customs, praise of the bride and groom, laudatory epithets, and sincere wishes. Also joy and good cheer. Examples: Catullus, 1, 56; Statius, *Silvae*, 1, 2; Claudianus on the marriage of Honorius. This type is both heroic and lyric.

12. *Apobateric*. In this genre of poetry those going away take their leave of those remaining. Its subject matter: the cause and the means of departure, sorrow and regret because of parting, best wishes to those remaining, and other things proper to a parting. Examples: Ovid, *Tristia*, elegy 3. Such poems can also be lyrical.

13. *Epibateric*. A poem by which those who have returned from a journey express their thanks to a deity and greet their fatherland and friends. Its subject matter: joy over the return and over the meeting with true friends, as well as other similar circumstances. I have not come across an example of it. It may be composed in hexameters and in stanzas.

14. *Propemptic*. By this type of poem those who are seeing off travelers express their best wishes. Subject matter of this type: landscape surrounding the road, observation of the winds and signs of weather, and sincere assurances of friendship. Examples: Horace, 1, ode 3; Tibullus, elegy 3; Statius, Book 1, poem 2.[34]

15. *Syncharetic* (*Eucharetic*). Another name for this type of poetry is *euphemic*. By this poem one greets those who have returned to their fatherland or else guests that have arrived. Examples: Claudianus on Honorius' return. This poem can also be composed in stanzas.

16. *Epinician*. A solemn poem with which poets greet the conqueror of enemies. Examples of this: Ovid, *Ex Ponto*, 2, elegy 1. There are also lyric poems of this type.

17. *Soteric*. A poem expressing greetings upon the deliverance from a severe illness. Example: Statius, Book 1, poem 4. It is also composed in stanzas.

18. *Epideictic* or *panegyric*. Noble benefactors and glorious deeds

are praised with this poem. Almost the whole work of Claudianus represents an example of it. It is both heroic and lyrical.

19. *Eucharistetic.* A poem bringing gratitude for a good deed. Examples: Virgil, eclogue 1; Horace, Book 1, odes 10, 21, 26, 36; Book 3, odes 3, 22, and Book 4, ode 9. This poem exists in the lyrical as well as in the heroic style.

20. *Aeonic.* With these poems, after the turn of each century, we narrate and describe notable events which have taken place during all this time, express our gratitude to God, our Protector, and praise our defenders and benefactors. Examples of this poem: Horace, *Epodes*, the last ode; Catullus, Book 1, poem 33. Such poems are lyrical as well as heroic.

21. *Skoliac* or *symposiastic.* A great banquet is described, exalted, and glorified by this poem. I have not happened to see a verse example of it anywhere, except in the writings of Horace and Boileau-Despréaux. It can be either lyrical or heroic.

22. *Proseuchetic.* A poem by which we either ask something of God or make some vows to him, or ask something from most exalted persons. It can be composed either in hexameters or in stanzas. An example of it is in Sarbievius,[35] Book 20, all of which is well worth reading.

23. *Apologetic.* This is a story told by beasts or inanimate creatures talking among themselves for the sake of correcting human mores and for the rooting out and destruction of immoral customs. Examples of these poems can be found in Phaedrus, who composed Aesopian fables in iambic senarii. In our language these fables can be composed in all kinds of verse lines, but it seems that it is not entirely unfitting to compose them in stanzas.

24. *Parnasus, Phoebus, Muses: Their Names and Duties* (Translated, from the hexameters of Ausonius in tetrameters).

Клиа точны бытия
В память предает поя
Мелпомена восклицает,
И в Трагедии рыдает.
Талиа, да будешь прав:
Осмехает в людях нрав.
Пажить, равро жатву серпа,
Во свирель гласит **Эвтерпа**

Гуслей **Терпсихора** звук
Соглашает разный вдрук.
Эрата смычком, ногами,
Скачет также и стихами
Урания звезд предел
Знает свойство и раздел.
Каллиапа всех трубою
Чтит Героев всезлатою.
Упражняясь наконец
В преклонении сердец
Полигимния нарядно,
И, вещает все, изрядно.
Движет превыспренный **Ум**
Муз сих, купно оных шум:
Посредине **Феб** сам внемлет,
А собою все объемлет.

CONCLUSION

25. This guide, short as it may be, is, in my opinion, entirely sufficient to explain the whole procedure of composing our verse, because it is complete. Nothing pertaining to this has been omitted; everything is presented and explained in the clearest possible manner. Every informed reader can see that this method of composing our verse is the same as was published in 1735, but amended and supplemented. There has been a rumor for some time that [supposedly] the lovers of our versification are complaining about it, in particular, because it is explained in such a way that they do not know whom to follow and on what to base their work. It may be that they complain about the inconsistency of our present versification because in our regular and essential verse lines they now see, in addition to trochees, also the iambic feet, while my method written at that time presented only the trochee. They also see alternation of verse lines, while the first method hardly mentioned it at all, except by name, and in actuality used it only in songs; they see, finally, feet in all the short verse lines which did not exist in such lines according to that other method of mine. I admit sincerely that in all this my method written at that time was insufficient, which is why in the present one all these shortcomings are corrected by means of emendation and supplementation. However, let those interested not think that this method differs from the first

one, since it is based on the very same tonic quantity of syllables which is the soul and life of our whole versification.[36] Whether one actually uses a trochee, an iamb, a dactyl, or an anapest, in all these verse feet that syllable is long on which the stress falls. Let the iamb be preferred, for some are favorably disposed to it; however, the iamb, too, is established in all our present verses on my quantity of syllables, as can be seen in works of versification now published, and as is proposed by this method. True, this whole method is composed in different words (except for the technical terms) and in a different order, but the foundation is still the same, and therefore it itself is the same, only, I repeat, amended and supplemented. I think that everyone is allowed to review his work, supplement it, amend it, and present it to the public in perfected form.

VI

Concluding Remarks

THE BASIC premises of the theory of versification elaborated by Trediakovskij and Lomonosov remained unchallenged throughout the eighteenth and nineteenth centuries, although in poetic practice there were numerous and significant deviations from and contributions to it. An extensive reconsideration of metrical theory came only in the early years of the twentieth century. At that time, attention was directed, among many other matters, to the varying intensities of stress, to the interrelation between word stress and intonational or phraseological stress; careful studies were made of the actual distribution of accents in traditional iambic or trochaic lines for the purpose of discovering a rhythmic reality which was not adequately described by traditional, and obsolete, notions like that of the substitution of pyrrhic feet for iambs and trochees.

In the survey that follows we will not concern ourselves with these new developments in the twentieth century, for in their great complexity and importance they go far beyond the framework of our topic. Our discussion of nineteenth-century versification must also remain very limited, for the changes that occurred then were in essence preliminary developments preparatory to the new verse structures of the twentieth century and can therefore be most profitably analyzed in that context.

Consequently, what follows is no more than a brief general description of the evolution of the syllabo-tonic system as it was reflected in the actual versification practice of the eighteenth and, to some extent, the nineteenth century.

128

In the most rudimentary outline, the Russian syllabo-tonic theory, as it emerges from the treatises of the reformers, adapted the terminology describing Greek and Latin metrics to a language having no quantitative oppositions, but possessing a strong accentual stress (with some secondary lengthening of the stressed vowel). In the system developed by Trediakovskij and Lomonosov, verse lines were divided into feet, a foot consisting of a syllable bearing, at least potentially, the word stress and one (in binary feet) or two (in trinary feet) unstressed syllables. While Trediakovskij preferred feminine rhyme, Lomonosov was the first to advocate the use of masculine and dactylic rhymes in addition to the feminine, allowing a certain systematic variation of all three kinds of rhyme within a single poem or stanza.

The reason for the extended success of the syllabo-tonic system in Russia, and the concomittant decline of the earlier syllabic system must be sought in the relationship between the theoretical norms of the new system and the living Russian language.

In the actual composition of poetry, Russian poets had to learn to organize their native language into the new metrical patterns. Here the properties of the Russian language exercised their influence, and therefore the real development of the metrics of written poetry could be only an approximation of the theoretical norm. Indeed, as soon as the reform of versification was established, another "reform" began which realized a compromise between the theoretical rules and linguistic reality.

The key factor in the tension between the syllabo-tonic rules and the realities of the Russian language is the ratio, close to 2:1, of unaccented to accented syllables as against a theoretical 1:1 ratio in binary meters Trediakovskij was willing to take this into account, allowing, in his terminology, the substitution of pyrrhic feet for iambs and trochees, but Lomonosov initally regarded pyrrhic feet as an "imperfection" to be avoided; while recognizing that pure iambic verse lines were "rather difficult to compose," he nevertheless attempted to write in pure or nearly pure iambics at the beginning.[1] Eventually he recognized that his "slips of the pen," unintended pyrrhic feet in his iambs, reflecting an important characteristic of the Russian language, did not destroy the rhythmic pattern; in his later poetry he used pyrrhic feet consciously and freely.

This step taken by Lomonosov is in a sense characteristic of the later developments of Russian metrics, for many of the subsequent changes in the structure of syllabo-tonic verse originated from experiments with the omission of stresses and even of syllables from verse feet.

Another important factor in the formation of the actual structure of Russian verse was the choice made by Russian poets among the various meters available in the syllabo-tonic system. Lomonosov, even though he advocated in his treatise the use of a wide variety of meters, wrote mostly in iambics and won fame with his solemn odes written in iambic tetrameters. This meter came to dominate the odic genre in the eighteenth century. Odes in four-foot iambics were written by Nikolaj Popovskij (c.1730–1760), the most immediate disciple of Lomonosov's literary work; by Jakov Knjažnin (1742–91), by Mixail Xeraskov (1733–1807), and by other poets. Even Sumarokov, although he did not like to consider himself Lomonosov's pupil and on one occasion said that he "wrote verses at a time when the public had not yet heard Lomonosov's name,"[2] composed most of his odes in iambic tetrameter. Another example of the genre was Aleksandr Radiščev's (1749–1802) famous ode, *Vol'nost* (Freedom), written in 1781–83, traditional in terms of metrics, if highly unorthodox in content.

Not all the odes were written in the meter established by Lomonosov. Some poets, for instance Vasilij Petrov (1736–99) sometimes used iambics with a variable number of feet per line,[3] and Trediakovskij and Sumarokov wrote odes in trochaic tetrameters, Nevertheless, four-foot iambics were clearly the dominant meter in the ode.

Another iambic meter which became popular in the eighteenth century was the hexameter. One of the earliest examples of this meter in Russian poetry was a translation by Lomonosov of an ode by one of the German members of the Russian Academy, Wilhelm Junker, written to celebrate the coronation of Empress Elizabeth in 1742. Both the German original and the Russian translation are in iambic hexameter. Mixail Xeraskov in his article "Rassuždenie o rosiijskom stixotvorstve" (A discussion of Russian versification), written in 1772, said: "The translation made by Lomonosov in 1742 of G. F. Junker's verse on the coronation of Empress Elizabeth taught us how to create true iambic verse."[4] Thus the name of Lomonosov again emerges as that of the forerunner of the most important verse forms in the eighteenth century.

Russian poets considered iambic hexameter as the Russian equivalent of the French alexandrine; it was, however, actually derived from German adaptations of this French meter, syllabic by nature. Like the French alexandrine, the Russian hexameter was used in epic poetry and in tragedy. Lomonosov wrote his tragedies and his unfinished epic *Petr Velikij* (Peter the Great; 1760–61) in iambic hexameters, and Sumarokov followed this example in his tragedies. Tragedies and heroic epics in iambic hexameters were written later in the century by Xeraskov, Knjažnin, and others. In the last third of the eighteenth century this meter spread also to mock heroic epics, such as the *Elisej ili razdražennyj Bax* (Elisej or exasperated Bacchus; 1771), by Vasilij Majkov (1728–78).

The iambic hexameter was also the dominant "background" meter for another form of verse which became widespread late in the eighteenth century—the "free iambics" (*vol'nyj jamb*), i.e. iambic verse with lines of varying length. This form, bringing verse closer to the intonations of colloquial speech, was especially characteristic of the fable. A similar form existed in French poetry and was developed to a high degree of perfection in the fables of La Fontaine. French verse, however, being syllabic, could not serve as a perfect model for the Russians who were working in the context of the syllabo-tonic verse.

The Russian free iambics, abandoning the equal number of feet per line, destroyed the structural balance of the syllabo-tonic system, with the result that other elements had to be used to establish a new balance.[5] One such compensation was that enjambement disappeared almost completely from the free iambics; varying in length, the lines could easily be made to coincide with syntactic units. The line came to be a unit of thought, an intonational unit, rather than a metrical one.

One may also observe a change in the function of the rhyme in free iambics. In regular syllabo-tonic verse the rhyme is rhythmically constant, occurring at regular intervals. In free verse its occurrence is irregular, since the lines vary in length. The effect of the rhyme is therefore one of "surprise" and of emphasis on the rhyming word.

Sumarokov wrote a number of fables in free iambics, but the fable as a genre having free iambic meter as its instrument found its fullest development in Russian poetry in the works of Ivan Andreevič Krylov (1769–1844).

The use of the free iambic verse spread from fables to other genres, notably the mock heroic *Dušen'ka* by Ippolit Bogdanovič (1743–1803), completed in 1775, as well as, with Deržavin, to lyrical verse. Aleksandr Griboedov (1795–1829) used free iambics with remarkable effectiveness in his famous comedy, *Gore ot uma* (Woe from wit; 1824). Although in free iambic verse the lines could be of any length, one finds a marked predominance of six- and five-foot lines. In Griboedov's comedy, forty-four percent of the lines are in iambic hexameter.[6] Iambics did not dominate Russian poetry to the exclusion of other kinds of meter. One may expecially note the work of Sumarokov, who was generally inclined to experiment with the new syllabo-tonic metrics. He wrote some odes in trochaic tetrameters[7] and also used trinary meters, mostly in light verse or in poems which did not have a strictly canonized form, such as the spiritual odes.[8] He also introduced the amphibrach into Russian verse, justifying this step by the peculiar argument that there should be five kinds of verse feet because human beings have five senses.[9]

Gavriil Deržavin (1743–1816), Russia's greatest eighteenth-century poet, was also one of the boldest experimenters in verse forms and genres. Early in his career he attempted to imitate Lomonosov's solemn odes in style and in metrics; but later he wrote odes in trochaic tetrameters, as Sumarokov had done before him, or even mixed binary and trinary meters, including also the free iambics, within a single poem. In general, however, Deržavin's experiments in versification did not initiate a new school or movement and, while greatly admired, he remained in his own time an isolated figure.

More immediate influence on Russian versification was exerted by sentimentalist-preromantic poets, such as Nikolaj Karamzin (1766–1826) and, in particular, Vasilij Žukovskij, (1783–1852). Karamzin was very familiar with Western European poetry of the early romantic period; he knew Klopstock and Macpherson's *Ossian*. Much of his poetry is of a bucolic, contemplative nature which was alien to the spirit of Russian classicism. He also departed from the earlier tradition in metrics in that he often composed his verse in dactyls and trochees, rather than in iambics. He experimented with the then unusual unrhymed verse.

Žukovskij, often called "the father of Russian romanticism," is best remembered for his translations or adaptations of Gray, Byron, Southey, Schiller, Uhland, Wieland, Goethe,[10] and other English and

German poets. Žukovskij often adapted the verse structure of his models, thus introducing new elements into the Russian syllabo-tonic tradition. He was especially precise in reproducing the great variety of stanzaic structures found in the originals, many of which were not previously known to Russian poetry.

On the other hand, Žukovskij hesitated to introduce meters which were unorthodox in Russian poetry, such as the German and English ballad meter.[11] In general, the omission of stresses, so common in Russian binary meters, was practically nonexistent in the trinary meters.[12]

Žukovskij also popularized blank verse through his translations of dramatic works, such as Schiller's *Die Jungfrau von Orleans*, rendered in the unrhymed iambic pentameters of the original. Finally, Žukovskij contributed much to the return of the trochee as a meter worthy of serious Russian poetry; after Trediakovskij's attempt to introduce his "heroic" line, trochees had been used mainly for light verse, except for a few odes by Sumarokov and Deržavin.

Toward the end of the eighteenth century, iambic hexameter declined as the meter of heroic narrative poetry. This Russian alexandrine began to seem monotonous and inadequate for works of epic dimensions.[13] In searching for a new metrical form, attention was drawn to the dactylic-trochaic hexameters which Trediakovskij had already used in his *Tilemaxida*—an adaptation in verse of Fénelon's *Les Aventures de Télémaque*. Trediakovskij's epic poem was never appreciated and was soon forgotten. Later, however, in 1790, in his famous *Putešestvie iz Peterburga v Moskvu* (Journey from St. Petersburg to Moscow), Radiščev alluded to the meter used by Trediakovskij: "I would like Homer to appear among us not in iambics, but in verse like his own, in hexameters."[14] Somewhat later, about 1801, further half-serious, half-mocking comments on Trediakovskij's work and his hexameters followed, entitled *Pamjat' daktiloxoreičeskomu vitjazju* (Tribute to the dactylic-trochaic hero). In this Radiščev defended Trediakovskij's pioneering efforts in this meter. Karamzin and other Russian poets of the time expressed their interest in reviving the dactylic-trochaic hexameter. Here again German poetry, especially Klopstock's *Messias* and his theoretical article, *Vom deutschen Hexameter*,[15] served as an important stimulus for the new interest in the ancient meter.

This renewal of interest in the hexameter soon brought rich fruit through the efforts of Nikolaj Gnedič (1784–1833), who translated the *Iliad* (published in 1829), and of Žukovskij, who followed with his translation of the *Odyssey* (1823–42). Both translations used the dactylic-trochaic hexameter, and both achieved unsurpassed excellence as Russian poetry in this meter. Gnedič's verse contains a fairly large number of trochaic feet substituted for dactyls, whereas Žukovskij's translation is almost entirely in regular six-foot dactyls.[16] It should be mentioned, however, that Žukovskij wrote several folk tales in the hexameter, using so many trochaic substitutions that the effect is almost one of "rhythmical prose." Quite possibly Žukovskij sought to approach the tonic meter of the Russian folk epics, thus bringing the ancient Greek measure and the Russian folk rhythm closer together.

The achievements of the preromantic and romantic poets, especially Žukovskij, prepared Russian poetry for the next, very creative and original stage of development which reached its peak in the work of Aleksandr Pushkin (1799–1837), the greatest Russian poet of the nineteenth century and perhaps of all time. Much of Pushkin's poetry is in iambic tetrameters; in this respect it worked a return to classicism and to the tradition that began with Lomonosov. This "conservatism," however, was a renewal and a continuation of a tradition. "The basic trait of his work," said B. Tomaševskij, "is that he knew how to be original while he was continuing the tradition."[17] Thus, in iambic tetrameter he developed the famous "Onegin stanza," used with great effect in his "novel in verse," *Eugene Onegin*, a complex sonnet-like stanza consisting of three quatrains with three different rhyme patterns and a couplet. Turning from the formal definition of meter to the actual distribution of accent, one may note that in his iambic tetrameter, Pushkin's distribution of stress differs considerably from that of Lomonosov.[18]

Pushkin and other poets of his time used the iambic tetrameter not only in narrative poetry, but also in other genres, so that for a time this meter again dominated Russian versification. A smaller proportion of Pushkin's poetry is in six- and five-foot iambics, in trochaic tetrameters, and in other meters. While Pushkin was quite conservative in the use of syllabo-tonic meters, he made some bold experiments in imitating the tonic meters of folk verse.

Some of Pushkin's contemporaries showed a much greater interest in experimentation with verse forms than Pushkin himself did. Mixail Lermontov (1814–41) frequently used trinary meters, thus reducing the hegemony of the iambic tetrameter. Lermontov often experimented with unusual rhythmic effects. In some of his poems various rhythmic devices—intonational emphasis, caesura, etc.—are used in such a way that a rhythm is created which is independnet of the theoretical meter.[19]

Other poets of the nineteenth century, for instance, Evgenij Baratynskij (1800–44) or Fedor Tjutčev (1803–73), tended to continue and expand individual experimentation with syllabo-tonic metrics, aiming at greater flexibility and expressiveness. They used mostly bisyllabic feet, but the alternation of stressed and unstressed syllables was frequently disrupted. Later in the century, the trinary meters were given a prominent place, notably in the poetry of Nikolaj Nekrasov (1821–77) who also wrote imitations of folk verse. Afanasij Fet (1820–92) often used trinary meters and experimented with a variety of stanzaic structures.

On the whole, however, the main body of poetry written during the nineteenth century adhered to the syllabo-tonic rules. It was only in the twentieth century that the various departures from the established metrics led to the development of new principles of versification.

Much attention was given throughout the nineteenth century to the metrics of folk verse. In very general terms, the attempts of the early theoreticians to apply the concepts of classical metrics to oral poetry were followed by efforts to define the rhythmic structure of oral poetry in its own terms, as a system substantially different from that of the metrics of written or "learned" verse. While the scholars were investigating the metrics in Russian oral poetry, the poets were writing a good deal of verse in which the folk themes, language, imagery, and the rhythmic structure were quite successfully imitated.[20] This activity engaged the attention of many of the major poets of the late eighteenth and nineteenth centuries, such as Karamzin, Žukovskij, and later Pushkin, Lermontov, and Nekrasov. Other poets, especially Aleksej Kol'cov (1809–42), achieved their greatest fame as imitators of folk verse. They were particularly successful in short and long trochaic lines, for example, the so-called *kamarinskij* verse. An important and influential source of folk verse was the collection of old Russian epics and songs by Kirša Danilov (first published in 1804).

NOTES

NOTES TO I: INTRODUCTION

1. According to P. M. Štokmar, *Issledovanija v oblasti russkogo narodnogo stixosloženija*, p. 45, the term "syllabo-tonic" was invented by a Russian critic, N. Nadeždin, in the nineteenth century. Other Russian authors have sometimes used different terms. For instance, V. N. Peretc, a noted nineteenth-century Russian authority on versification, called it the "metro-tonic" system. In English, too, this system is not always called "syllabo-tonic"; Boris Unbegaun calls it "syllabo-accentual."

2. For a concise description of the Russian syllabo-tonic system see Boris Unbegaun, *Russian Versification*, pp. 11–14.

3. See Zizanij's rules of versification in Richard Burgi, *A History of the Russian Hexameter*, pp. 18–19.

4. For more details on the life and work of Maxim the Greek in Russia, see N. K. Gudzy, *History of Early Russian Literature*, Susan Wilbur Jones, tr. (New York, 1949), pp. 326 ff., and D. Čizevskij, *History of Russian Literature from the Eleventh Century to the Baroque* ('S-Gravenhage, 1960), pp. 291–300.

5. Burgi, pp. 20–21.

6. See *ibid.*, chapter 2, for traces of Zizanij's and Smotrickij's systems in Russian poetry of the time. Especially interesting is the discovery by V. N. Peretc, mentioned by Burgi on p. 28, of a number of "religious verses composed entirely in accordance with Smotrickij's rules."

7. See Unbegaun, pp. 1 ff.

8. Ad. Stender-Peterson, ed., *Anthology of Old Russian Literature*, p. 339.

9. On Polonization in these countries, see E. Karskij, *Geschichte der weissrussischen Volksdichtung und Literatur*.

10. Jan Trzykadłowski, "Rytmotwórcza funkcja akcentu w wierszu staropolskim," introduction to Karol Wiktor Zawodziński, *Studja z wersyfikacji polskiej*, pp. xxvi–xlvii.

11. See Maria Dłuska, *Studia z historii i teorii wersyfikacji polskiej*, I, 216 ff.

12. *Ibid.*, p. 206.

13. Manfred Kridl, ed., *An Anthology of Polish Literature*, p. 25.

14. See I. P. Eremin, "Simeon Polockij—poet i dramaturg," in Simeon Polockij, *Izbrannye sočinenija* (Moscow–Leningrad, 1953), p. 240.

15. D. Blagoj, *Istorija russkoj literatury XVIII veka*, 2d ed., p. 4.

16. Petr Pekarskij, *Istorija Imperatorskoj Akademii Nauk v Peterburge*, II, 4.

17. In his short autobiographical sketch, written in 1754, Trediakovskij speaks of his poverty and dependence upon Russian diplomatic representatives abroad for material survival. See A. Kunik, ed., *Sbornik materialov dlja istorii Imperatorskoj Akademii Nauk v XVIII, veke*, I, xiii–xiv. Trediakovskij's old alma mater, the Slavo-Greco-Latin Academy, refused him any help when he turned to it in 1727, accusing him of leaving the school without permission and even of obtaining a false passport for this purpose (Pekarskij, p. 7).

18. This feeling is noticeable in Trediakovskij's *Lettre d'un Russien à un de ses amis sur la nouvelle versification Russe*, written in 1736. It is available in Russian translation in Trediakovskij, *Stixotvorenija*, pp. 354–57. The speech Trediakovskij delivered on the opening of the Assembly also reflects such feelings. See *Sočinenija Trediakovskogo*, I, 266–67.

19. Trediakovskij defended his views fiercely but unsuccessfully, reacting to Lomonosov's letter with a long, involved letter of refutation. This letter was never sent to Lomonosov, and was subsequently lost. See *Sočinenija M. V. Lomonosova*, ed. A. Suxomlinov, III (St. Petersburg, 1895), *Primečanija*, pp. 4–5.

20. For Trediakovskij's own account of this incident, see *Sočinenija Trediakovskogo*, I, 796–801.

21. This particular argument was submitted to the reading public for judgment. Each author wrote his own version, a paraphrase in verse of Psalm 143. Lomonosov and Sumarokov wrote in iambs, and Trediakovskij, in trochees. *Sočinenija M. V. Lomonosova*, III, *Primečanija*, pp. 220, 237.

22. Pekarskij, pp. 183, 195–97.

23. A number of Trediakovskij's homes and lodgings burned down; the fires occurred in 1738, 1747, and 1794.

24. Pekarskij, appendix VI, pp. 250–57.

25. *Ibid.*, pp. 208–9.

26. For a discussion of Trediakovskij's skill in using the Russian hexameter, see Burgi, pp. 31–68.

27. V. K. Trediakovskij, "Mnenie o načale poezii i stixov voobšče," *Sočinenija Trediakovskogo*, I, 194 note.

28. "O drevnem, srednem i novom stixosloženii rossijskom," *ibid.*, p. 739.

29. A. F. Hilferding, *Onežskie byliny*, St. Petersburg, 1873.

30. A. X. Vostokov, *Opyt or russkom stixosloženii.*

31. P. D. Goloxvastov, *Zakony stixa russkogo narodnogo i našego literaturnogo.*

32. Kiril Taranovski, *Ruski dvodelni ritmovi*, See esp. pp. 49–58, 356, and 369.

33. Roman Jakobson, "Studies in Comparative Slavic Metrics," *Oxford Slavonic Papers*, III (1952), 21–26, and "The Kernel of Comparative Slavic Literature, "*Harvard Slavic Studies*, I (1953), 1–71.

34. Quoted by L. I. Timofeev, *Očerki teorii istorii russkogo stixa*, p. 316.

35. Two copies of the play have recently been found—one in Vologda, Russia, and another in Lyons, France. The title of the French publication is: *La Comédie d'Artaxerxès (Artakserksovo dejstvo) présentée en 1672 au Tsar Alexis par Gregorii le Pasteur.* Texte allemand et texte russe, publiés par André Mazon et Frédéric Cocron (Paris, 1954); that of the Russian edition: *Artakserksovo dejstvo. Pervaja p'esa russkogo teatra XVII v.*, ed. with an introduction by I. M. Kudrjavcev (Moscow–Leningrad, 1957).

36. Burgi, p. 35.

37. Paus, "Praxis pietatis Melica," manuscript No. 1.16.7.20, Biblioteka Akademii Nauk, Leningrad.

38. See V. N. Peretc, *Iz istorii razvitija russkoj poezii XVIII veka*, p. 284.

39. See B. Tomaševskij, *Stilistika i stixosloženie*, p. 326.

40. L. V. Pumpjanskij, "Trediakovskij," *Istorija russkoj literatury*, Vol. III, *Literatura XVIII veka*, Part One, p. 224.

41. Kunik, p. xix.

42. L. I. Timofeev, "Sillabičeskji stix," *Ars Poetica*, II (1928), 37–71.

43. *Ibid.*, pp. 67–68.

44. A. V. Pozdneev in a recent study, "Die tonischen Elemente im russischen syllabischen Vers," *Zeitschrift für slavische Philologie*, XXVIII no. 2, (1960), 405–12, indicates that studies of song collections in manuscripts of the seventeenth and eighteenth centuries show a rather high incidence of regular stress distribution in various types of verse, including the syllabic. However, as Pozdneev himself acknowledges, the theory of syllabo-tonic versification as such was developed in Russia by Trediakovskij and Lomonosov.

45. Cf. this statement by Martin Opitz: "Nachmals ist auch ein jeder verss entweder ein iambicus oder trochaicus; nicht zwar das wir auff art der griechen un lateiner eine gewisse grösse der sylben können inn acht nehmen; sondern das wir aus den accenten onnd dem thone erkennen, welche sylbe hoch onnd welche niedrig gesetzt soll werden," *Buch von der deutschen Poeterey*, p. 40.

46. Tomaševskij, "Problema stixotvornogo ritma," *Literaturnaja mysl'*, II (1923), 5–6.

47. See Taranovski, *Ruski dvodelni ritmovi*, p. 50.

48. V. Trediakovskij, "O drevnem, srednem i novom stixosloženii rossijskom," *Ežemesjačnye sočinenija k pol'ze i uveseleniju služaščie*, June (1755), p. 497.

49. *Ibid.*, p. 498. Some scholars (I. Timofeev, I. Rozanov) think that this booklet was a collection of poems by the Serbian poet Iv. Gundulić (1588–1638). These poems show a clear trochaic tendency, but since they were written in octosyllabic lines they would not be directly relevant to Trediakovskij's choice of regular trochees in his heroic 13-syllable line.

50. Tomaševskij, *Teorija literatury, Poetika*, 6th ed., p. 99.

51. For a brief but lucid description of this area and its special position, see B. N. Menšutkin, *Russia's Lomonosov*, Jeanette Eyre Thal and Edward J. Webster, tr., pp. 7–11.

52. See Pekarskij, pp. 308–11.

53. An example is Lomonosov's much-praised translation from the French of the Italian opera *Clemenza di Tito*, which played at the court and had political overtones flattering to the new empress, Elizabeth. *Ibid.*, p. 323.

54. Lomonosov wrote solemn odes on such occasions as the visits of foreign dignitaries to Russia, the birthdays of royal personages, and the coronation of Empress Elizabeth (1742). He also translated Psalms and ancient authors: Homer, Virgil, Anacreon, Ovid, Seneca, etc. On occasion he wrote poems encouraging scientific and industrial endeavor, for instance, his letter to Šuvalov on the advantages of glass (1752). He also wrote tragedies: *Tamira and Selim* (1750) and *Demofont* (1752). Of his lyrics, the best-known are the "Morning and Evening Meditations on the Greatness of God" (1743).

55. See Grigorij Gukovskij, *Russkaja poezija XVIII veka*, pp. 19 ff.

56. Menšutkin, p. 137.

57. See P. N. Berkov, *Lomonosov i literaturnaja polemika ego vremeni, 1750–1765*, p. 54.

58. Some attempts have been made to relate Lomonosov's ideas on versification to the metrics of Russian folklore. See Hilferding, p. xlvii, and P. N. Berkov, "Lomonosov i fol'klor," *Lomonosov, Sbornik statej i materialov*, II, 107–29.

59. E. Ja. Dan'ko, "Iz neizdannyx materialov o Lomonosove," *XVIII vek*, II (1940), 248–75, provides detailed references to various German authors from which Lomonosov had apparently borrowed his specific ideas. Gottsched's *Versuch einer kritischen Dichkunst* (Leipzig, 1730) and *Ausfürhliche Redekunst* (Leipzig, 1736) contributed much not only to Lomonosov's ideas on versification but also to his monumental works on rhetoric, written in 1744 and 1748.

60. *Aug. Ludwig Schlötzer's Öffentliches und privat-Leben von ihm selbst beschrieben* (1802), p. 218; quoted in A. Suxomlinov, ed. *Sočinenija M. V. Lomonosova*, Vol. I, *Primečanija*, p. 58.

61. For Suxomlinov's analysis of such similarities see *ibid.*, pp. 41 ff.

62. *Ibid.*, pp. 11–13.

63. Tobias Huebner, *Poetisches Handbuch* (1742), p. 272; quoted by Dan'ko, p. 272.

64. Timofeev, *Očerki teorii i istorii russkogo stixa*, p. 315, mentions that in the first odes of Lomonosov (four-foot iambs) there are 70.5 percent pure iambics and the remaining 29 percent have only three stresses per line. His trochees (also four-foot) are 32 percent pure, 55 percent with three stresses per line, and 13 percent with only two stresses.

65. Gottsched, *Versuch einer kritischen Dichtkunst*, p. 390; quoted in Dan'ko, p. 268.

66. The originator of this theory seems to have been Kantemir's friend and biographer, Abbé Gouasco, whose book *Satyres du Prince Cantemir, Traduites du Russe en François; avec L'histoire de Sa Vie* (London, 1749 and 1750), served as the starting point and main source for most subsequent biographies of Kantemir.

67. *Ibid.* (1750), p. i.

68. See L. V. Pumpjanskij, "Očerki po literature pervoj poloviny XVIII veka," *XVIII vek*, I (1935), 83–85.

69. Soviet biographers, for instance, F. Ja. Prijma in his introduction to Antiox Kantemir, *Sobranie stixotvorenij* (2d ed.), p. 6, say that long-standing friendly relations between the Moldavians and the Russians, as well as the desire of Demetrius Kantemir to liberate his Christian country from Turkish rule, were the main reasons for his defection to the Russian side. However, other sources, such as Marcelle Ehrhard, *Un Ambassadeur de Russie à la Cour de Louis XV. Le Prince Cantemir à Paris* 1738–1744), p. 15, indicate that various double-dealings of the Turkish rulers with respect to the taxation of Kantemir's estate, etc., also contributed to this decision.

70. *Ibid.*, pp. 16–21.

71. M. I. Radovskij *Antiox Kantemir i peterburgskaja Akademija Nauk*, p. 17, mentions that a document has been preserved from which it can be seen that Kantemir was one of the very first students at the newly established Academy. He seems to have been there between 1724 and 1725 (see Prijma, pp. 7–8). Gouasco, p. xij, even reports that Kantemir was elected Member of the Academy; "l'élut bientôt por un de ses membres, dans l'espérance de l'avoir un jour pour son chef."

72. Prijma, p. 9.

73. Soviet scholars (for instance, D. Blagoj) always emphasize the frustration suffered by Kantemir because he could not have his satires printed during his lifetime, supposedly due to their timely and dangerous political content. Actually, the small Russian reading public of the time did know his works, which were circulated in manuscript copies. The quick, favorable reaction of Feofan Prokopovič to Kantemir's first satire demonstrates that manuscript copies did get around.

74. Ehrhard, p. 23.

75. Demetrius Kantemir had asked Peter I to give the Kantemir estates to his most deserving son; the decision as to which of Demetrius' sons deserved the inheritance was to be made by Peter I himself. But soon after the death of Demetrius, Peter I himself died without having made his decision, and so Konstantin, the eldest son of Demetrius, took possession of the estates, although his father seems actually to have favored Antiox. See Gouasco, pp. xix–xxvj; Ehrhard, p. 23; and Prijma, p. 15.

76. This appointment may have actually been a form of "honorary exile"; Anna Ioannovna's gratitude to Kantemir was not especially profound, since she did not like his barbed political satires. However, there is also reason to believe (see Erhhard, p. 26) that Kantemir was happy with his appointment.

77. Gouasco, p. xlvij, says: "Sa maison étoit le rendezvous des savants, attirés par sa réputation et par l'accueil gracieux qu'il leur faisait." The "savants," at least according to Pumpjanskij ("Očerki po literature," p. 89), were somewhat behind the times, for they remained in the comfortable afterglow of the Italian Renaissance instead of keeping abreast of new social and political movements in Europe. This point is also made by Professor Aleksandrenko in his introduction to L. N. Majkov, *Materialy dlja biografii kn. A. D. Kantemira*, p. vi.

78. Prijma, p. 20.

79. Ehrhard, p. 30.

80. At this time Kantemir probably met Gouasco, who was also in Paris in 1738. For a description of Gouasco's background and personality, see R. J. Morda Evans, "Antioch Kantemir and His First Biographer and Translator," *The Slavonic and East European Review*, XXXVII (No. 88, December, 1958), 186–87. Mr. Morda Evans raises doubts that Gouasco was actually the translator of Kantemir's satires, pointing out the probability that the life of the poet and the translations of his satires were as much the work of Heinrich I. Gross, Kantemir's protegé in Paris and his successor as the minister to France, as that of Gouasco.

81. Ehrhard, p. 26.

82. For a description of Kantemir's relations with Montesquieu, see M. P. Alekseev, "Montesk'e i Kantemir," *Vestnik Leningradskogo Universiteta*, No. 8 (1955), and also Prijma, p. 22.

83. Kantemir's illness seems also to have contributed to his longing to escape the stormy political life and to retire to an "ivory tower" existence, although it is doubtful that he would have found it in the Academy of Sciences.

84. Ehrhard, p. 188. It seems that Kantemir had thought of becoming the president of the Academy as early as 1731 (Prijma, p. 15).

85. Gouasco, p. lv.

86. Concerning the time and the circumstances of Kantemir's contact with Trediakovskij's "Method" of 1735, see introductory remarks to Kantemir's "Letter," pp. 78–79.

87. Trediakovskij took advantage of this statement of Kantemir at a much later date to imply that the latter was, in effect, a dilettante:

As for the most recent of our versification systems, which appeared in 1744 and has been formulated by a certain person, even though the author with his praiseworthy ratiocinations showed the great incisiveness of his inventive power to the learned Russian society, nevertheless, if one were to eliminate from his system all the unnecessary circumlocutions, side-steppings, and distortions, then everyone would see that it leads straight to nothing but the middle [syllabic] versification, that is, versified prose. The author himself reveals on how strong a ground he stands at the end of ≠ 63 by saying: "If anyone asks me the reason for all this, I cannot show anything except that my ear advises me to take these precautions."

Trediakovskij, "O drevnem, srednem i novom stixosloženii rossijskom," *Ežemesjačnye sočinenija*, pp. 509–10.

In a way, this remark sounds like a sort of "revenge," for Kantemir, in the introduction to his "Letter," praised Trediakovskij with a grain of irony for his sharp-wittedness and zeal but not for his accomplishment.

88. S. M. Bondi, "Trediakovskij, Lomonosov, Sumarokov," introduction to Trediakovskij, *Stixotvorenija*, p. 100.

89. *Cf.* Boris Unbegaun, pp. 6–7:

Polish syllabic verse, made up of words whose accents fall on the penultimate syllable, inclined to the trochaic rhythm. Kantemir, in trying to introduce a pattern of more regular rhythm in syllabic verse, finished, as could have been expected, by emphasizing still further its trochaic cadence. From this stage it was but a short step to a pure trochaic line, excluding the stress from even syllables. This step was taken within Kantemir's lifetime by his contemporary Vasily Trediakovsky.

90. Pumpjanskij, "Očerki po literature pervoj poloviny XVIII

veka," pp. 87–88, even professes to see a whole school of "neo-syllabic" verse which followed the Italian pattern, and he includes Kantemir and Feofan Propokovič among the members of that school. However, he cites no evidence to show that there was indeed an "Italian school" of Russian syllabic poets.

91. See Tomaševskij, *Teorija literatury*, p. 85.

92. Blagoj, *Istorija russkoj literatury*, p. 122.

93. See Timofeev, *Očerki teorii i istorii russkogo stixa*, p. 290.

94. This continued development in the practice of Russian poets is also noted by Alexander Adamczyk, "Russische Verskunst, ein geschichtlicher Überblick," *Münchener Beiträge zur Slavenkunde*, IV (1953). See especially p. 180, where Adamczyk points out that Trediakovskij's reform did not really amount to any revolution in Russian versification.

95. It has been noted by many scholars that Trediakovskij's heroic line was not in actuality a hexameter. For instance, C. L. Drage, "Trochaic Meters in Early Russian Syllabo-Tonic Poetry," *The Slavonic and East European Review*, XXXVII (No. 91, June, 1960), 364, states:

Care is needed in the interpretation of Trediakovskij's list of trochaic lines. It appears to be a list from dimeter to hexameter; but in fact only the three shortest of the lines which he gives are the lines as ordinarily understood. His "trochaic pentameter" and "trochaic hexameter" are both, as he terms them, hypercatalectic. This ought to mean that they are longer than the normal line by one short syllable. But he says expressly that the extra syllable is a long one. Since this syllable must constitute an extra foot, this means that his "trochaic pentameters" and "trochaic hexameters" are really hexameters and heptameters, respectively.

96. K. Taranovski, pp. 47–48, notes that the only form in which Trediakovskij's 13-syllable line continued to exist in Russian poetry is a four-foot trochee, resulting from making two lines out of Trediakovskij's two hemistichs: As an example, Taranovski quotes the following lines from Aleksej Tolstoy:

Колокóльчики мой,
Цвéтики степнне

97 *Sočinenija Trediakovskogo*, I, 329–30.

98. Cf. Tomaševskij, *Russkoe stixosloženie. Metrika*, p. 48.

99. For a very thorough analysis of Trediakovskij's hexameters see Burgi, chapter III.

100. Trediakovskij, "K čitatelju," *Sočinenija Trediakovskogo*, I, xxiii–xxiv.

101. *Ibid.*, II, xlvii–xlviii.

102. Trediakovskij, "O drevnem, srednem i novom stixosloženii rossijskom," p. 125.

103. Tomaševskij, "Problema stixotvornogo ritma," *Literaturnaja mysl'*, p. 125.

NOTES TO II: TREDIAKOVSKIJ'S METHOD OF 1735

1. The Russian translation reads: "Stixotvorčestvu nas Bog tokmo naučaet/ i svjatoj oxotu v nas plamennu raždaet." Much later Trediakovskij translated the same Latin lines once more, in his preface to *Tilemaxida*, and this time kept much closer to the original. The Russian of the second translation is: "Est' Bog v nas; ego sotrjaseniem my plameneem/ Semja svjaščena uma imeet stremlennost' sija" (There is a God in us; He sends us the shock that sets us on fire/ And this striving has in it the sacred seeds of mind). *Sočinenija Trediakovskogo*, II, vii.

2. After the publication of this treatise there was some response from the young poets of the time. Sumarokov, then still a student in the Cadet Corps, wrote some congratulatory verses to the empress in 1740 in Trediakovskij's thirteen-syllable "trochaic hexameter" (Kunik, p. xxi). In 1739 Trediakovskij was requested to comment upon the value of an ode written by Vytynskij, a professor at the Xar'kov Academy, which was written according to the new system. The most important follower of Trediakovskij seems to have been the poet Mixail Sobakin, who in 1738 wrote a poem of birthday greetings to Empress Anna Ioannovna in Trediakovskij's heroic verse (see P. N. Berkov, "U istokov dvorjanskoj literatury XVIII veka. Poet Mixail Sobakin," *Literaturnoe nasledstvo*, No. 9–10 (1933), pp. 421–32).

Also, one of the earliest works of Lomonosov—a translation of an ode by Fénelon in four-foot trochees, done in 1738—shows clear traces of Trediakovskij's influence both in the meter and in the use of "poetic license" as explained by Trediakovskij in this treatise (see *Sočinenija Lomonosova*, Vol. I, *Primečanija*, pp. 12–13).

3. Yet when Lomonosov presumed to "correct and supplement" Trediakovskij's treatise in his letter on Russian versification Trediakovskij replied with a long defense of his own treatise. A comment by A. Kunik on Trediakovskij's letter to Lomonosov (which is now lost) indicates how strongly Trediakovskij felt about his new method. (The letter was written immediately after the cruel beating Trediakovskij had suffered at the hands of Minister Volynskij.)

Reading [Trediakovskij's] report about the beating administered to him and knowing that the Academician Duvernois was barely able to prevent a gangrene in his wounds, one cannot help but believe that the patient was seriously preparing to die. In this case, the letter of Trediakovskij to Lomonosov, sent by him on the next day, that is, February 11, to the Chancellery of the Academy to be forwarded to Freiberg, deserves special attention. Trediakovskij, on his deathbed, wanted to defend his greatest intellectual accomplishment from the attacks of other persons who only as a consequence of his "Method" had begun to understand clearly the form of Russian verse. (Kunik, p. xlvii)

Later in his life Trediakovskij repeatedly insisted that the new "tonic" Russian versification had been introduced by him in 1735.

4. Peretc (*Iz istorii russkoj pesni*, pp. 53–54) points out that almost all the old Latin textbooks of poetics used in Russia at the end of the seventeenth and the beginning of the eighteenth century started with a definition of the subject matter in poetry and of the means of presenting it (in verse), as, for instance, in the following passage from *Triumphus Poeseos:* "Materia poeseos res omnes tam verae quam fictae; quia de omnibus rebus tam veris quam fictis poesis potest versibus formare." Trediakovskij continued to hold to the clear distinction between versification and poetry. For instance, in his article "Opinion on the Beginning of Poetry and Verse in General, "written in 1755, he states: "That which is depicted with paint is something entirely different from the paint itself; in the same way poetry is certainly not verse. Verse is similar to paint, and poetry to that which has been depicted with it" (*Sočinenija Trediakovskogo*, I, 181). This attitude differs from that of most of Trediakovskij's contemporaries, who differentiated between poetry and prose, but less clearly between poetry and versification. Thus, while Trediakovskij regarded both Barclay's *Argenis* and

Fénelon's *Télémaque* as poems "in prose," Lomonosov described them as "tales" or "stories": "an extensive description of some action which contains examples and teachings on politics and morals [is called] a 'tale' (povest'); such are Barclay's *Argenis* and Fénelon's *Télémaque*" (Lomonosov, "Kratkoe rukovodstvo k krasnorečiju," 1748, in *Sočinenija M. V. Lomonosova*, III, 207).

One might also point out that at the end of his "New and Brief Method" Trediakovskij included the French "romances," one of which he mistakenly thought to be Barclay's *Argenis*, among the examples of epic poetry, even though they were written in prose.

5. The word *jazyki* used by Trediakovskij means "languages," but also "nations" in the ethnic rather than political sense.

6. The reference here is to Smotrickij's grammar, in which the rules on quantitative Russian versification were elaborated. The reasons why Smotrickij's system became known as "Maximian prosody" may be that Smotrickij included in his grammar many excerpts from the works of Maxim the Greek together with his own passages without identifying himself as the author of the latter. For a detailed discussion of this problem, see P. M. Štokmar, *Bibliografija rabot po stixosloženiju*, pp. 177–82. As Štokmar also observes, Trediakovskij here does not actually attribute this grammar to Maxim the Greek; he may have realized that the sections on versification were the work of Meletij Smotrickij. (See also p. 3.)

7. Trediakovskij is referring here to a passage in Horace's *Epistles*, II, 1:

> Si foret in terris, rideret Democritus, sen
> Diversum confusa genus panthera camelo.

Trediakovskij's attitude toward "Maximian prosody" points up the fact that he was actually the first Russian theorist of versification to devise rules for practical use rather than for a theoretical understanding of versification in general, as Smotrickij did. The 1721 edition of Smotrickij's grammar actually contains a note to the effect that the intent of the rules on versification was to acquaint students with classical (Greek and Latin) versification. (See Peretc, *Iz istorii russkoj pesni*, p. 21.)

8. The reference is to syllabic verse such as that composed by Antiox Kantemir and Feofan Prokopovič.

9. The Russian term translated here as "verse line" is *stix*, from the Greek *stichos*. The Latin term *versus* signified a recurring pattern of lines, as distinguished from prose, which went "straight on." (See William Beare, *Latin Verse and European Song*, p. 20.)

10. B. Tomaševskij (*Stilistika i stixosloženie*, p. 316) comments on Trediakovskij's use of the word "letters" and points out that the term denoted "what we would call 'phonemes' but the concept of phoneme was lacking in the eighteenth century, and instead of it there was the concept of 'letter' in which the sound and the symbol denoting that sound were confused."

11. It is possible that Trediakovskij understood the term "foot" not in the present meaning of a unit of scansion consisting of a certain number of syllables with one stress in some fixed position within that unit but, as it was sometimes in France, simply as a "unit of two syllables." As Tomaševskij points out, "In this sense the term 'foot' (*pied*) was preserved in French literature until the nineteenth century, and even now one may hear the definition of the twelve-syllable alexandrine as a 'vers de six pieds' " ("Problema stixotvornogo ritma," p. 5). This explains why Trediakovskij permitted only bisyllabic feet in 1735. The three-syllable "foot" was not given recognition by French theorists.

12. The Russian term *polstišie* is a loan translation from Greek, like the French *hémistiche*.

13. The Russian term is *presečenie*, "cutting off." In modern Russian terminology this word has been replaced by the word *cezura*.

14. Trediakovskij must have been aware that in normal prose speech some monosyllabic words, enclitics and proclitics, remained unstressed, but he apparently chose to ignore this fact. Very likely, his insistence that all monosyllabic words must be counted "long" indicates that he still basically adhered to the syllabic style of declamation in solemn poetry, with each syllable of a verse line fully articulated, whether stressed or not; Lomonosov, on the other hand, took normal speech into account when devising his rules with respect to monosyllabic words. (See Lomonosov's "Letter," p. 72.)

Even later, when Trediakovskij did recognize the need to take the accentuation of normal speech into consideration in verse, he was willing to do so only on condition that "short" monosyllabic words be described as "poetic license." The system of hyphens which

Trediakovskij introduced later to indicate enclitics and proclitics—the monosyllabic words that are counted short—was perhaps really an attempt to surround this "disorder" with special rules, to give it formal status; he had already accounted for omissions of stress in strong positions by means of the formal admission of pyrrhic feet into Russian versification.

15. Here Trediakovskij is alluding to the advantages of his "tonic" system over the quantitative Russian metrics devised by Zizanij and Smotrickij. For one thing, Greek and Latin were dead languages, and it was hard to decide with assurance which syllables in these languages were actually pronounced long. For another, in transplanting the principle of syllabic length into Russian versification one was forced to be completely arbitrary, so that quantitative metrics could not help but be conjectural and twice removed from the original system. Trediakovskij, on the other hand, was basing his system on the Russian of his day.

It may be noted that, if Trediakovskij makes a sharp distinction here between the qualitative and the tonic principles, elsewhere he expresses the thought that Greek length was associated with pitch. In his 1752 introduction to the paraphrase of Psalm 143, which he translated in trochees in competition with Lomonosov and Sumarokov, Trediakovskij states (*Sočinenija Trediakovskogo*, II, 331):

In spite of the fact that their quantity of syllables is not tonic but measured in time, that is, consisting in either a slow or a rapid pronunciation, their length and brevity, distributed in time, cannot possibly do without the heightening and lowering of voice (pitch) in the organization of a line.

Incidentally, Trediakovskij's assertion that the whole strength of his system consisted in this "tonic length and brevity" of syllables evoked a sardonic comment from Sumarokov:

I do not know of a shorter method to become a poet than by learning to read and to recognize what a foot is; this science is the easiest of all and demands only that one write and give what one has written to the printers. This new and brief method has already been adopted to some extent.

("K nesmyslennym stixotvorcam," quoted in Berkov, *Lomonosov i literaturnaja polemika ego vremeni*, p. 247.)

16. Lomonosov in his letter on versification (see p. 73) insisted that pyrrhic feet should not be allowed in iambic lines, and one finds very few "accidental" pyrrhic feet in his early verse; but later he abandoned

his stand and used pyrrhic feet freely. Sumarokov, like Trediakovskij, seems to have seen from the very beginning that some pyrrhic feet would have to be tolerated in Russian verse:

The examples of pyrrhic feet are quite numerous, and the fewer of them there are, especially at the caesura, the purer is the verse. But the very beauty of a verse work sometimes demands them; thus it is better to keep a beautiful verse with a pyrrhic foot at the caesura than to weaken its meaning and feeling.

(Sumarokov, *o stoposloženii*, quoted in Taranovski, *Ruski dvodelni ritmovi*, p. 35.)

However, in Sumarokov's poetry the pyrrhic feet sometimes occur at the caesura, which Trediakovskij insisted should always be masculine, and Trediakovskij attacked him for having pyrrhic feet in this position, particularly in his tragedies:

A great many of his iambic hexameters are faulty in their construction because they do not mark the caesura with an iamb . . . . Of the many hexameters written by the author in *Xorev, Hamlet,* and the *Epistles* without an iambic caesura, the following from *Xorev,* and others like these, are faulty in their construction:

Отéц твой вóинством// вéсь гóрод окружáет . . .
Щедрóта пóздняя// разгнéванных небéс . . .
Смешéнна с кáзнию// и лютою напáстью . . .
Хотя и нéкую// чáсть вóльности имéю . . .

(Trediakovskij, "Pis'mo v kotorom soderžitsja rassuždenie o stixotvorenii, ponyne na svet izdannom ot avtora dvux od, dvux tragedij i dvux epistol, pisannoe ot prijatelja k prijatelju, 1740, v Peterburge," in *Stixotvorenija,* p. 389.)

Trediakovskij is speaking here of Sumarokov's iambics (by 1750 he had already accepted this meter as suitable for heroic verse), but the same exclusion of pyrrhic feet at the caesura applied, in Trediakovskij's view, to his heroic 13-syllable line, where the seventh—caesura—syllable had to be long.

17. The Russian word *rifma* (rhyme) is connected with the word rhythm and with the concept of number (of arithmetic). Trediakovskij points out here that rhyme is not related to "numbers," as rhythm was called in Latin and Greek, but to like-sounding endings only (cf. Tomaševskij, *Stilistika i stixosloženie,* p. 316). Later, in the preface to the 1752 edition of his works, he himself pointed out the incorrect

usage of the Russian term *rifma:* "[The classical hexameter] does not at all allow in its final position *consonance* with the next line which we now incorrectly call rhyme (*rifma*), that is, number, according to the Greeks, instead of the correct term homoeoteleuton (similar ending)." (*Sočinenija Trediakovskogo*, I, xliv)

18. The Russian term, *perenos*, means literally "carrying over." In present-day Russian usage the French term *enjambement* is often used. One will note that Trediakovskij calls the enjambement a "defect"; in his new system the integrity of a verse line was of paramount importance. Enjambement which covers only a part of the second line tends to blur the boundary between lines. As Tomaševskij points out, "In condemning the enjambement—the 'carrying over' of the sense in the terminology of Trediakovskij—he gave a definite expression to the demand that phrase units should coincide with metrical units." ("Problema stixotvornogo ritma," *Literatunaja mysl'*, p. 18). When the enjambement is carried to the end of the next line, there is at least a distich as a recognizable metrical unit, and Trediakovskij does not object to this (Rule VI). Incidentally, the Polish school texts on versification also allowed enjambement if it remained within the confines of a distich (see Peretc, *Iz istorii razvitija russkoj pesni*, p. 59).

19. This is another instance of Trediakovskij's treating phonetics in terms of "letters." He is considering the contact between the final *j* of an adjectival ending, in his example *každyj* with the initial *i* of the following word *imeet*. Normally, an initial *i* is not iotized in Russian. The pronunciation *ji* of the initial *i* does occur, however, although it is not standard. Trediakovskij obviously regarded this pronunciation as standard; hence *každyj jimeet*. To avoid a geminated *j*, Trediakovskij prescribes the elision of the first *j*: *každy jimeet*.

20. In his dislike of the iamb, Trediakovskij is in sharp disagreement with Lomonosov, who praised this meter in his "Letter" (see p. 75) and used it for all his odes. Some scholars were puzzled that Trediakovskij, having such a low opinion of iambic feet, allowed them at all. Bondi ("Trediakovskij, Lomonosov, Sumarokov," *Trediakovskij, stixotvorenija*, p. 95, note) offers the following tentative explanation.

If the pyrrhic foot and even the spondee do not violate the trochaic pattern of the verse, then the iambs would undoubtedly be a dissonance in them. How to explain their admittance in the new verse? Probably an important role was played here by the pedantry of the inventor. Having "discovered" feet he, apparently, wanted to have *all* types of bisyllabic feet represented in his "hexameter" and "pentameter." . . . Another consideration is also possible. The point is that in Trediakiovskij's "hexameter" the variation of the rhythm with the iamb *in some cases* does not sound so bad at all, expecially in the second hemistich.

A much more important point, however, is that Trediakovskij does not set up a rigidly exclusive system but merely proposes a hierarchy of feet from good to middling to poor.

21. In conforming to the tradition of the earlier Russian poets who wrote in syllabic verse, Trediakovskij clearly indicated that his reform was not intended to change the basic syllabic principle, but merely to organize it better by introducing further tonal constants; in this he differed considerably from Lomonosov and from his own revised treatise (1752), even if he did not admit this change in his thinking.

22. Trediakovskij has revised this line (from Kantemir's satire entitled "*Na xuljaščix učenie*" or "*K umu svoemu*" to make it conform to the meter of his 13-syllable heroic line. He discusses the changes made and the reasons for them later in the present treatise.

23. Trediakovskij insists that the caesura is necessary in order to regain one's breath after the first seven syllables. In this connection Lomonosov observed in his letter on versification that human breath is not that weak, and no one would run out of breath on the thirteenth syllable when speaking the lines in a normal voice. But Trediakovskij apparently had in mind here and elsewhere in this treatise that "art of reading verse" in which the French, Arabs, and Turks were supposedly so proficient. If we remember that for Trediakovskij a verse is "sung," that is, recited in a special manner, separating each syllable clearly, we may conceive that Trediakovskij had in mind a declamation in which the rising pitch at the caesura syllable played a central role. Trediakovskij may also have based his statement on a literal interpretation of what Ronsard called "repos ou reprise d'haleine" in French versification terminology.

24. Trediakovskij probably allows the caesura to separate a noun from the two adjectives qualifying it because the two adjectives are enough to form a "center of gravity" of their own, establishing the second hemistich as a separate and complete rhythmical unit of this line.

25. Kantemir took quite the opposite position with respect to elision (see "Letter of Xariton Makentin," ≠ 23, p. 86), maintaining that such an elision contributes to a smoothness in the flow of voice.

26. In indicating "syllable length" in Kantemir's line Trediakovskij is quite consistent with his doctrine that all monosyllabic words must be "long," i.e. stressed. The word *tol'*, while it usually has no stress in the line, can be stressed; thus Trediakovskij marks it "long," obtaining a spondee in the first foot. Lomonosov thought otherwise on this point (see his "Letter," p. 71).

27. The term "bandura players" was a barb aimed at the Ukrainian poets who wrote in syllabic verse (a bandura is a Ukrainian musical instrument). At the time when the Ukrainian and South Russian poetry was spreading its influence among Great Russians, it had acquired secular content, sometimes of fairly frivolous nature, which would explain Trediakovskij's term "songsters." These secular songs and poems in syllabic verse had become rather popular among the Great Russians. For a detailed discussion of this development see Peretc, *Iz razvitija russkoj pesni*, chapter V. Since many of the instructors at the Slavo-Greco-Latin Academy, which Trediakovskij attended, were of Ukrainian or Belorussian origin, Trediakovskij was familiar with this type of poetry. He referred to it quite interestingly in the preface to his translation of Tallemant's *Voyage à l'ile d'amour*, published in 1730:

It may turn out that you will not be satisfied with the sense of my verse [*virši*]. Therefore I beg you to accept kindly at least the rhyming [*rifmy*— Trediakovskij seems here to be using this term more in the sense of "versification"], since this is the true Russian verse, on which point I refer you to all the versifiers of the *Spasskij Bridge* [the location of the Academy], even though they cannot be of much use to me with their testimony concerning the measure of feet, quantity of syllables, the caesura, and the type of verse, because they do not consider these rules in expounding their argumentations and, to speak the truth, perhaps do not even know them.

(Trediakovskij, *Stixotvorenija*, p. 325)

Trediakovskij translated the songs in the *Voyage* into syllabic verse with short lines and often a quite regular distribution of stress.

28. In the letter to Stählin, written in 1736, Trediakovskij provided the following translation of the Russian lines given in this example:

L'or est plus précieux que l'argent, la vertu surpasse l'or.
Rien n'est égal á elle; et la souveraine c'est Dieu même.

(Pekarskij, p. 56)

29. Trediakovskij takes up an extensive discussion of short lines later on in the treatise, where he says that he would have included the discussion in its proper place, but the pages where it should have been inserted were already at the printer's. Since Trediakovskij now turns to poetic license and rhyme, one may surmise that the "proper place" for the discussion of short lines would have been right after he had finished discussing the meter of the long lines and of the Sapphic stanza.

30. The Russian form *dovol'nyj* is a "long" (attributive) adjective, nominative singular. *Dovol'ny*, on the other hand, is normally the nominative plural of the same adjective in its "short" (predicative) form. Therefore it is clear how a careless use of this "poetic license" could result in a confusion between nominative plural and singular.

31. In paragraphs I to IX Trediakovskij lists under the common term "poetic license" not only arbitrarily distorted (truncated or abbreviated) forms, but also forms that were actually used either in Church Slavonic or Old Russian, or in regional speech.

Such forms as *piš́eš́i* (paragraph I), *bud'*, *bolš'* (paragraph, III), or the vocatives in paragraph VIII are actually obsolete Church Slavonic or Old Russian forms and thus could not be described strictly as poetic license. *Mja*, *tja* (paragraph II) are old short Church Slavonic enclitics. The form *meždu* (paragraph III) is Church Slavonic, but it has been accepted in common usage with the result that the actual Russian form *mež* produces an archaic impression and has been listed by Trediakovskij as "poetic license." The vocatives *Bože* and *Gospodi* are used interchangeably with *Bog* and *Gospod'* even now; the same is true of the old instrumental forms such as *soveršennoju pravdoju* (paragraph V)—these occur in poetry and sometimes in formal speech, while the "abbreviated" instrumental *soveršennoj pravdoj* is now standard.

On the other hand, Trediakovskij includes here some truly arbitrary changes of form for the sake of meter or for some other reasons. Among these are *sčinjaju* (paragraph VII) instead of *sočinjaju* and *o vosklicani* (paragraph V), instead of *o vosklicanii*, etc.

32. Trediakovskij quotes here "fixed epithets" which occur frequently in Russian oral tradition. It is indicative of the general attitude

of the time toward folk poetry that he limits their use in written poetry to unimportant and facetious verse. Lomonosov made a marginal note at this place on his own copy of Trediakovskij's treatise, supplying another such fixed epithet: *kalena dubrava*. See Berkov, "Lomonosov i fol'klor," p. 108.

33. The direct object of a negative verb in Russian generally takes the genitive case instead of the accusative in a positive statement. Trediakovskij regards as an extreme poetic license, to be avoided if at all possible, the use of the accusative with negative verbs. In his two examples:

(1) *Vody* is the subject, *ne gasjat* the predicate, and *plamen'* the direct object; the latter is modified by *serdečnyj*. In the accusative form the phrase *plamen' serdečnyj* fits into Trediakovskij's metrical scheme:

Воды пламень не гасят// ваши тем сердечный

x́ x x́ x x́ x x́// x́ x x́ x x́ x

The genitive *plamenja serdečnogo*, with its two additional syllables, disrupts the meter.

(2) In the second example, with the negative predicate *ne možno*, the object is the infinitive *syskat'* with its own object, *vnutrennij pokoj;* this is the accusative form; the genitive, *vnutrennego pokoja*, would violate the meter. In modern usage the use of the accusative with negative verbs is perfectly permissible; in the early nineteenth century Pushkin expressed his preference for the accusative in constructions of the type illustrated in Trediakovskij's second example.

34. As P. N. Berkov (*Lomonosov i literaturnaja polemika ego vremeni*, p. 28) points out, *z* [for *iz*] *glubiny duši*, also *meju* [for *imeju*] *sposob*, are Ukrainianisms, brought into Russian verse during the time of Ukrainian and South Russian influence. Trediakovskij's objections to them were directed toward the elimination of Ukrainianisms from Russian literary language. *Bregu* or *stregu* are Church Slavonic nonpleophonic forms. Trediakovskij does not permit *ostrožno* because this is a Polish word.

35. Trediakovskij is considering two, actually unrelated, matters here and taking a strong stand on both: he is against the abolition of grammatical rhymes which are, indeed, plentiful in Russian, and he insists on the phonetic, not orthographic, nature of the rhyme. This

latter view, it may be noted, was expressed by French Authorities as early as the seventeenth century. See, e.g., quotation from Claude Lancelot in Grammont, *Le Vers Français*, p. 347:

Lancelot disait déjà au milieu du XVII siècle: "La rime n'est pas autre chose qu'un même son et non pas mémes lettres. Car la rime n'étant que pour l'oreille et non pour les yeux on n'y regarde que le son et non l'écriture: ainsi *constans* et *temps* riment très bien."

36. Trediakovskij's insistence on the immutability of the 13- and 11-syllable lines clearly indicates that he was attempting not so much to devise an entirely new system of metrics as merely to organize the stress pattern within the existing syllabic lines. Trediakovskij has nothing to say in support of his view other than to refer to tradition.

37. Here again Trediakovskij remains within the syllabic system by refusing to admit any other rhyme except the feminine for serious poetry.

38. In his copy of Trediakovskij's treatise, Lomonosov made a rather ungracious marginal remark on this passage: "This is true, because it passes through the innards."

39. Kantemir expressed an opinion on folk verse in a commentary to his translation of Horace's first epistle to Augustus (Book 2):

For their amusement those coarse shepherds and farmers used to exchange insults in verse and thus were the initiators of versification. It is not hard to judge how coarse was this verse produced by the elemental movement of nature in the peasants deprived of all art and without any forethought. We ourselves have much verse of this type which is the invention of our simple people and from which we may form judgments about the earliest Roman verse.

(*Sobranie stixotvorenij, p.* 496)

Kantemir then goes on to quote a few lines from a Russian historical song. Thus Kantemir and Trediakovskij agreed that folk verse was coarse. Kantemir, however, did not show any interest in its metrics, whereas Trediakovskij, having "discovered" verse feet in folk poetry, declared that the prosody of folk poetry was the source of his new system.

40. Trediakovskij's references here to "our most ancient native poetry, that of the plain folk" as the main source of his own "new hexameter and pentameter" are not very specific. In a later work

("Mnenie o načale poezii i stixov voobšče," *Sočinenija Trediakov-skogo*, pp. 194 ff.), Trediakovskij elaborated on his conception of ancient native poetry, trying at the same time to substantiate his notion that it was tonic and composed in feet. In Trediakovskij's opinion, the first to compose verse were priests, in Russia the pagan priests of the pre-Christian era. Unfortunately, no sample of this pagan poetry, Trediakovskij admits, has been preserved. However, Trediakovskij continues, "it is even now apparent from peasants' songs that our most ancient verse . . . consisted of feet, was unrhymed, and had tonic quantity in the syllables [i.e., in Trediakovskij's terminology, a "quantitative" difference in pitch, not in length] . . . the feet were for the most part trochees, or trochees with dactyls . . . [a listing of the various classical meters follows]." To illustrate this, Trediakovskij produces several examples of folk poetry, with all due apologies for quoting such vulgar material. These samples are labeled by Trediakovskij, in a highly artificial and even arbitrary fashion, as trochees, trochees with dactyls, dactyls, etc. Of the six examples, only one is defined as a trochee; but even if it is a trochee (which is doubtful), it is a trochaic tetrameter with, moreover, unrhymed dactylic endings:

$$\acute{x}\, x/\, \acute{x}\, x/\, \acute{x}\, x/\, \acute{x}\, x\, x$$

This meter is very remotely related to Trediakovskij's "heroic" verse, a trochaic hexameter with its obligatory coupled feminine rhyme. And, perhaps more important, in its developed expression, Trediakovskij's attitude toward native poetry was that ideally regular forms existed in remote antiquity; that this perfect, if rather mythical, poetry was corrupted, but was still reflected in uneducated oral folk poetry which Trediakovskij attempted to force into the norm of syllabo-tonic metrics.

S. I. Bomštein, in his article "Trediakovskij the Philologist and Folklore" (*XVIII vek*, V [1962], 249–72) makes the point that Trediakovskij tended to attribute to Russian folk poetry such verse feet as he himself had come to accept at various stages in his career. Thus, in 1735, when he disliked the iambs and rejected ternary meters altogether, he spoke merely of the "various feet" in folk verse. On the other hand, in the 1750s, when he had become convinced that all verse feet proposed by Lomonosov were suitable, he named them specifically and provided examples from Russian folk songs.

41. "Alternation" here means the use of both feminine and masculine rhymes and "mixed" rhymes in some pattern other than coupled rhymes, such as a b a b or a b b a, etc. "Mixed" rhymes could obviously be all feminine, and Trediakovskij saw no objection to them.

42. Trediakovskij wrote this ode to celebrate the taking of Danzig by Russian forces on June 19, 1734, in the course of a war with Poland. It was the first solemn ode written in Russian. The ode is written in nine-syllable lines, using varied rhyme schemes.

43. The metric patterns of the two are as follows:

1. x́ x/ x x/ x́ x   a F
   x́ x/ x́ x/ x́   b M
   x́ x/ x́ x/ x́ x   a F
   x x/ x́ x/ x́   b M
2. x x́ x/ x x́ x   a F
   x x́ x/ x x́   b M
   x x́ x/ x x́ x   a F
   x x́ x/ x x́   b M
   x́ x x́/ x x́ x   c F
   x x́ x/ x x́   d M
   x x́ x/ x x́ x   c F
   x x́ x/ x x́   d M

In these examples Trediakovskij not only alternates masculine and feminine rhymes, but also, in the second, uses the amphibrach, one of the ternary meters he condemned. He explains that he wrote these verses to French tunes and that in both French and German songs the rhythm of the melody follows the rhythm of the lyric. Thus Trediakovskij, in these examples, was reproducing, or endeavoring to reproduce, the rhythm of some French poetry as reflected in the rhythm of a song.

It may be noted that the "song," in the eighteenth century a marginal, noncanonical genre, but one free of the declamatory pomposity of the canonical genres, was largely the source of both the rhythms and the language of later lyrical poetry.

44. The sonnet, by Jacques Valée Des Barreaux (1599–1673), beginning with the lines: "Dieu, tes jugements sont remplis d'equité/ Toujours tu prends plaisir à nous être propice," was quite well known in its time. To Voltaire, however, it seemed "aussi médiocre que fameux."

The lines by Boileau to which Trediakovskij is referring are as follows:

Un sonnet sans défaut veut seul un long poème
Mais, en vain mille auteurs y pensent arriver
Et ce heureux phénix est encore à trouver!
(Boileau, *L'art poetique*, Chant II, 94–96)

45. Vincent Voiture (1594–1648), one of the great wits of the time of Cardinal Richelieu. His quatrains, rondeaux, etc. were very popular with the refined French society of his day.

46. The Latin quotation is from Horace, *Ars Poetica*, lines 97–98:

Telephus et Peleus cum pauper et exsul uterque
Proicit ampullas et sesquipedalia verba

47. In Russian the Epistles of the Apostles are called "messages" (*Poslanija*). Hence, Trediakovskij's term *epistola*, to distinguish the poetic epistle from *poslanie*.

48. The reason for this apology for using the names of pagan gods may be the denunciations by the Orthodox Church of the new secular literature which was spreading throughout Russia from the south. Moreover, Trediakovskij knew that he had been accused of "godlessness" before.

49. Henriette de Coligny Comtesse de La Suze (1618–73), a minor French poetess, was praised by Boileau for her elegies.

50. Gukovskij (*Russkaja poezija XVIII veka*, pp. 48–52) discusses the difficulties Trediakovskij had in describing the genre of elegy. The elegies of Countess de La Suze, rather *précieux* in their style, dealt with erotic *motifs*, and this is why Trediakovskij had to apologize again for the treatment of love in his own elegies and to assure the reader that "legitimate" love was his theme. There was also a native tradition of poetry approaching the genre of elegy to which belonged some of the works of Simeon Polockij, or the extensive monologues of the heroes in the school dramas. Gukovskij thinks that by using the Greek term to define elegy Trediakovskij simply "cut the Gordian knot."

The lines quoted by Trediakovskij are from Ovid, *Amores*, II, 9.

51. The reference is to Corinthian bronze, mentioned in the works of several ancient authors, such as Petronius Arbiter, *Cena Trimalchionis*, section 50, second half; Pliny the Elder, *Natural History*, 34 (chapter 3) 6–8; and Plutarch.

52. Trediakovskij's definition of the ode in his "Considerations on Odes in General," attached to the "Ode on the Taking of Danzig," read as follows:

The word "ode" comes from the Greek ὠδή, which in our language means "song." But in actuality, an ode is a group of stanzas, consisting of even (or else, uneven) lines in which one describes, always and without exception, a noble, important matter which occasionally can also be tender and pleasant, in highly poetic and noble words. From this description of the ode it can be seen that it does not differ from epic poetry in the nobility of material and loftiness of language. The difference is in the brevity of the ode and also in the kind of verse line used, because the ode is never written in a hexameter or in a verse having six-unit meter.

(Sočinenija Trediakovskogo, I, 278)

53. The redundant arguments that follow were intended to prove that lines with an even number of syllables are not "regular" and that short lines need not be divided. But actually this argumentation does not prove anything and is perhaps the most confused and contradictory part of the whole treatise. It apparently reflects Trediakovskij's confusion as to the place of short lines in Russian poetry. His intention was to reform the 13- and 11-syllable lines of syllabic poetry, since these were to be used for epic poetry and all other important genres except the ode. However, once having started his deliberations on the long lines, Trediakovskij saw that it was also necessary to comment at least on the preferable forms of short lines, in the light of his reform of the long lines.

54. Trediakovskij's reasoning, obviously spurious, is presented in a somewhat clearer fashion earlier in the treatise (Corollary to Rule I, p. 42). Trediakovskij's main reason for condemning trinary meters seems to be that "trinary meters" meant to him primarily the Greek or Latin hexameter, predominantly dactylic, but admitting binary feet as well, and therefore having a variable number of syllables. From Trediakovskij's syllabic premises, this was inadmissible. Nor, apparently, was he able to conceive of regular dactylic or other trinary verse, without binary feet and with the desired constant number of syllables.

55. Literally: "because of I don't know what attractive"; this is a characteristic Gallicism: "Je ne sais quel . . . ."

56. Aside from the rhyming words: *glatki, slatki*, the proverb also

makes use of repetitions of consonants (*p*rostoj, *p*rjaniki). Another example of such devices found in Russian folk proverbs would be the following (taken from Y. M. Sokolov, *Russian Folklore*, Catherine Smith, trans., p. 278): "I chEst', nE chEst', koli nEchEgo Est' (Even honor is not honor when there is nothing to eat.)" Not only the vowel *e* is repeated, but also the consonant *c* (*ch*), and the consonantal combination *st'*.

57. Trediakovskij's argument that the lines with an odd number of syllables are "regular," because they can have a caesura syllable contradicts his earlier position that short lines do not need a caesura in the first place. Clearly, the only way out of the difficulty was to extend the principle of division into feet to the short lines and to discard the notion of caesura as the organizing element of such lines.

58. One of the epigrams, "About a man who, having achieved honor, became so proud that he was inclined to neglect his previously equal friends," goes as follows:

> О! сударь мой свет! как ты уж спесив стал!
> Сколь ни заходил, я не мог тя видеть:
> То спишь, то нельзя, я лишь ходя устал.
> Ты изволил сим мя весьма обидеть.
> Нужды, будь вин жаль, нет мне в красовулях;
> Буде ж знаться ты с низким перестал
> Как к высоким всё уже лицам пристал;
> И к себе притьти позволь на ходулях.

> Oh, Sir, my light! how snobbish you've become!
> Whenever I came, I could not see you:
> Either you are sleeping or don't receive: I simply got tired of walking.
> Thus you have chosen to insult me completely.
> I don't want (if you begrudge me wine) your drinking glasses
> And if you no longer wish to know people of low station,
> If you have now attached yourself to great people,
> Then allow me to come visit you on stilts.

This epigram is interesting for two reasons. One is that Lomonosov used some of the words in it for a vicious lampoon in verse on Trediakovskij. Two lines from this poem by Lomonosov make fun of Trediakovskij's rhymes *xoduljax-krasovuljax* in the epigram. The passage goes as follows:

Уже за тридцать лет ты записной дурак,
Давно изгага всем читать твои синички,
Дорогу некосну, вонючие лисички;
Никто не поминай нам подлости ходуль
И к пьянству твоему потребных красовуль.

For more than thirty years now you have been on record as a fool
Everybody has long been sick of reading about your titmice,
About your miserable roads, your stinking foxes;
No one should even mention the vulgarity of your stilts
Or the drinking glasses needed for your carousing.

        (Quoted by Berkov, *Lomonosov i literaturnaja polemika*, p. 226)

The "miserable roads" and the rhyme *sinički-lisički* refer to another poem by Trediakovskij.

Another interesting feature of Trediakovskij's epigram is that it provides examples of masculine rhymes (lines 1, 3, 6, 7), which he permitted in facetious poetry. The epigram is written in 11-syllable lines, and some of the lines with masculine rhyme lose their trochaic stress pattern completely. For instance, the following line (the stresses are placed in accordance with Trediakovkij's rule that all monosyllabic words are to be counted as long):

Тó спишь/ тó нé/ льзя́,// я́ лишь/ ходя́/ устáл

The whole line consists of spondees, with two iambs at the end. B. Tomaševskij (*Stilistika i stixosloženie*, p. 324) makes the following comment on this epigram: "It can be understood what made things difficult for him. He did not know any other means of achieving a masculine rhyme except by changing the trochee to the iamb, and the result was a cacophony, as in this epigram."

59. François Joseph de La Grange-Chancel (1677–1758). Wrote for the theatre but now is mostly known for his satirical odes.

60. Pierre Corneille, the famous tragedian, and his brother Thomas Corneille (1625–1709).

61. Bernard le Bovier Fontenelle (1657–1757). His *Entretiens sur la Pluralité des Mondes* was translated by Kantemir in 1730 and caused a stir in Russia because of its supposedly atheistic content. Trediakovskij is referring to him here as a theoretician of versification, apparently because of his *Réflexions sur la Poétique*.

62. Mathurin Regnier (1573–1613), a satirist. His work was praised by Boileau.

63. Actually, much more than "poetic license" is involved in the change made by Trediakovskij in Kantemir's line. The basic point is that these changes in wording turn the old syllabic 13-syllable line into Trediakovskij's new "hexameter." Kantemir's line

Уме слабый, плод трудов//не долгой науки

has the following stress distribution:

$$\underline{x\,\acute{x}}\ \underline{\acute{x}\,x}\ \underline{\acute{x}}\ \underline{x\,\acute{x}}//\ \underline{x}\ \underline{\acute{x}\,x}\ \underline{x\,\acute{x}\,x}$$

Trediakovskij changed this line to read:

Ум толь слабый плод трудов//краткия науки

The trochaic cadence in the first hemistich was continued in the second, producing the "heroic hexameter":

$$\underline{\acute{x}\ x}/\ \underline{\acute{x}\ x}/\ \underline{\acute{x}\ x}/\ \underline{\acute{x}}//\ \underline{\acute{x}\ x}/\ \underline{x}\ \underline{x}/\underline{\acute{x}\ x}$$

This shows that Trediakovskij did not conceive of his "hexameter" as an entirely new kind of verse, but merely as a revision or "correction" of the old syllabic line.

As for the "poetic license" in Kantemir's line, the vocative *ume* would indeed be an example according to paragraph VIII, p. 48. But Trediakovskij introduces a form as archaic as the vocative *ume:* the *genitive* feminine *kratkija*, where Kantemir had the modern form *kratkoj*.

64. This remark about Kantemir indicates that Trediakovskij intended his treatise for the former's consideration, hoping, no doubt that Kantemir in his treatise would accept him as tutor in matters of versification. When Kantemir disputed many of the points of Trediakovskij's theory, Trediakovskij's enthusiasm for Kantemir cooled considerably. An example of this change of attitude is his evaluation of Kantemir's treatise (see p. 144). In the essay ("O drevnem, sred-nem . . .," *Sočinenija Trediakovskogo*, pp. 782–83), after having asserted that Russians were better syllabic poets than the Ukrainians and other non-Russians (Kantemir was of Moldavian origin), and after having quoted some verses of the Russian poet Buslayev, whom he praised greatly, Trediakovskij makes the following remark:

Indeed, if the respected author who has recently written some booklet about our versification, Mr. Abbé Gouasco, as it is rumored, rightly or wrongly, could have seen all this which I have now, not on the basis of rumor or indirect reports [presented], he would undoubtedly, to his credit, change many things in this booklet of his and would issue a more correct and more truthful edition.

Since there is no record of anything else published by Gouasco on Russian versification, one must assume that this "booklet" is *Satires du Prince Cantemir.* Gouasco's name does not appear in this book, which explains Trediakovskij's reference to "rumor". Gouasco had high praise for Kantemir's poetry and some words of disparagement concerning Trediakovskij's efforts.

There are some traces left of a correspondence beween Kantemir and Trediakovskij, and it is possible that they had discussed versification.

65. Jean-Baptiste Rousseau (1670–1741) and, apparently, Edme Boursault (1638–1701), who was active in the theatre and wrote some successful comedies. He gained notoriety as an enemy of Molière.

66. These lines are from Boileau's "Discours au Roi" (1665), lines 55–56.

NOTES TO III: LOMONOSOV'S LETTER ON RUSSIAN VERSIFICATION

1. Unlike Trediakovskij, Lomonosov left no other major works on versification, although he did write on poetry and rhetoric. He apparently intended to include a special book on versification as the third part of his *Rhetoric*, but it was never completed. In 1751, in reporting to the Academy on his activities during that year, Lomonosov wrote that he "dictated to the students the beginning of my third book on eloquence, dealing with versification in general." See D. K. Motol'-skaja, "Lomonosov," *Istorija russkoj literatury,* III, 312. No traces of this work have been preserved, unless the few outlines for the study of rhythm in folk verse done by Lomonosov were, as P. N. Berkov has surmised, a preparation for his book on poetics and versification. See Berkov, "Lomonosov i fol'klor," pp. 107–29.

2. Lomonosov may have followed Johann Christoph Gottsched, who said, complaining about attempts to force German versification into Greek and Latin molds: "Wir müssen aber unsere Dichtkunst in ihre eigene Landesart kleiden und sie nicht nach dem griechischen oder Lateinischen Gehör zwingen" ("Praschen's gründliche Anzeige

von Verbesserung der deutschen Poesie," *Beyträge*, Vol. II [1733]; quoted in *Dan'ko*, "*Iz neizdannyx materialov o Lomonosove*," p. 265).

3. Lomonosov's second point, that the limitations of other nations' metrics must not be allowed to impoverish the Russian system, is a thrust at Trediakovskij, who excluded trisyllabic feet and the alternation of rhymes because they did not exist in the old syllabic poetry based on Polish tradition.

4. As a general position, this statement agrees with Trediakovskij's view that syllable "length" should be understood as stress (Definition V, p. 40). In fact, this is the main principle that the two treatises have in common. Motol'skaja (p. 301) is even of the opinion that it was Trediakovskij and not the Germans who taught Lomonosov the "tonic principle." S. M. Bondi ("Trediakovskij, Lomonosov, Sumarokov," p. 60) also states: "On the foundation given by Trediakovskij's 'Method' a new and more radical reform of versification was being proposed." Since both the German sources and Trediakovskij's treatise were in agreement on the definition of the stressed syllable as "long," there seems to be no way of distinguishing which particular source Lomonosov followed, and no need to do so. It is even possible that Trediakovskij also goes back to Gottsched indirectly, if we remember his possible conversations about versification with the German poets at the Academy.

5. Macvej Strikovskij (1547–*c*.1582), a Polish author of historical chronicles who became known in Russia in the seventeenth century. The paragraph in Smotrickij to which Lomonosov is referring runs as follows: "Matfij Strijkovskij, a Samoite canon, a trustworthy compiler of Slavic chronicles, in the book of his chronology writes that glorious Ovid, the Latin poet, was in exile among the Sarmatian people and mastered their language to perfection, wrote poetry or verse in a Slavonic dialect instead of his own pure and gracious language" (quoted by Burgi, p. 21). The theory that the ancient Sarmatians were Slavs kept recurring in both Russian and, especially, Polish writings.

6. Lomonosov's spelling for the place of Ovid's exile is Tomy. It is not exactly clear where this place was, but it seems to have been located somewhere near the present city of Constanza, Rumania; in all likelihood Slavs did not inhabit the area.

7. This is actually the first time that a Russian hexameter was written according to the syllabo-tonic principle, that is, with stress

substituting for syllable length. Lomonosov, however, did not use this meter, preferring iambic tetrameter for most of his poetry. It remained for Trediakovskij to develop fully such hexameters and pentameters, as he did in his *Tilemaxida*.

The example of pentameter given by Lomonosov does not seem to fit the meter it purports to illustrate. Since there are six stresses in each line of the "pentameter," the lines would seem to read rather like hexameters.

8. Tomaševskij (*Teorija literatury*, p. 79) scans Smotrickij's quantitative hexameter in the following manner:

Са́рма́т/ски́ но̆во̆/ра́стны̄/я̆ му́̄/зы̄ сто́пў/ пӗрвў, etc.

As can be seen, the line consists of six four-morae feet (with one mora missing in the last foot). The sign | indicates ictus, which only incidentally corresponds to the word stress which I have marked here with the sign /. Such a hexameter is so artificial in Russian that one can perceive no rhythm in attempting to read the line in Smotrickij's manner, as interpreted by Tomaševskij. Of the three reformers of versification only Kantemir made even a tentative suggestion that a quantitative meter might perhaps work in Russian (see Kantemir's treatise, p. 81).

9. Lomonosov explicitly differs from Trediakovskij's view that all monosyllabic words must by definition be counted as long. It is significant that he cites examples from everyday speech to show that some monosyllabic words remain unstressed. This brings Lomonosov's poetic diction closer to the normal spoken language. This difference in attitude accounts for the divergent readings of the line from Trediakovskij's first elegy, printed in the second part of his treatise of 1735. Trediakovskij scanned the line as follows:

не́ возмо́жно се́рдцу а́х!// не́ име́ть печа́ли

This is his heroic 13-syllable line with trochaic scansion. Lomonosov obtains his scansion by counting the monosyllabic particle *ne* both times as short, but *ax*, an interjection, as "long," that is, stressed. The "pentameter," as scanned by Lomonosov, has both bisyllabic and trisyllabic feet—a meter which Trediakovskij was not prepared to accept at the time he wrote his first treatise.

Lomonosov was quite correct in regarding the particle *ne* as un-accented; his reading of the line as an iambic-anapestic pentameter, however, is questionable, although possible. Actually his correction makes pyrrhic feet out of two feet read by Trediakovskij as trochees.

10. It is this division of monosyllabic words into three main cate-gories with respect to their "length" that indicates Lomonosov's dependence upon the ideas current in contemporary German theories of versification. Gottsched (*Beyträge*, II, 144–45, quoted in Dan'ko, "Iz neizdannyx materialov," p. 267) had the following to say about the versification rules expounded by the German theoretician Prasch:

Prasch behauptet dass etliche einsylbige Wörter ihrer Natur nach lang, etliche kurz, etliche frey (ancipites) waren, dass ferner wiederum etliche nur zufälliger Weise lang oder kurz waren, nach dem sie an einem Orte stunden oder mit anderen vereinigt wurden.

Nach Praschen's Meinung sind vollkommen und beständig lang von einsylbigen Wörtren:

"Die Nennworter die ein Wesen oder dessen Eigenschaft anzeigen, als Mann, Baum, Blut.

"Die eigenen Namensworter (besser Namen), als Mars, Styx, und vornehmlich der Name Gott."

As Dan'ko points out, Lomonosov's *Xram*, *svjat*, and *Bog* are always long for the same reason that "Gott" is long in Prasch. Lomonosov's examples, however, seem to show that he had a clear understanding of proclitic and enclitic word groups in Russian.

11. Here Lomonosov clearly states his opposition to Trediakov-skij's view that trisyllabic meters are not suitable for Russian verse—a view expressed several times in the 1735 treatise: in Part I, Defini-tion III and Corollary 3, as well in as Part II. At the same time Lomonosov indicates that he is not following the Germans alone. The point is that Lomonosov's reform places Russian versification within the syllabo-tonic tradition instead of the French, Polish, and Italian syllabic tradition.

12. Both a set number of syllables and a strict commitment to the regular alternation of stress do violence to the natural flow of speech. The divergent views of Lomonosov and Trediakovskij find their expression in their preferences for one restriction over the other. It seems that Lomonosov feared the verse would lose its cadence if the regular alternation or at least the mixing of the same types of feet

was not precisely adhered to. Therefore one may say that he depended on the purity of verse feet throughout the line to produce the desired cadence and rhythm. Trediakovskij, on the other hand, felt that such cadence was the result of several factors taken together (see Rule IX, p. 46). Lomonosov saw that if one took advantage of Trediakovskij's theoretical permission to substitute any bisyllabic foot for any other in any position in the line, the whole point of tonic metrics would be lost and the verse would again return to the syllabic system. Since his attention is directed towards pointing out Trediakovskij's errors, he does not take into account the latter's insistence on esthetic, not formal, grounds that the trochaic foot is by far the best for Russian verse.

In actual practice, Trediakovskij limited himself mostly to the substitution of a pyrrhic foot for a trochee (except occasionally, when he permitted an iambic substitution), and thus his lines generally kept their trochaic beat. Lomonosov himself realized very quickly that such substitution did not destroy the metrical pattern and used it in his own verse.

13. In choosing these particular lines of Boileau to support his point, Lomonosov imitated the argument of Gottsched, *Versuch einer Kritischen Dichtkunst* (1742), p. 390, quoted in Dan'ko, pp. 268–69:

Bey dem allen wollen die guten Franzosen es nicht begreifen, dass ihre Sprache lange und kurze Sylben habe. . . . Z. E. die erste Zeile aus des Boileau Ode auf die Eroberung Namurs:

> Quelle docte et sainte yvresse!

wird von allen Franzosen als eine trochaische von vier Füssen ausgesprochen.

14. The examples given by Lomonosov, with their bisyllabic and trisyllabic feet of the same type freely mixed, may give the impression that in this he was not unlike Trediakovskij, who also, at least in theory, permitted the mixing of feet, even if he would not allow trisyllabic meters. However, the two authors were following two different principles. For Trediakovskij a foot was a two-syllable unit, and he allowed substitution of any two-syllable foot for any other (including, theoretically, that of an iamb for a trochee), provided that the masculine caesura and the feminine ending were preserved (Rule I, p. 42).

Lomonosov, on the other hand, felt that a sequence of falling-rising or rising-falling feet (e.g., iamb-trochee; anapest-dactyl) would disrupt the beat of the line. Therefore he allowed only the combinations of either two falling (trochee, dactyl) or two rising (iamb, anapest) meters, as his examples show, except in "free and irregular verse."

15. Here Lomonosov not only questions Trediakovskij's arguments about the need to catch one's breath in the middle of a long line, but also seems to doubt the absolute need for a caesura. This was a quite unorthodox position, considering that French, Polish, Russian, and Italian long lines, as well as Greek and Latin verse, contained a caesura. One possible explanation of this may be that Lomonosov took little interest in the long epic line and in the problems of caesura connected with it, even though he was the first Russian poet to give examples (in this treatise) of a true syllabo-tonic imitation of the Greek hexameter.

16. The Russian text has "trochees" (*xorei*) instead of the expected "iambs" (*jamby*). This would contradict Lomonosov's principle of not mixing feet which are, as he said of trochees and iambs, "opposed to each others," and is obviously a mistake. One must remember that the "Letter" was printed from a copy of the original manuscript.

Lomonosov's preference to iambs and anapests directly contradicts Trediakovskij, who preferred trochees. In his deliberations upon "whom and in what it is better to follow," Lomonosov apparently decided in favor of his German sources. *Cf.* Gottsched "Mann ist also im Deutschen vor Alters fast bey den jambischen allein geblieben, weil dieselbe unserer Sprache an natürlichsten sind" (*Versuch einer Kritischen Dichtkunst*, p. 385; quoted in Dan'ko p. 272).

17. Lomonosov's statement that the iambs are especially suited for solemn odes contains the germ of a future argument he had with Trediakovskij and Sumarokov concerning the "emotional" value of iambs and trochees. Here again Lomonosov was apparently influenced by the opinions of German theoreticians, for instance, the statement by Hübner in his *Poetisches Handbuch* (1742), p. 24 (quoted in Dan'ko, p. 272), "VI. Die jambischen Verse steigen demnach gleichsam in die Höhe," or, concerning the trochees and dactyls, Gottsched's remark: "Sie klingen an sich selbst sehr lustig und springend und sind daher zur Abwechslung in Cantaten oder anderren musicalischen Stücken sehr bequem" (*Versuch einer Kritischen Dichtkunst*, p. 385). The ode

Lomonosov mentions here is, of course, the "Ode on the Taking of Xotin."

One may note that neither Lomonosov nor Trediakovskij made any mention of amphibrachs in their treatises, although examples of Russian amphibrachs written by Paus already existed (see Unbegaun, p. 49). The reason for the omission of the amphibrach might be that both Lomonosov and Trediakovskij could only conceive of verse feet as either "ascending" (iambs, anapests) or "descending" (trochees, dactyls). The amphibrach, being an "ascending-descending" verse foot, did not seem to fit into their systems.

In opposition to Trediakovskij, who would only admit feminine, i.e., trochaic, rhymes for serious poetry, Lomonosov here attributes "noble" qualities to masculine and dactylic rhymes as well. Russian syllabic versification, while it definitely preferred feminine rhymes, sometimes permitted masculine and dactylic rhymes also, and certainly Kantemir had no theoretical objections to them.

19. In stating in his 1735 treatise that iambic rhymes are suitable only for works of facetious content, Trediakovskij may have been thinking of the "iambics" of Horace, which were satirical and humorous. Lomonosov, on the other hand, probably felt that his position found support in the German theoreticians of versification, Gottsched, for instance, referred to the iambic rhymes as "Pfeile" and "Donnerschläge."

20. The reference here is to Trediakovskij's epigram; see the notes to his treatise of 1735 (pp. 162–63).

21. When Lomonosov was writing his treatise there was already a movement in Germany opposed to rhyme in poetry. Gukovskij (*Istorija russkoj poezii XVIII veka*, pp. 104–5) points out that this movement arose out of the desire for liberation from Gottsched's influence and his laws of versification.

22. This sarcastic reaction of Lomonosov to Trediakovskij's rather ponderous attempt to be witty in his 1735 treatise was later reechoed in a special epigram written by Lomonosov:

> I had a fine husband, whom I married long ago,
> Nevertheless I have to stay without him—a grass widow.
> Stivelius assured me that my husband was thin and weak,
> That a helpless, vulgar, old, decrepit blackamoor was he;
> He said that all ways to married life were closed to me,

That my legs were crooked and trembling.
I really thought I was like that myself—
A good-for-nothing perennial widow.
Nevertheless, now the whole of Russia has been convinced
That I, Russian poetry, am a beauty,
That my lawful husband is a lad to be envied,
And that he has put an end to my misfortunes.

(Translated from *Sočinenija Lomonosova*, II, 287)

In this edition Suxomlinov includes this epigram among Lomonosov's works written in 1764, but Berkov (*Lomonosov i literaturnaja polemika*, p. 96) gives 1751 as the date of composition.

The name Stivelius was first given to Trediakovskij by Sumarokov in the latter's *Epistle on Versification*, in a passage where Lomonosov was compared with Pindar and Malherbe, whereas Stivelius supposedly knew only how to lie. Since Stivelius was a well-known synonym for learned pedantry and stupidity, Sumarokov's readers immediately understood that Trediakovskij, who had such a reputation, was intended. The name Stivelius comes from Stifelius (or Stiefel), a well-known German mathematician (1488–1567) who had a reputation for pedantry. The Danish playwright Holberg used this name mockingly in one of his comedies, and apparently Sumarokov borrowed it from a German translation of Holberg's works. See *Sočinenija Lomonosova*, II, *Primečanija*, 389–99.

23. It has not been established whether these examples of verse were composed by Lomonosov during the writing of the treatise or before. However, it seems unlikely that he could have written them without knowing the work of the German poets and theoreticians; it is therefore probable that these poems were written either at the time the treatise was composed or not more than two or three years before. According to the documents contained in Kunik, ed., pp. 92–115, Lomonosov did not know any German when he left for Marburg in 1736, and his first letter written in German dates from 1737.

NOTES TO IV: KANTEMIR'S LETTER ON RUSSIAN VERSIFICATION

1. Kantemir's "measured verse" purports to apply to Smotrickij's metrics (see p. 3), which, unlike those of Trediakovskij and Lomonosov, Kantemir refuses to dismiss without further experimentation. It

is, however, practically impossible to reconstruct the meter Kantemir had in mind in the example he gives, if only because certain vowels in Smotrickij's system could be either long or short.

2. This refers to a passage in Trediakovskij's treatise of 1735, and specifically to the phrase "laughing Democritus" (see the 1735 "Method", p. 38).

3. The five lines are 13-syllable syllabic verses, written according to the rules stated by Kantemir in $\#$ 25 ff. of this treatise, except that they are unrhymed. In addition to feminine endings, the regularity of stress manifests itself in the pre-caesural stress, either: x x́// in lines 1, 4, and 5, or: x́ x x// in lines 2 and 3.

4. Kantemir is apparently referring to Trediakovskij's statement in Definition VI of the 1735 treatise: "the French poetry, which is the same as ours, except for certain substantial qualifications" (see p. 40). Kantemir's statement also seems to imply that Trediakovksij considered rhyme an essential element of Russian verse. Actually, Trediakovskij did point out in his first treatise (p. 61) that, while rhyme was the best ornament of Russian verse, it was not something "so essential that without it verse could not be called verse."

5. Other Russian writers of the eighteenth century, including Trediakovskij, were familiar with the practice of using Church Slavonic words in order to elevate ordinary prose to the level of poetic speech. In 1757 Lomonosov organized this usage into a formal system in his *Predislovie o pol'ze knig cerkovnyx*.

According to Lomonosov, there are three "styles" of writing in Russian: a high style, which employs noble Church Slavonic words which are not used in Russian but which Russians understand and in which solemn odes, heroic epics, etc. ought to be written; an intermediate style in which one may use those Church Slavonic words that are familiar to every educated Russian, and which is suitable for such genres as drama, and, finally, a low style in which one uses the common expressions of ordinary Russian speech and which is suitable for comedy, satire, etc.

Kantemir's satires, which constitute the main body of his poetic work, often contain colloquialisms of the kind that Lomonosov might have described as belonging to the "low style."

6. These are 13-syllable lines, with coupled feminine rhymes and a caesura after the seventh syllable.

7. In admitting (like Lomonosov) not only feminine, but also masculine and dactylic, rhymes, Kantemir is in substantial disagreement with Trediakovskij. Trediakovskij's position was determined both by the Polish origins of the syllabic tradition and by his preference for the trochee (a feminine rhyme is a trochaic foot). Kantemir is not bound by the trochaic cadence and, in this instance, rather paradoxically, he is less influenced by the syllabic tradition than Trediakovskij.

The terms describing the three types of rhyme were apparently borrowed by Kantemir from Italian. The "blunt"—masculine (*tupye*)— rhymes are called *tronchi* in Italian, the "simple"—feminine (*prostye*)—*piani*, and the "gliding"—dactylic (*skol'zkie*)—*sdruccioli*. See Francesco Flamini, *Notizia Storica dei Versi e Metri italiani dal Medioevo ai Tempi nostri*.

8. Kantermir's term "conjunct vowels" (*priprjažno-glasnye*) may be misleading. The two symbols, ъ and ь, represented reduced vowel sounds, but at a much earlier time than Kantemir's. In his day they were written following consonants in certain positions, in particular the final position, merely as signs indicating the palatalization or nonpalatalization of the preceding consonant. Present-day spelling still uses ь for palatalization in final position, but not ъ to indicate nonpalatalization. Thus, to use his example, *poklon-zvon* rhyme because of the identity of the last syllable which ends in a nonpalatalized *n*; *zvon-von'* do not rhyme because of the palatalization (here shown by an ') of the final *n* in the second word, but not in the first.

9. Phonetically *d*, *b*, *ž* (voiced) equal respectively *t*, *p*, *š* (unvoiced) when in final position or before other unvoiced consonants, by assimilation; thus *vodka* is pronounced *votka*, and rhymes with *glotka*. But Kantemir's examples assuming assimilation before *n* [*nužnyj-vozdušnyj*] are not standard. Finally, the example *droglyj-issoxlyj* reflects the standard pronunciation of *g* as voiced fricative *x* (*h*) by educated Russians in Kantemir's time. On this latter point Tomaševskij (*Russkoe stixosloženie. Metrika*, p. 92) makes the following observations: In the eighteenth century *g* in literary speech had the same pronunciation which we now hear in South Russian dialects: the fricative *g* (*h*). It corresponded to the unvoiced consonant *x*. Kantemir, in establishing correspondences between consonants in rhymes, points to *x* as a sound which rhymes with *g*.

10. The three oppositions with which Kantemir concerns himself here are not oppositions between monophthongs and diphthongs. First pair: the Russian symbols transcribed in this text as *a* and *ja* (one symbol, not a digraph, in Russian) stand, the first for *a* and the second, if initial or postvocalic, for *ja*, and in postconsonantal position for *a* but with palatalization of the preceding consonant. Second pair: *e* and *ě* are identical in sound value and were distinguished only orthographically. Third pair: *i* and *y* are allophones of the same phoneme, but phonetically are not identical. Consequently, in the case of *a* and *aj* and of *e* and *ě*, there is no "poetic license" involved (except from the standpoint of the "visual rhyme"). Rhymes consisting of *y* and *i* may be regarded as approximate rhymes consecrated by a well-established tradition (cf. V. Žirmunskij, *Rifma, ee istorija i teorija*, p. 131). Roman Jakobson ("The Kernel of Comparative Slavic Literature," p. 23) writes on this point:

No Russian or Polish literary epoch, and no poetic school has cast doubt on the equivalence of the front unrounded *i* and the back unrounded *y* for exact rimes: *bil—byl*. Not a single artist, however refined his riming technique, has sought to avoid such rimes. This equivalence is a natural result of the fact that the Polish and Russian *i* and *y* are nothing but the contextual variations of one and the same phoneme—a high unrounded vowel, as Baudouin de Courtenay astutely observed.

11. The "conjunct vowels," as pointed out before (see n. 8), are not vowels at all.

12. As can be seen from the examples izve*st*nyj, te*sn*yj, Kantemir must obviously have meant "between two consonants."

13. Infinitives with final *i* (e.g., *pisati* in Kantemir's example) are an older variant of the form *pisat'*.

14. The grammatical rhymes, including those of verb infinitives ending in -*ati*, to which Kantemir is objecting here, were frequently used in earlier Russian versification. Kantemir's statement is in striking contradiction to Trediakovskij's defense of grammatical rhymes in his 1735 treatise: "There is no reason to choose a particular part of speech; it is only necessary to select a sound which would not be disagreeable to the ear and which would sound like the ending of the preceding line, regardless of the part of speech" (see p. 50).

15. The transposition of stress for the purpose of obtaining a rhythmical organization of the line is a common feature of Russian folk

songs. Kantemir, apparently, was thinking not of folk songs, but of the arbitrary shift of word stress to the penultimate syllable found in Russian syllabic poetry to conform to the rule of feminine rhyme. R. Jakobson ("The Kernel of Comparative Slavic Literature," pp. 59–60) makes the following remarks concerning this practice of the Russian syllabic poets:

Although this limitation in riming was accurately sensed as a Polonism unwarrantable in Russian and Ukrainian poetry, the rule persisted. Sometimes it even forced an arbitrary shift of the stress to the penult—compare Simeon's rimes *ostávi-jávi* (<*javí*), *télo-zélo* (<*zeló*).

It is difficult to judge with confidence just how much Kantemir may have transgressed against his own rules in this respect, because on some words the stress may have differed from that used today. However, Timofeev (*Očerki po teorii*, p. 295) professes to find several examples of arbitrary transposition of stress in the rhymes of Kantemir, such as *ótec—kónec* (instead of *otéc—konéc*) or *zvezdámi—molnijámi* (instead of *mólnijami*), etc. Trediakovskij also allowed transposition of stress, provided that irregular stress was marked to warn the reader (see 1735 treatise, p. 49).

16. This statement seems to imply that Kantemir never seriously considered the possiblity of legitimizing by rules the quantitative verse, of which he gave an example in 1, where the line has fifteen syllables. In setting the maximum number of syllables per line at thirteen he is in full agreement with Trediakovskij and with the syllabic tradition. It is interesting, however, that Kantemir gives official status to lines with an even number of syllables, which Trediakovskij did not do. Nevertheless, in Kantemir's own poetry there were very few short lines, or lines with an even number of syllables. The great majority— 81 percent— of his verse (according to Timofeev, *Očerki*, p. 308) was written in the heroic 13-syllable line.

17. Actually, as can be seen from the elaboration of his rules in the following paragraphs, Kantemir did not mean that the two compulsory stresses could occur anywhere at all in each line, but rather that there must be in each line two stresses in constant position (one in relation to the caesura and the other to the rhyme).

18. This definition of a "long" syllable is very similar to that of Trediakovskij (the treatise of 1735, Definition V, corollary 2, p. 40). All three authors (Kantemir, Trediakovskij and Lomonosov) are thus

unanimous in accepting the principle that Russian stress serves as a substitute for the long syllables of Greek and Latin poetry.

19. Here Kantemir takes issue with Definition VII and Rule IV of Trediakovskij's treatise of 1735 (see pp. 41–45). In the first place, he mentions the poetry of five nations (significantly omitting France) where enjambement is used, apparently attempting to bolster his argument by referring to other than Latin poetry, in which the use of enjambement was justified by Trediakovskij on the grounds that the Latins did not have rhyme. Kantemir could hardly be impressed by French poetry, Trediakovskij's main authority, for he found its lines with coupled rhymes and without enjambement monotonous. L. V. Pumpjanskij ("Očerki po literature pervoj poloviny XVIII veka") believes that Kantemir, in effect, is fighting on the Italian side against the French versification theorists as much as he is opposing Trediakovskij. In Pumpjanskij's opinion, Kantemir's statement that ·"enjambement is allowed" sounds like a direct contradiction of Boileau's rule (*L'Art Poëtique*): 'Et le vers sur les vers n'osa plus enjamber." Pumpjanskij (p. 99) even thinks that this whole paragraph is translated from an Italian treatise or textbook on versification, without, however, giving credit to the Italian source.

In his poetry Kantemir used enjambement frequently and even increased its use when he rewrote his satires to make them conform to his own new rules. L. I. Timofeev (*Očerki po teorii*, p. 290) gives the following percentage of enjambements in the first and second versions of Kantemir's first five satires:

Satire	1	2	3	4	5
First version	8.0	9.3	13.0	13.5	10.4
Second version	18.0	24.0	18.8	22.8	23.0

In his use of enjambement Kantemir was in accord with the poetic practice and theory of his friend Feofan Prokopovič. Prokopovič in his *De Arte Poetica*, Part II, chapter 3, says: "As in scanning by feet a word should cross over from one foot to another, so let thought be carried over from one line to another; thus, although divided by lines, the thought will nevertheless unite a number of lines together, until the thought as well as the poem is completed at the same time." (*De Arte Poetica*, in Feofan Prokopovič, *Sočinenija*, p. 285.) Prokopovič also followed this precept in his own verse, sometimes linking three or four lines with enjambements.

20. The Russian term translated here as "elision" is *slitie*, meaning, perhaps, "blending." Kantemir's use of this term seems to be the same as Trediakovskij's (see Definition IX, p. 41 and n. 19, p. 152).

21. Kantemir here obviously refers to Trediakovskij's changing of the first line of Kantemir's satire *K umu svoemu*. Trediakovskij quotes this line, corrected according to his notions of meter, several times in the 1735 treatise, beginning with Rule I, as a fine example of his (i.e., Trediakovskij's!) heroic line (see also n. 62 to Trediakovskij's 1735 treatise). There are actually three versions of the line involved. Kantemir's first version was: "umé slábyj, plód trudóv// nedólgoj naúki." Trediakovskij changed this syllabic line to read as it is quoted here, explaining at the end of his 1735 treatise (p. 66) his reasons for changing it to a "heroic hexameter" of his own invention. Kantemir himself, however, rewrote the line later in the following manner: "umé nedozrélyj, plód// nedólgoj naúki." One detects Kantemir's annoyance with Trediakovskij's presumption in "correcting" his poetry, and this was obviously why he chose this particular line to demonstrate the unpleasant effect of repeating the same consonants. Incidentally, Trediakovskij wrote "um tol' slabyj" and not "um tak slabyj," as here.

22. Although Kantemir is much less elaborate here than Trediakovskij (in Rule III of the 1735 treatise), they both adhere to the same basic principle: the caesura must not interrupt a unit of thought. This rule together with the establishment of a compulsory pre-caesural stress by both authors, contributes to the organization of the two hemistichs as self-contained metrical units. Trediakovskij, conceiving of the caesura as a rest "to catch one's breath," naturally wished to avoid that kind of syntactic structure in a line which would work against this pause. Kantemir, whose long line was based on the rhythmic balance of two compulsory stresses, feared that caesura enjambement might weaken the first stress (*cf*. L. I. Timofeev, "Sillabičeskij stix," *Ars poetica* II, 49).

23. This line is quoted by Kantemir somewhat inaccurately from his own satire. It should read: *Tot v sej žizni liš' blažen, kto malym dovolen*. See Antiox Kantemir, *Sobranie stixotvorenij*, p. 147.

24. Paragraphs 28 and 29 express Kantemir's basic ideas concerning she metrical pattern of the 13-syllable line. In certain important ways this conception echoes Trediakovskij's: the seventh syllable must be

stressed (producing the masculine caesura), and the line must have a feminine rhyme. The two authors differ in that Kantemir allows, as an alternate choice, the fixing of an obligatory stress in the first hemistich on the fifth syllable, which produces the dactylic caesura. The masculine and dactylic caesura was also frequent in the German Alexandrine of the seventeenth and eighteenth centuries. It is not likely, however, that Kantemir had any thorough knowledge of German poetry.

25. Kantemir allows the use of the feminine caesura in the dodecasyllabic line, while permitting only the masculine or the dactylic in the 13-syllable line. The stress distribution in Kantemir's first example (with the feminine caesura) resembles that of the Italian *dodecasillabo dattilico*. The metrical scheme of this Italian line is the following: x/ x́ x x/ x́ x// x/ x́ x x/ x́ x (see Rocco Murari, *Ritmica e Metrica razionale italiana*), and that of Kantemir's example: x x́ x x x́ x// x x́ x (x́) x́ x. We see that the second, fifth, eighth, and eleventh syllables are stressed in both. The difference is, of course, that the Italian verse, by excluding the first syllable (anacrusis) from the number of feet, obtains a dactylic sequence, with the caesura cutting the second dactyl; while Kantemir does not have verse feet and also allows extra stresses.

26. In placing the caesura after the fifth syllable in this verse line, Kantemir agrees with Trediakovskij, who places the caesura in the same position in his pentameter (see "Method," 1735, p. 47).

27. Kantemir's rules on the 11-syllable line place the obligatory stress on the same syllables as in the Italian endecasyllabics which belong to the type called *versi minori* and have stresses on the fourth and tenth syllables (see John Purves, *A First Book of Italian Verse*), e.g.:

la/scio/lo/fé/le e/ro/ per/ dol/ci/ pó/mi

(Dante, *Inferno*, 16,61)

Kantemir did not necessarily borrow this from the Italians, for the structure is also that of the Polish 11-syllable line—feminine rhyme, caesura after the fifth syllable, and pre-caesura stress on the fourth, as in the following lines by Jan Kochanowski:

W Tobie ja sámy,// Panie, szłowiek smútny,
Nadzieję kładę ;// Ty racz o mnie rádzić

(Psalm 7:1,2)

28. The main metrical differences between the 11-syllable line which Kantemir discusses in # 33 and the line he calls "Catullian

endecasyllabic" are: 1) the caesura, which in the 11-syllable line follows the fifth syllable, is placed in the "Catullian endecasyllabic" after the sixth, and 2) in the "Catullian endecasyllabic" the precaesural stress is dactylic, while in the 11-syllable line it is trochaic.

It is difficult to make a comparison between Kantemir's "Catullian" and the phalaecean or hendecasyllabic of Caius Valerius Catullus, since the Latin line is metrical, that is, has verse feet in addition to a set number of syllables in this special line. Insofar as comparison is possible, the similarity between Kantemir's line and that of Catullus is not exact. Kantemir's line has the following metrical scheme:

x x x x́ x̆ x̆// x x x x́ x̆
1 2 3 4 5 6   1 2 3 4 5

and the hendecasyllabic of Catullus,

$$//\stackrel{\perp}{-}\stackrel{\smile}{-}|-\smile\smile|\stackrel{\perp}{-}|\smile|\smile|-\smile|\stackrel{\perp}{-}\smile//,$$

as in lines

Lūgēte, Ō Věněrēs// cŭpīdĭnēsquĕ (Catullus, 3, 1)
Pāssēr mōrtŭŭs ēst// mĕaē pŭēllaē (Catūllus, 3, 3).

See Elmer Truesdell Merrill, ed., *Catullus* (College Series of Latin Authors) (Boston, 1893), p. xlii.

As we can see, the caesura occurs after the sixth syllable in both Catullus' and Kantemir's line. Also, the obligatory stress on the fourth syllable in the second hemistich coincides with the practice of Catullus. In the first hemistich, however, one of the main characteristics of the phalaecean is that the second foot is a dactyl, i.e. the third syllable of the hemistich is long, and not the fourth, as Kantemir postulates. Finally, in the phalaecean the caesura commonly divides a trochaic foot, so that the sixth syllable is stressed, whereas Kantemir states that it should be without stress.

29. The "friend Nikita" referred to in the example is Prince Nikita Jurjevič Trubeckoj, who is apparently also the "friend" mentioned in the title of the treatise. The preface to the treatise probably served as a kind of introductory letter to Trubeckoj and was not altogether a literary device (see also introductory remarks to the treatise, p. 79). In March, 1743, Kantemir actually sent Trubeckoj a manuscript of his satires and other poems, reworked according to his new rules of versification, that is, after the versification treatise had already been sent. A copy of this manuscript, made at the Academy in 1755,

entitled *Satires and Other Verse of Prince Antiox Kantemir with Historical Notes,* also contains a letter by Kantemir to Trubeckoj in which he comments on the revision of his works in about the same manner as he does in the verse example here (see Antiox Kantemir, *Sobranie stixotovrenij,* pp. 434 and 525).

30. In accepting lines with an even number of syllables as fully legitimate forms of Russian verse, Kantemir differs substantially from Trediakovskij. The key point is, of course, the concept of the caesura. Kantemir regarded it merely as a pause and saw no need for a special caesura syllable, as did Trediakovskij.

31. The second variant of Kantemir's decasyllabic line resembles the French pentameter in that it also stresses the fourth syllable as a tonic constant. The obligatory stress on the ninth syllable (rather than the tenth, as in French pentameter) is in the tradition of syllabic poetry with its feminine rhymes.

32. The obligatory stresses on the seventh and tenth syllables in this line produce a dactylic foot plus a stressed syllable. If Kantemir's suggestion that a stress be put on the first syllable as well is followed, the whole line acquires a dactylic cadence.

33. The metrical scheme of the nine-syllable line, as described by Kantemir, closely resembles one of the main patterns of the Italian *novenario giambico,* a nine-syllable line with the following metric structure:

$$- \cup \Big|\cup \underset{\cup\,-}{\acute{}}\Big\|\Big| - \cup \Big|\underset{\cup\,-}{\acute{}}\Big|^{} \cup$$

and Kantemir's:

x́ x x x́// x́ x x x́ x
x́ x x x́// x́ x x x́ x

See Pier Enea Guarnerio, *Manuale di Versificazione italiana,* p. 44). As can be seen, the fourth and eighth syllables must be stressed, while stress on the first and fifth syllables (as in Kantemir) is optional Guarnerio (p. 45) quotes a Piedmontese song in which some lines have precisely the stress pattern used by Kantemir in his example: "Áme-me, mí, dóna Lombárda." The Italian *novenario giambico* also permits a caesura after the fifth syllable, which is what Kantemir has in the second, reversed, example of a masculine line. The *novenario,* however, has feminine endings only.

34. Kantemir's scheme for the nine-syllable line without caesura perfectly resembles a regular dactylic trimeter. It may be remembered that his ten-syllable line without caesura also tends towards dactyls.

35. The eight-syllable lines given in the example are in effect regular trochees. Kantemir's description of this line closely resembles that of the Italian *ottonario*, which either may be a regular trochaic tetrameter or may substitute an iamb for a trochee in the first and third feet, but must in any case have stresses on the third and seventh syllable, just as Kantemir demands (see Murari, *Ritmica e Metrica razionale italiana*, p. 31). An example of such an Italian line from the first half of the eighteenth century is the following:

> La stagión de'fiori amíca
> x x x́ x x x x́ x
>
> > (Pietro Metastasio, "L'Estate: canzonetta
> > composta dale' Autore in Roma l'anno 1742")

The significance of the Italian model may be limited, however, by the fact that the trochaic octosyllable with strong down-beats on the third and seventh syllables is also common to other European versification patterns, such as those of Medieval Latin and German. It is characteristic of Russian folk verse as well, and Russian song collections from the seventeenth and eighteenth centuries contain many examples of this pattern.

36. The second version of the eight-syllable line is another instance of a regular dactylic trimeter. The third variant of the eight-syllable line (# 54, below) has an amphibrachic stress distribution: x x́ x x x́ x x x́ in the first line.

37. Kantemir reproduces here his example of the 12-syllable line (# 31), dividing each line in two.

38. In the example, the four-syllable verse is a trochee with some inversions.

39. Kantemir's claim that in devising his rules of metrics he was guided by his "ear" alone cannot be accepted without qualifications. His knowledge of Russian, Italian, French, and Polish poetry undoubtedly influenced his formulation of many specific rules for various lines. Nevertheless, it is not possible to trace the origin of all his rules to Russian or foreign theory or practice of poetry, and in such instances one has little choice but to accept Kantemir's own explanation that he was guided by his sense of rhythm.

Kantemir's shorter lines, in particular, tend to have a rather regular beat, approximating syllabo-tonic meters. The reason for this is that the shorter the line, the higher the ratio of fixed to free stresses. Actually, when Kantemir prescribes two stresses to a line, he simultaneously regulates at least four syllables, or more, since at least one syllable next to the stressed one must be "short." Therefore, in a shorter line relatively little room is left for rhythmical variations.

This, however, does not fully explain the appearance in Kantemir's compositions of regular or nearly regular trochaic, iambic, etc. lines. Kantemir himself pointed out an additional reason for this regularity by saying that his "ear" told him how to distribute stress. It does seem that he had a well-developed sense of rhythm, at least in the short lines, which are much more melodious than Trediakovskij's.

It is interesting that both Kantemir and Trediakovskij achieved regularity of stress, although in opposite kinds of lines; Trediakovskij, proceeding from the verse foot as the basic entity, regularized the beat of the heroic lines and the pentameters, whereas Kantemir, taking the line as his basic entity, achieved regularity in the short lines. Kantemir used some of the short lines in his translations of Anacreontic verse.

40. The dot used by Kantemir in addition to the signs of length and brevity obviously stands for syllables which may be either long or short.

41. Both Kantemir and Trediakovskij essentially agreed that monosyllabic words must by their nature be "long," that is, stressed. However, Kantemir allowed some of them to remain unstressed as a matter of "poetic license," whereas Trediakovskij, at least in 1735, was not willing to do this. It may be true in a limited sense that all monosyllabic words are stressed, but only if one regards them in isolation; in context, however, and metrically only context matters, many Russian monosyllabic words are used enclitically or proclitically and must be unaccented.

42. In calling the Russian forms in # 69 "contractions" or "abbreviations," Kantemir shows that he was unaware of certain principles of Russian morphology. *Vek* and *čelovek* are not "contracted" genitive plurals (instead of *vekov, čelovekov*), but genitive plural nouns with zero suffixes, coinciding with the nominative singular. There was vacillation in Kantemir's time between the zero and -*ov* endings for the genitive plural in the case of a number of nouns. Both endings were in use, and Kantemir apparently regarded one as a "full" and

another as a "contracted" form. In modern Russian usage *vekov* and the zero form *čelovek* prevail. Kantemir makes a somewhat similar mistake in considering the adjectives *čist* and *sladok* as "contracted" adjectives. They are the so-called short adjectives (predicative in modern Russian terms). The present "long" (attributive) adjectives were formed in the Common Slavic period by means of adding the old third person demonstrative pronoun to the original ending (*j*; *cf.* Lithuanian *jis, ji*).

43. Here again, the form *rogi* is not an "abbreviation" of the instrumental plural but an older type of this form which, it is true, also happens to be shorter that the newer *rogami*.

44. Kantemir here sanctions the confusion of two prepositions, *s* and *iz*. The standard Russian form is *iz* (out of, out from); the use of *s* was due to Belorussian or Ukrainian influence.

45. Both the *-ee* and *-ej* endings of the short comparative adjectives are standard in modern Russian.

NOTES TO V: TREDIAKOVSKIJ'S SECOND
TREATISE ON VERSIFICATION, 1752

1. In the 1752 edition of his treatise Trediakovskij once more makes a distinction between verse and prose rather than between prose and poetry. He held that poetry could be written in prose as well as in verse. In an essay entitled "Opinion on the Beginning of Poetry and Verse in General" he wrote:

There are many opinions concerning the origins of poetry; however, not a single one concerning the beginnings of verse, for many of those writing about the origins of poetry sometimes confused it with verse. Our language is very conducive to this since a poem is called a creation in verse (*stixotvorenie*), although actually the true concept of poetry does not have to do with the composition of verse but with creation, invention, and imitation.

(*Sočinenija Trediakovskogo*, I, 181–82)

Lomonosov, on the other hand, would probably have called "rhetoric" what Trediakovskij called "poetry," while the term "poetry" itself was for Lomonosov approximately identical with the term "verse." In the 1748 version of his *Rhetoric* he wrote:

Speech can be expressed in two ways, in prose and in poetry (*poema*). Prose is speech whose parts do not have a precisely determined meter and order of syllables. . . . Poetry (*poema*) consists of parts determined by a certain meter and has precisely ordered its syllables according to their stress and pronunciation.

(Sočinenija Lomonosova, III, 87)

Trediakovskij's differentiation of poetry resembles the views of certain French authors, for instance, Ronsard:

Car toute ainsi que le bout de l'orateur est de persuader, ainsi celui du Poëte est d'imiter, inventer & representer des choses qui sont, qui peuvent estre, ou qui les ancients ont estimé veritables. . . .

(Ronsard, "Abbregé de l'Art Poëtique François,"
Pierre de Ronsard, Œuvres Complètes, XIV, 13)

2. In 1735 Trediakovskij apparently believed that an equal number of syllables per line constituted a necessary, if not sufficient, element of Russian verse, at least in the heroic and 11-syllable line. In cases of conflict with another verse technique this principle of a set number of syllables per line always prevailed, as it did, for instance, when Trediakovskij condemned the "alternation" of verse lines. In 1752, however, he evidently realized that parisyllabism is not essential to Russian verse and is not even an essential element of verse in general, since the figure of the isocolon occurs in prose as well.

3. Trediakovskij methodically stripped away all those elements of verse which appeared secondary to him until only regular stress distribution remained. However, regular intervals between stresses may also occur in prose; many prose authors have unintentionally written groups of words which can be scanned in verse feet. Theoretically, all the technical characteristics of verse could be put on an equal footing; and the choice of one as the "essential" feature distinguishing verse from prose is arbitrary, or rather, it defines only a particular system of versification, not the general concept of verse.

Sone contemporary Russian scholars are inclined to define verse not in terms of any one technical characteristic but in terms of the task the versifier sets himself—a task which is different from that of the prose writer. This is, for instance, the way Tomaševskij approaches the problem in his book *Russkoe stixosloženie. Metrika*, pp. 7–8:

It is impossible to give a precise objective definition of verse; it is impossible to note the basic characteristics which differentiate verse from prose. Verse we *recognize* by means of direct perception. . . . The basic characteristic of verse language is that sound language (*zvukoreč*) is organized according to goals pertaining to sound (*po zvukovomu zadaniju*). To say it more precisely: *the goals pertaining to sound dominate in verse over those pertaining to meaning.*

4. Having established the recurrence of stress at regular intervals as the essential characteristic of verse, Trediakovskij was led to accept all types of bisyllabic and trisyllabic feet as equally valid units for metrical organization.

Although he claimed that both treatises were formulated on the same principle, there seems to be a difference. In 1735 a verse foot was defined as a *group of syllables* (actually of two syllables only), preferably with a stress on the first syllable. In 1752 the verse foot becomes a *stress* combined with a certain number of unstressed syllables. One may note that the pyrrhic foot is now treated separately, as poetic license (# 18). In this Trediakovskij moved closer to Lomonosov in his understanding of what constitutes a verse foot.

Moreover, in the first treatise Trediakovskij understood his task as one of organizing the rhythm of the 13-syllable line; in 1752, on the other hand, he endeavored to establish the essential characteristics of any line of verse.

5. Trediakovskij here retreats from the position he held in 1735 (that monosyllabic words must always be "long"—see Definition V, Corollary 1, p. 40) only as a concession to hard necessity, without showing any inclination to reconsider the principle itself. His statement that all monosyllabic words are "by their nature long" seems to point an accusing finger at Lomonosov's treatise, where some of these words were considered "by nature" long and others short (see Lomonosov's "Letter," p. 72). Actually, what Trediakovskij is yielding to as "unavoidable license" is linguistic reality.

6. The reasons Trediakovskij gives in this paragraph for allowing trisyllabic feet are the same as those cited by Lomonosov in his treatise (see Lomonosov's "Letter," p. 73). However, by mentioning his own translation of *Argenis*, where trisyllabic feet are used in conjunction with bisyllabic ones in the verse passages, Trediakovskij implies that a rule of versification acquires real meaning only after it has proved itself in actual usage. In spite of his theoretical statements and the few examples he supplied, Lomonosov wrote almost entirely in iambics.

Thus, Trediakovskij believed that he himself was really the first to introduce trisyllabic feet into Russian versification. In the preface to his translation of *Argenis*, Trediakovskij concedes to Lomonosov the honor of having first introduced iambic verse, but on the basis of the latter's odes rather than the rules stated in his "Letter."

7. The reference is obviously to his first treatise, the "Method" of 1735. Throughout his career Trediakovskij was anxious to reassert his claims to priority in the development of the syllabo-tonic system in Russia.

8. It is typical of Trediakovskij's "geometrical mind" that he should cite his own definition of verse as the reason why the monometer cannot be called verse.

9. In effect Trediakovskij is offering here four "heroic hexameters," only one of which—the dactylic-trochaic—is a true imitation of the Greek and Latin epic line. Technically, priority in the introduction of this hexameter belongs to Lomonosov, who was the first to give examples of it in his "Letter."

10. The acceptance of all three kinds of rhyme naturally follows the acceptance of the iambic and dactylic feet. It is a clear step away from the syllabic tradition, where the rhyme—always feminine—was not understood in terms of feet at all and where it served as a metrical constant.

11. This trochaic "hexameter," which was the mainstay of Trediakovskij's old system, postulated in the treatise of 1735, had actually become superfluous since the new, true dactylic-trochaic hexameter was introduced. However, apparently in the interests of "completeness," he kept it here as well, and even furnished a masculine variant by means of simple reversal of the hemistichs. The fact that he permits a feminine caesura in his new variant of the old 13-syllable line, seems to imply a change in attitude of Trediakovskij's part, namely, that a masculine caesura while an absolute necessity in iambic lines, may be omitted from trochaic lines. It is also interesting that in order to continue regarding this line, in either of the two forms, as a hexameter, Trediakovskij had to allow the implication that a stressed syllable alone may not constitute a verse foot, even an incomplete one. Thus, even in 1752 Trediakovskij did not completely abandon the view of a verse foot as a group of two syllables, whether stressed or not (as in 1735), in favor of the concept of the stress as the essential part of a

verse foot. The definition in chapter I, # 11, of this treatise, that a tone *together with* its interval constitutes a foot clearly implies that both stressed and unstressed syllables are equally essential components of a verse foot.

It can be inferred from the example of trochaic hexameter with feminine rhyme given in # 10 that Trediakovskij even in 1752 held to the notion that the "caesura" was at the same time a "long" syllable and a pause, and that it was not included in the number of feet (compare Introduction, p. 17) and the 1735 treatise, p. 43 as well as n. 23, p. 153). When, due to a reversal of hemistichs, this syllable was removed from its central position in the line, as in the masculine trochaic hexameter (second example, # 10), Trediakovskij still did not count it as one of the feet in the line.

On the other hand, when Trediakovskij discussed other heroic lines, including trisyllabic feet, he included the "caesura syllable" in a verse foot that counted in the scanning of the line, even if this contradicted his basic notion. In the iambic hexameter (# 15, p. 107) the stressed syllable is part of the third foot, in the dactylic-trochaic hexameter (see examples for # 19 and # 20, pp. 108–9) this syllable is part of a trochaic foot which straddles the caesura, etc. In one instance (# 9, p. 112, the dactylic-trochaic pentameter), Trediakovskij even gave this syllable the value of one half of a foot, the other half being the final stressed syllable. It seems that in 1752 Trediakovskij tried to solve this problem of the caesura as best he could in each instance, disregarding the ensuing confusion and contradictions.

12. In 1735 Trediakovskij clearly distinguished between the mixing of rhymes of the same kind (e.g., a F b F a F b F) and the alternation of different kinds of rhymes (e.g., M F M F), objecting strenuously to the latter. In paragraphs 11 and 12 of this chapter, however, he seems to allow the terminology to become confused. The alternation of feminine and masculine rhymes is now called mixed rhyme as well. The parenthetical sentence at the end of # 12 which states that such mixing is called combining of verses is in striking contrast to the treatise of 1735 where much effort was expended on denouncing just such an alternation (see p. 51).

Actually, there was no need for Trediakovskij to gloss over this contrast, for now he had found a way to make a masculine 13-syllable line, thus removing his previous main objection to the alternation of rhymes, the violation of the parisyllabic principle. Moreover, this principle itself lost its importance in the over-all design of his versification treatise of 1752, for now Trediakovskij introduced new types of heroic verse which did not have to be parisyllabic.

13. Since there can be no pause between a monosyllabic word "completing a thought" and the word preceding it, the caesura is carried one syllable further. As a rule all monosyllabic words in Trediakovskij's system are "long", and thus one would have a masculine caesura, as in the feminine trochee, in this way destroying the principle of reversed hemistichs which Trediakovskij applied in order to obtain his masculine trochees. Actually, Trediakovskij warns against the use of enclitic monosyllabic words after the caesura; the words he lists are generally not enclitic.

14. The attitude toward enjambement is the same as in the 1735 treatise; if the lines have a set number of syllables, the enjambement is a fault. The formula seems to be this: rhymed lines permit only limited enjambement (that is, only one kind—the one which extends through the whole second line), and unrhymed lines permit any kind of enjambement.

15. Trediakovskij seems to identify iambics with German versification in the same way as syllabic verse was identified with Polish versification. German poetry used other meters, and Trediakovskij certainly knew this. It seems, however, that in pointing out the German origins of this meter, he specifically had in mind Lomonosov's odes and theoretical statements, which, he thought, were direct imitations of German poetry and versification techniques. Toward the end of his career Trediakovskij apparently decided that Lomonsov should be given credit for introducing this meter into Russian poetry, providing it was made clear that he, Trediakovskij, was the original reformer of Russian versification according to syllabo-tonic principles. In the first version of his preface to the translation of *Argenis* Trediakovskij wrote:

Iambic verse was introduced into our versification by *Professor Lomonosov after* I had already introduced the trochaic. . . . *Professor Lomonosov* at that time had already sent me a letter from Freiberg concerning this verse. . . .

When Lomonosov protested that he had sent his letter on the rules of Russian versification not to Trediakovskij personally, but to the

Russian Assembly as a whole, Trediakovskij was forced to delete the references to Lomonosov from his preface. (See Kunik, ed., *Materialy dlja istorii* . . ., pp. xlii–xliv.)

As for the iambic caesura, Trediakovskij here differed radically from both Lomonosov and Sumarokov, since the latter admitted pyrrhic feet at the end of the first hemistich. As Kiril Taranovski (*Ruski dvodelni ritmovi*, pp. 104–5) points out, Trediakovskij treated six-foot iambs as the equivalent of the French alexandrine; the first and third parts of Boileau's *L'Art Poétique* were translated by Trediakovskij in this iambic meter. Therefore, he probably introduced the masculine caesura into his "iambic hexameter" under the influence of the French alexandrine. German six-foot iambics did not invariably take a masculine caesura.

16. Trediakovskij's translation of Fénelon's *Les Aventures de Télémaque* was written in this dactylic-trochaic meter, and it may be said that this work (*Tilemaxida*) is Trediakovskij's greatest achievement in poetry.

17. Charles Rollin. See Introduction, p. 9.

18. André Dacier, French philologist (1651–1722); the translations he commented upon were those of his wife, née Anne Lefebvre, a distinguished Hellenist and Latinist.

19. Since in the Greek hexameter a spondee instead of a dactyl is usually possible in all feet except the fifth, Trediakovskij substitutes a trochee as an alternative to a dactyl in all these feet. Trediakovskij did not seem to see any particular difficulty in substituting the trochee for the classical spondee in adapting this heroic meter to Russian poetry. Later, however, there was considerable doubt about the propriety of such substitution. Richard Burgi (*History of the Russian Hexameter*, pp. 62–63) summarizes the pro and contra of the issue as follows:

> Purists in Russia, as in Germany, will object that freely mixed dactyls and trochees cannot be accepted as the accentual counterpart of the classical hexameter. They will argue that, if the accented sound is the equivalent of the long vowel and the unaccented sound represents the short vowel of classical metrics, then, logically, the spondee must be rendered by two accented sounds, the trochees being an unwarranted distortion. These were, in the main, the arguments offered by the distinguished philologist and translator, Professor Zielinski, at the beginning of this century.

The argument, however, is posited on two essential fallacies, namely, that a stressed sound is equal to two unstressed sounds as in quantitative prosodic system a long equals two shorts. The entire quantitative prosodic system is built on the equivalence of one short to one-half of the long. In accentual metrics there is no such opposition of isochronic components, but only an opposition of ictus to non-ictus. The second fallacy is the irrational conviction that a parity must exist between an accentually stressed sound and a quantitatively long sound. A tonic system of metrics has no exact equivalent for any feature of a system of metrics built on quantity, because each system is based on completely different attributes of speech-sound. An accent is a dynamic sound serving as a nucleus around which less intensive syllables are organized.

20. N. V. Peretc (*Iz istorii razvitija russkoj poezii*, p. 65) criticizes Trediakovskij's lack of originality and points out that in the matter of the spondee Trediakovskij followed almost literally Meletij Smotrickij, and also a Latin textbook written by the Jesuit Emmanuel Alvares (1586), which contains this statement: "Quintus pes nunnumquam spondeus est, unde versus spondaicus appelatur, quo vel rei alicuius gravitas et amplitudo, vel ingens moeror, animique angor vel aliud declarator."

Peretc's criticism is hardly fair. The task Trediakovskij undertook was primarily that of introducing his countrymen to the traditional classical theories he had learned. In this particular case, however, he did follow Alvares too closely and was misled by him, for in classical verse the substitution of a spondee for a trochee in the fifth foot is quite rare.

21. This statement indicates that Trediakovskij's disapproval of rhyme was largely confined to the epic meter. On one occasion he actually specified the types of poetry where rhyme could be used properly:

But let those who have taken a passion for rhymes not get upset that I have, so to speak, deprived them of two domains in versification. Their homeland with respect to rhyme still remains quite large and manifold, namely, in epigrams, satires, elegies, epistles, and odes.

(Introduction to *Tilemaxida, Sočinenija
Trediakovskogo*, II, lxviii)

22. This new type of meter had apparently been developed by Trediakovskij in the interests of "symmetry" and completeness. The

trochaic-dactylic and the trochaic hexameters making one pair, the anapestic-iambic hexameter would serve as a counterpart to the iambic. There seems to be no model for this structure of the anapestic-iambic hexameter in classical verse, and therefore one may assume that Trediakovskij devised the scheme himself, although, to be sure, Lomonosov had included the possibility of such verse in his "Letter."

23. Trediakovskij used his masculine trochaic pentameter in translating the Eunuchus by Terence. He compared this meter with the Latin *senarius:* "In my translation I have used the trochaic pentameter, for it seemed to me most similar to the Latin *senarius*" introduction to *Evnuch*, quoted by L. B. Modzalevskij, " ' Evnux' V. K. Trediakovskogo," *XVIII vek*, p. 313). W. Beare (*Latin Verse and European Song*, p. 133), gives the following diagram of the Plautine iambic *senarius:*

```
  ᴗ ᴗ ᴗ ᴗ │ ᴗ ᴗ ᴗ ᴗ │ ᴗ ᴗ ┊ ᴗ ᴗ │ ᴗ ᴗ ᴗ ᴗ │ ᴗ ᴗ ᴗ ᴗ │    ᴗ
   ─    ─  │  ─    ─  │  ─  ┊  ─  │  ─    ─  │  ─    ─  │ ᴗ ─
        ᴗ  │      ᴗ   │     ᴗ    │      ᴗ    │      ᴗ   │
```

If the position of the long syllable is reversed so as to obtain a trochaic sequence, a similarity appears between this meter and Trediakovskij's feminine pentameter: two trochaic feet and then a long syllable followed by caesura, and a trochaic foot at the end, for which a pyrrhic cannot be substituted. And yet, Trediakovskij insisted that his verse was a pentameter, even though it had six stresses, comparable to the six feet of the *senarius*. To be sure, in what would be the third foot of *senarius* Trediakovskij does not have a second, unstressed syllable, and therefore, according to his principles, this position does not constitute a foot. The iambic *senarius*, as well as the iambic and trochaic *septanarius*, was used mostly for dialogue by Plautus and Terence.

24. K. Taranovski (*Ruski dvodelni ritmovi*, pp. 158–59) points out that this description of the iambic pentameter is the same as that of the French pentameter, which also has a caesura at the fourth syllable and two tonic constants at the fourth and the tenth syllables. In fact, Trediakovskij's iambic hexameter also has the caesura in the same position as the French alexandrine. *Cf.* Ronsard, *Abbregé de l'Art poëtique* . . ., p. 26: "Les vers communs sont de dix à onze syllabes, les masculins de dix, les foeminins d'onze, & ont sur la quatriesme

syllabe leur repos ou reprise d'aleine ainsi que les vers Alexandrins sur la fin des six premières syllables." It could be added that Trediakovskij's insistence on the masculine caesura in his "trochaic hexameter"— the 13-syllable line which constituted the main accomplishment of his 1735 reform—may also be due to French influence (see p. 150, n. 15).

25. The example of the pentameter is the second of the two lines above. According to Trediakovskij, the dactylic-trochaic pentameter consists of two dactyls (for which trochees or pyrrhic feet may be substituted), the caesura (one accented syllable before a word boundary), two more dactyls and one accented syllable; the caesura and the final syllable are rated one half foot each, giving with the four dactyls the five-foot line. This "dactylic-trochaic pentameter" is given the same name in all European metrics, despite the fact that it has six stresses.

26. Trediakovskij's reference to Quintilian's *Institutionis Oratoriae*, VI, iv, is apparently incorrect, for Quintilian does not discuss metrics in this part of his work; moreover, the work does not contain any discussion of the metrics of poetry as such. Trediakovskij must have had in mind the following passage from IX, iv, 109 of the *Institutionis*: "Non quidem optime est sibi iunctus anapaestos, ut sit pentametri finis, vel rhythmos qui nomen ab eo traxit: *Nam ubi libido dominatur, innocentiae leve praesidium est;* nam synaeloephe ut duae ultimae syllabae pro una sonent" (*The Institutio Oratoria of Quintilian*, with an English translation by H. E. Butler [London, 1922], III, 568).

The end of the prose sentence quoted by Quintilian scans as follows:

... innocentiāe/ lĕvĕ praēsĭdĭum ēst

thus producing two anapests which, according to Quintilian (as Trediakovskij points out), constitute the ending of a pentameter.

Quintilian makes the above reference to the last two feet of the pentameter in a discussion concerned with the rhythmics of oratorical prose, but Trediakovskij apparently supplied the description of the full line using common knowledge of the Latin pentameter as his basis. Normally the structure of the Latin pentameter in heroelegiac verse is as follows:

See W. Beare, p. 78.

One may easily see that the two schemes (Trediakovskij's and Quintilian's) describe the same distribution of strong and weak positions in different terms, those used by Trediakovskij hardly offering the advantage of clarity (the first two feet, identical in both schemes, are disregarded):

Trediakovskij: $- - - -/\acute{x}//\ \acute{x}\ x\ x/\ \acute{x}\ x\ x/\ \acute{x}$
Quintilian: $- - - -\ -/\acute{x}\ \acute{x}/\ x\ x\ \acute{x}/\ x\ x\ \acute{x}$

In both schemes a word boundary is required between the first two consecutive stressed (or long) syllables.

27. There is a difference between Trediakovskij's later concept of the Sapphic stanza and the example of that stanza given in the treatise of 1735. There the first line of a Sapphic stanza reads as follows:

Силы/ в сереб/ре//всяк ску/пой не/знает

forming this metric pattern:

$$\underline{\acute{x}\ x/}_{1}\ \underline{x\ x/}_{2}\ \underline{\acute{x}//}\ \underline{\acute{x}\ x/}_{3}\ \underline{\acute{x}\ x/}_{4}\ \underline{\acute{x}\ x}_{5}$$

The line has in the third position a stressed syllable which precedes the caesura and also completes the word, thus, according to Trediakovskij's rules, dividing the line into two hemistichs.

In 1755 Trediakovskij had an argument with Sumarokov about the construction of the Sapphic stanza, during which he, without actually saying so, repudiated his earlier construction of a Sapphic stanza line. Sumarokov had criticized the metrics of the example given in # 28, and Trediakovskij's response was the following:

. . . for you say that according to this example of mine the Sapphic stanza consists in the first hemistich of the three first lines of two trochees, and for the caesura, which is unnecessary, a long syllable has been added to the two trochees. The second hemistich in the two first lines consists of one anapestic foot, one iamb, and one short syllable, which three syllables, even though they make up a foot, do not form a trochee.

All this, Dear Sir, is not so, and you were led to this faulty measuring which discovered hemistichs in my verses by the caesura, which you groundlessly suppose to be outside the number of feet and which you say, moreover, rather arbitrarily, is unnecessary. I, on the other hand, affirm and will prove to you clearly that my Sapphic verse line does not contain hemistichs and that it must have a caesura which is to be counted in the dactylic foot.

(Pekarskij, appendix VI, p. 250)

Apparently, Sumarokov scanned the example as follows: x́ x/ x́ x/ x́// x x x́/ x x́ (x), as opposed to Trediakovskij's scanning: x́ x/ x́ x/ x̂// x x/ x́ x/ x́ (x). Sumarokov must have attempted to read the example given in ≠ 28 according to Trediakovskij's construction of the Sapphic stanza in the treatise of 1735 and then found a breakdown of the meter in the second hemistich, instead of reading the lines according to the new rules in which, as Trediakovskij goes on to explain, there are no hemistichs, for the long syllabe in the third position, while it completes the word, does not complete but begins a dactylic foot, and a caesura which cuts across a verse foot does not, according to Trediakovskij, divide the line into two hemistichs. The metrical pattern of the Sapphic stanza Trediakovskij used in 1752 follows rather closely the Greek Sapphic stanza, which is as follows: x̄ x̆/ x̄ x̄/ x̆ ; x̆ x̆/ x̄ x̆/ x̄ x̄ (cf. Beare, p. 85).

28. In his preface, Vol. I, pp. lxxv–lxxvi, Trediakovskij gives the following explanation of why the Russian Horatian stanza cannot have spondees in the first two lines:

In these first two lines we cannot put a spondee in place of the usual trochee as we also cannot substitute an iambic foot because of the following long syllable which constitutes the caesura. The very nature of word stress does not allow two long syllables in one word, and always to select words with a long final syllable for the sake of the iamb and then end the caesura with a one-syllable word means deliberately to abandon the beauty of verse by putting two caesurae in a row.

29. In his reformed verse, as described in his treatise of 1735, Trediakovskij also used the feminine rhyme almost exclusively, thus following the Polish practice stemming from Polish accentuation. Trediakovskij fails to mention here that in this respect, at least, his reformed verse of 1735 did not advance beyond blind imitation of the Polish model.

30. There may be an element of paradox in Trediakovskij's growing dislike of rhyme, for the very principle of verse rhythm based on stress, which Trediakovskij advocated in the present treatise, made rhyme possible. According to Beare, p. 255: "As long as stress was ignored in verse, modern rhyme, which depends on it, was obviously impossible; it is the recurrence of stress, not of verse-ictus, which is needed for rhyme." The reason why Greek and Latin verse was not,

on the whole, rhymed, is not only that rhyme would interrupt the epic flow of narrative with "ungainly neighing," as Trediakovskij once put it, but also that the classical verse did not take stress into account and thus could not develop a rhyme. It was only in the Middle Ages—Trediakovskij's "Gothic times"—that Latin verse began to be rhymed; this became possible when vulgar Latin substituted stress for length.

31. It is perhaps indicative of the state of flux of the Russian language in the eighteenth century that Trediakovskij no longer attempted, as he did in 1735, to list the allowable deviations from traditional norms, which he called "poetic license," but instead refers to poetic practice, allowing it to establish new standards.

32. In his listing of poetic genres Trediakovskij imitates the Polish textbooks on versification written in Latin and used in Kiev and other Ukrainian and South Russian schools. Only the arrangement of the material is different, for the present treatise includes items which in the Polish textbooks would go under various separate categories of classification. For instance, a book entitled *Aurifodina Poetica*, by the Jesuit Professor Smarzewski, published in 1704, had a considerable number of different methods of classifying verse: according to authors (Sapphic, Horatian, etc.,) according to meter, to number of syllables, to content, etc. See Peretc, *Iz istorii russkoj pesni*, p. 47.

33. Trediakovskij was in general agreement with the opinion then prevalent in France and Germany that poetry had originated with simple shepherds and other rural folk. In his article "Opinion on the Beginning of Poetry and Verse in General," following Fontenelle, he points to a specific person who before the flood was inspired by God to create poetry. Trediakovskij's (and Fontenelle's) source was, apparently, Genesis, 4: 21: "And his brother's name was Jubal: he was the father of all such as handle the harp and the organ."

34. Trediakovskij's reference to Statius is evidently wrong. *Silvae*, I, ii, is an Epithalamium in honor of Stella and Violentilla. There is, however, a propemptic poem—"Propempticon Maecio Celeri"— in Statius (*Silvae*, III, ii).

35. Latinized form of Maciej Sarbiewski (1595–1640), a Polish Jesuit monk who wrote exclusively in Latin and was often referred to as the Christian Horace because of his successful imitations of Horace's odes. Sarbiewski also wrote a book on poetics which Trediakovskij may have known.

36. This is Trediakovskij's major argument in support of his contention that the 1752 treatise is in all essential respects the same as the 1735 treatise. And indeed, due credit must be given to Trediakovskij, for he was the first to state that a regular pattern of stress distribution should serve as the basis of Russian versification.

NOTES TO VI: CONCLUDING REMARKS

1. Lomonosov's ode to Ioann VI Antonovič, written in 1741, contains, according to B. Tomaševskij (*Stilistika i stixosloženie*, pp. 357–, 58), only five lines with pyrrhic feet out of a total of 210 lines. The earlier versions of his "Ode on the Taking of Xotin" (which have not come down to us) in all likelihood also contained only occasional lines with pyrrhic feet; those, in all probability, were due to oversight.

2. Quoted by Berkov, *Lomonosov i literaturnaja polemika ego vremeni*, p. 68.

3. Cf. Gukovskij, *Istorija russkoj poezii XVIII veka*, p. 46.

4. Xeraskov, "Rassuždenie o rossijskom stixotvorstve," first published, with introduction, by P. N. Berkov, *Literaturnoe nasledstvo*, No. 9–10, p. 293. We must remember that Lomonosov's "Ode on the Taking of Xotin" had not been published.

5. Cf. Timofeev, "Vol'nyj stix XVIII veka," *Ars Poetica*, II (1928), 75.

6. Tomaševskij, "Stix 'Gorja ot uma," *Stix i jazyk*, p. 150.

7. E.g., his *Oda Gosudarine Ekaterine Vtoroj na den' eja roždenija 1768 goda Aprelja 21 dnja* (Ode to the Empress Catherine the Second).

8. E.g., his spiritual ode (*Protivu zlodeev*) (Against evildoers), 1759, written in anapestic trimeters.

9. Cf. Tomaševskij, *Stilistika i stixosloženie*, pp. 350, 380. Lomonosov did not refer to the amphibrach at all in his "Letter" of 1739, apparently because he thought in terms of "ascending" (iamb, anapest) and "descending" (trochee, dactyl) verse feet, and the amphibrach, being neither one nor the other, did not fit into his scheme (see n. 12 to Lomonosov's "Letter," p. 168). Trediakovskij again did not mention the amphibrach in 1752, while in 1735 he had rejected all trinary meters.

10. Cf. André von Gronicka, "Goethe and His Russian Translator—Interpreter V. A. Zhukovski (1783–1852)," *PMLA*, LXX (No. 1, 1955), 145–65.

11. Thus Goethe's "Erlkönig" was rendered by Žukovskij in regular amphibrachs:

> Wer reitet so spät durch Nacht und Wind?
> Es ist der Vater mit seinem Kind;
> x x́ x/ x x́/ x x́/ x x́
> x x́/ x x́ x/ x x́/ x x́

> Кто скачет, кто мчится под хдадною мглой?
> Ездок запоздалый, с ним сын молодой;

> x x́ x/ x x́ x/ x x́ x/ x x́
> x x́ x/ x x́ x/ x x́ x/ x x́

12. The stress ratio of nearly 2:1, as was pointed out before (p. 129), made it easy for Russian poets to maintain the "purity" of trinary meters.

13. See Burgi, pp. 89, 125.

14. Radiščev, "Pamjatnik daktiloxoreičeskomu vitjazju," in *Polnoe sobranie sočinenij*, I, 323.

15. Burgi, pp. 80–81.

16. For a comparative statistical analysis of the number of trochaic substitutions in the verses of Gnedič and Žukovskij, see Burgi, p.132.

17. Tomaševskij, "Strofika Puškina," *Stix i jazyk*, p. 222.

18. According to the tabulations of Tomaševskij and those of Andrej Belyj (Tomaševskij, *O stixe. Stat'i*, p. 106 and note; Belyj's figures are given in brackets), on the variants of the iambic tetrameter, the highest frequency (between 40 and 45 percent) in both Lomonosov and Pushkin belongs to the line:

> x   x́/ x x́/ x x/ x x́/ (x)

In other types, on the contrary, there are sharp differences; thus the line:

> x x́/ x x/ x x́/ x x́/ (x)

has a frequency of 24.4 percent [21.5 percent] in Lomonosov and only of 9.7 percent [5.4 percent] in Pushkin. Finally, counting together two kinds of line beginning with a pyrrhic foot:

x x/ x x́/ x x́/ x x́/ (x)

and

x x/ x x́/ x x/ x x́/ (x)

we have for Lomonosov a frequency of only 4.1 percent [2.1 percent] and for Pushkin 15.6 percent [18.5 percent].

19. For example, in his poem *Vyxožu odin ja na dorogu* (I go out alone upon the road), 1841, the theoretical meter is a five-foot trochee: x́ x/ x́ x/ x́ x/ x́ x/ x́ x/, but the omission of the first stress in most lines, strong caesura after the third syllable, and the intonational stress on the third are so dominant that the actual rhythm becomes: x x x́// x x́/ x x/ x x́/ (x). See Boris Ejxenbaum, *Melodika russkogo liričeskogo stixa*, p.115.

20. On the role of imitations of folk poetry in Russian literary works, see Alexander Adamczyk, "Russische Verskunst, ein geschichtlicher Überblick," *Münchener Beiträge zur Slavenkunde*, IV (1953), 179–201.

Bibliography

I. WORKS BY KANTEMIR, LOMONOSOV, AND TREDIAKOVSKIJ

Kantemir. *Sobranie stixotvorenij*. 2d ed. Leningrad: Sovetskij pisatel', 1956.

—— *Sočinenija, pis'ma i izbrannye perevody knjazja Antioxa Kantemira*, edited by P. A. Efremov, with notes and introduction by V. Ja. Stojunin. 2 vols St. Petersburg: Ivan Il'ič Glazunov, 1867–68.

Lomonosov. *Polnoe sobranie sočinenij*. Moscow: U.S.S.R. Academy of Sciences. Vol VII, Philological Works, 1952.

—— *Izbrannye filosofskie proizvedenija*, edited with an introduction by T. S. Vaseckij. Moscow, 1950.

—— *Sočinenija M. V. Lomonosova*, edited with explanatory notes by M. Suxomlinov. 4 vols. St. Petersburg; Imperatorskaja Akademija Nauk, 1891–98.

Trediakovskij. *Argenida*. John Barclay's *Argenis*, translated with an introduction by V. K. Trediakovskij. St. Petersburg: Imperatorskaja Akademija Nauk, 1751.

—— "O drevnem, srednem i novom stixosloženii rossijskom" *Ežemesjačnye sočinenija k pol'ze i uveseleniju služaščie*, June, 1755, pp.467–510.

—— *Sočinenija Trediakovskogo*. 2 vols. St. Petersburg: Alexander Smirdin, 1849.

—— *Stixotvorenija*. Moscow: Sovetskij pisatel', 1935.

—— *Izbrannye proizvedenija*. Moscow-Leningrad: Sovetskij pisatel', 1963.

II. SECONDARY WORKS

Adamczyk, Alexander. "Russische Verskunst, ein geschichtlicher Überblick," *Münchener Beiträge zur Slavenkunde*, IV (1953), 179–201.

Alekseev, M. P. "Montesk'e i Kantemir," *Vestnik Leningradskogo Universiteta*, No. 8 (1955).

Artakserksovo dejstvo. Pervaja p'esa russkogo teatra XVIIIv., edited with introduction and commentaries by I. M. Kudrjavcev. Moscow-Leningrad, 1957.

Beare, William. *Latin Verse and European Song: A Study in Accent and Rhythm*. London: Methuen & Co., Ltd., 1957.

Berkov, P. N. *Lomonosov i literaturnaja polemika ego vremeni, 1750–1765*. Moscow-Leningrad, 1936.

——"Lomonosov i fol'klor," in *Lomonosov, sbornik statej i materialov*, Vol. II, edited by A. I. Andreev and L. V. Modzalevskij. Moscow-Leningrad, 1946.

—— " 'Rassuždenie or rossijskom stixotvorstve', neizvestnaja stat'ja M. M. Xeraskova," *Literaturnoe nasledstvo*, No. 9–10 (1933), 287–94.

—— "U istokov dvorjanskoj literatury XVIII veka: Poet Mixail Sobakin," *Literaturnoe nasledstvo*, No. 9–10, pp. 421–32.

—— "Iz istorii russkoj, poezii pervoj tret'i XVIII v.," *XVIII vek*, I (1935), 61–81.

—— "Neispol'zovannye materialy dlja istorii russkoj literatury XVIII veka," *XVIII vek*, I, 327–76.

—— " 'Xor ko prevratnomu svetu' i ego avtor," *XVIII vek*, I, 181–202.

Blagoj, D. D. *Istorija russkoj literatury XVIII veka*. Moscow, 1945; 2d ed., rev., Moscow, 1951.

—— "Gavrila Romanovič Deržavin," in G. R. Deržavin, *Stixotvorenija* (Leningrad: Sovestkij pisatel', 1957), pp. 5–74.

Blok, Aleksandr, and Andrej Belyj. *Aleksandr Blok i Andrej Belyj, perepiska*, edited by V. N. Orlov. Letopisi Gosudarstvennogo literaturnogo muzeja, No. 7. Moscow, 1940.

Bomštejn, G. I. "Trediakoskij—fililog i fol'klor," *XVIII vek*, V, 249–72.

Budilovič, A., comp. *Lomonosov kak pisatel'. Sbornik statej dlja rassmotrenija avtorskoj dejatel'nosti Lomonosova*. St. Petersburg, 1871.

Bulič, N. N. *Sumarokov i sovremennaja emu kritika.* St. Petersburg, 1854.

Burgi, Richard. *A History of the Russian Hexameter.* Hamden, Conn.: The Shoe String Press, 1954.

Bykova, T. A. "K istorii russkogo toničeskogo stixosloženija (Neizvestnoe proizvedenie I. G. Sparvenfel'da)," *XVIII vek,* III, 449–53.

Casini, Tomaso. *Le Forme metriche italiane,* Florence: G. C. Sansoni, 1915.

Černov, S. "Literaturnoe nasledstvo M. V. Lomonosova," *Literaturnoe nasledstvo,* No. 9–10 (1933), 327–39.

Clarke, Charles Cameron. *Concerning French Verse: An Essay for English-Speaking Readers of French.* New Haven: Yale University Press, 1922.

Dan'ko E. Ja. "Iz neizdannyx materialov o Lomonosove," *XVIII vek,* II, 248–75.

Dłuska, Maria. *Studia z historii i teorii wersyfikacji polskiej.* 2 vols. Kraków, 1948–50.

Drage, C. L. "Trochaic Metres in Early Russian Syllabo-Tonic Poetry," *The Slavonic and Eastern European Review,* XXXVII (No. 91, 1960), 361–79.

Ehrhard, Marcelle. *Un Ambassadeur de Russie à la Cour de Louis XV. Le Prince Cantemir à Paris (1738–1744).* Lyon: BOSC Frères, 1938.

Ejxenbaum, Boris. *Melodika russkogo liričeskogo stixa.* Petersburg: Opojaz, 1922.

Eremin, I. P. "Simeon Polockij—poet i dramaturg," in Simeon Polockji, *Izbrannye sočinenija* (Moscow-Leningrad. 1953), p. 240.

Erlich, Victor. *Russian Formalism. History—Doctrine.* (Slavistic Printings and Reprintings, Leiden University, Book Four.) 'S-Gravenhage: Mouton & Co., 1955.

Flamini, Francesco. *Notizia storica dei Versi e Metri italiani dal Medioevo ai Tempi moderni.* Leghorn: Raffaelo Giusti, 1919.

Gerškovič, Z. I. "K biografii A. D. Kantemira," *XVIII vek,* III, 456–59.

—— "K voprosu ob evoljucii mirovozzrenija i tvorčestva A. D. Kantemira (Promblema 'devjatoj satiry')", *XVIII vek,* III, 44–64.

Goloxvastov, P. D. *Zakony stixa russkogo narodnogo i našego literaturnogo.* St. Petersburg, 1883.

Gottscheds Lebens-und Kunstreform in den zwanziger und dreissiger Jahren, edited by F. Brüggeman. (Deutsche Literatur, Sammlung literarischer Kunst-und Kulturdenkmäler in Entwicklungsreihen. Reihe Aufklärung.) Leipzig: Reclam-Verlag, 1935.

Gouasco. *Satyres du Prince Cantemir, traduites du Russe en François, avec l'Histoire de sa Vie.* London: Chez Jean Nourse, 1750.

Grammont, Maurice. *Le Vers Français, Ses moyens d'expression, son harmonie.* Paris: Eduard Champion, 1913.

Gronicka, André von. "Goethe and His Russian Translator-Interpreter V. A. Zhukovski (1783–1852)," *PMLA*, LXX (No. 1, 1955), pp.145–65.

Guarnerio, Pier Enea. *Manuale di Versificazione italiana.* Milan: Francesco Vallardi, 1913.

Gudzij, N. K. *Istorija drevnej russkoj literatury.* Moscow, 1938. English translation by Susan Wilbur Jones: *History of Early Russian Literature.* New York, 1949.

Gukovskij, G. *Russkaja poezija XVIII veka.* "Voprosy poetiki," installment 10. Leningrad: "Academia," 1927.

—— *Očerki po istorii russkoj literatury XVIII veka. Dvorjanskaja fronda v literature 1750-x godov.* Moscow-Leningrad, 1936.

—— "O 'Xore k prevratnomu svetu'," *XVIII vek*, I, 203–17.

Gundolf, Friedrich. *Martin Opitz.* Munich & Leipzig: Duncker & Humbolt, 1923.

Harkins, William E. *The Russian Folk Epos in Czech Literature, 1800–1900.* New York: King's Crown Press, 1951.

Hilferding, A. F. *Onežskie byliny, zapisannye Aleksandrom Feodorovičem Gil'ferdigom letom 1871 goda.* St. Petersburg, 1873.

Humiston, C. C. "A Comparative Study of the Metrical Technique of Ronsard and Malherbe," *University of California Publications in Modern Philology*, XXIV (1941), 1–180.

Ivanov, N. *Ob osnovanijax russkogo narodnogo i literaturnogo stixosloženija (Na pamjat' A. A. Potebne)*, Voronež, 1893.

Jakobson, Roman. "Bolgarskij pjatistopnyj jamb v sopostavlenii s russkim," in *Sbornik v čest' na Prof. L. Miletič* (Sofia: Macedonian Academy of Sciences, 1933), pp.108–17.

—— "Studies in Comparative Slavic Metrics," *Oxford Slavonic Papers*, III, 21–26.

204 *Bibliography*

—— "The Kernel of Comparative Slavic Literature," *Harvard Slavic Studies*, I, 1–71.

Jarxo, B. I. "Ritmika tak naz. 'Romana v stixax'," *Ars Poetica*, II, 9–37.

Johanneson, Fritz. *Die Bestrebungen Malherbes auf dem Gebiete der poetischer Technik in Frankreich*. Halle a/S: Fritz Johanneson, 1881.

Karskij, E. *Geschichte der weissrussischen Volksdichtung und Literatur*. Berlin & Leipzig: Walter de Gruyter & Co., 1926.

Kolmogorov, A. N. and A. M. Kondratov. "Ritmika poem Majakovskogo," *Voprosy jazykoznanija*, III, (1962), 62–74.

Kondratov, A. M. "Evoljucija ritmiki V. V. Majakovskogo," *Voprosy jazykoznanija*, V (1962), 101–9.

Kridl, Manfred, ed. *An Anthology of Polish Literature*. New York: Columbia University Press, 1957.

Kucerov, A. "N. M. Karamzin," in N. M. Karamzin and I. Dmitriev, *Izbrannye stixotvorenija* (Leningrad: Sovestkij pisatel', 1953), pp. 7–52.

Kunik, A., ed. *Sbornik materialov dlja istorii Imperatorskoj Akademii Nauk v XVIII veke*, Vol. I. St. Petersburg, 1856.

Majakovskij, Vladimir. "Kak delat' stixi," in *Polnoe sobranie sočinenij*, XII (Moscow, 1959), 81–117.

Majkov, L. N. *Očerki iz istorii russkoj literatury XVII i XVIII stoletij*. St. Petersburg, 1889.

—— *Materialy dlja biografii kn. A. D. Kantemira*. St. Petersburg, 1903.

Menšutkin, B. N. *Žizneopisanie Mixaila Vasil'eviča Lomonosova*. Moscow, 1937. English translation by Jeanette Eyre Thal and Edward J. Webster: *Russia's Lomonosov*. Princeton, 1952.

Modzalevskij, L. B. " 'Evnux' V. K. Trediakovskogo," *XVIII vek*. I, 311–26.

—— "Literaturnaja polemika Lomonosova i Trediakovskogo v 'Ežemesjačnyx sočinenijax'," *XVIII vek*, IV, 45–65.

Morda Evans, R. J. "Antioch Kantemir and His First Biographer and Translator," *The Slavonic and East European Review*, XXXVII (No. 88, 1958), 184–95.

Motol'skaja, D. K. "Lomonosov," *Istorija russkoj literatury*. Vol. III, *Literatura XVIII veka*, Part I (Moscow-Leningrad: The U.S.S.R. Academy of Sciences, 1941), pp. 264–348.

Murari, Rocco. *Ritmica a Metrica razionale italiana.* Milan: Ulrico Hoepli, 1927.

Opitz, Martin. *Buch von der deutschen Poeterey.* Halle a/S: Max Niemeyer, 1902. Reprint of first edition (1624).

Orlov, VI. 'Aleksandr Blok," in Aleksandr Blok *Stixotvorenija, poemy, teatr,* I (Moscow, 1955) v–lvi.

Pekarskij Petr. *Istorija Imperatorskoj Akademii Nauk v Peterburge,* Vol. II. St. Petersburg, 1873.

Peretc, V. N. *Iz istorii russkoj pesni.* Vol. I of *Istoriko-literaturnye issledovanija i materialy.* St. Petersburg, 1900.

—— *Iz istorii razvitija russkoj poezii XVIII v.* Vol. III of *Istoriko-literaturnye issledovanija materialy.* St. Petersburg, 1902.

—— *Očerki po istorii poetičeskogo stilja v Rossii.* Vol. IV of *Istoriko-literaturnye issledovanija i materialy.* St. Petersburg, 1905.

Pigarev, K. "F. I. Tjutčev," in F. I. Tjutčev, *Stixotvorenija, pis'ma,* I (Moscow, 1957), 3-32.

Plotkin, L. "A. V. Kol'cov," in A. V. Kol'cov, *Polnoe sobranie stixotvorenij,* 2d edition (Leningrad, 1958), pp.5–41.

Pozdneev, A. V. "Die tonischen Elemente im russischen syllabischen Vers," *Zeitschrift für slavische Philologie,* XXVIII, (No. 2, 1960), 405–12.

Prijma, F. Ja. "Antiox Dmitrievič Kantemir." (Introduction to Kantemir's *Sobranie stixotvorenij*). Leningrad, 1956.

Prokopovič, Feofan. *Sočinenija.* Leningrad: U.S.S.R., Academy of Sciences, 1961.

Pumpjanskij, L. V. "Trediakovskij," *Istorija russkoj literatury.* Vol. III, *Literatura XVIII veka,* Part I (Moscow-Leningrad: The U.S.S.R. Academy of Sciences, 1941), pp. 215–63.

—— "Kantemir," *Istorija russkoj literatury,* Vol. III, *Literatura XVIII veka,* Part I (Moscow-Leningrad: The U.S.S.R. Academy of Sciences, 1941), pp. 176–212.

—— "Očerki po literature pervoj poloviny XVIII veka," *XVIII vek,* I (1935), 83–132.

Purves, John. *A First Book of Italian Verse.* Edinburgh: Oliver & Boyd, 1930.

Pushkin, A. S. *Puškin, pis'ma,* edited by B. M. Modzalevskij, Vol. 1, Moscow-Leningrad, 1926.

Quintilian. *The Institutio Oratoria of Quintilian*, with an English translation by H. E. Butler. London, 1922.

Radiščev, A. N. "Pamjatnik daktiloxoreičeskomu vitjazju," in *Polnoe sobranie sočinenij* (Moscow, 1907), pp. 389–425.

Radovskij, M. I. *Antiox Kantemir i Petersburgskaja Akademija Nauk.* Moscow-Leningrad, 1959.

Ronsard, Pierre de. *Abbregé de l'Art poëtique François.* In *Œuvres Complètes*, Vol. XIV, critical edition with introduction and commentary by Paul Laumonier. Paris: Librarie Marcel Didier, 1949.

Schaffer, Aaron. *Georg Rudolf Weckherlin: The Embodiment of a Transitional Stage in German Metrics.* Baltimore: The Johns Hopkins Press, 1918.

Šengeli, G. *Texnika stixa.* Moscow, 1960.

Simeon, Polockij. *Izbrannye sočinenija*, edited with introduction and commentaries by I. P. Eremin. Moscow-Leningrad, 1953.

Sokolov, A. N. *Očerki po istorii russkoj poemy XVIII i pervoj poloviny XIX veka.* Moscow, 1955.

Sokolov, Y. M. *Russian Folklore*, translated by Catherine Ruth Smith. New York: The Macmillan Co., 1950.

Stender-Peterson, Ad., ed. *Anthology of Old Russian Literature.* New York: Columbia University Press, 1954.

Štokmar. M. P. *Bibliografija rabot po stixosloženiju.* Moscow, 1933.

—— *Issledovanija v oblasti russkogo narodnogo stixosloženija.* Moscow, 1952.

—— "Vol'nyj stix XIX veka," *Ars Poetica*, II, 117–67.

Sumarokov, A. P. *Izbrannye proizvedenija*, with introduction by P. N. Berkov. Leningrad: Sovetskij pisatel', 1957.

Taranovski, Kiril. *Ruski dvodelni ritmovi.* Belgrade: The Serbian Academy of Sciences, 1953.

—— Review of P. M. Štokmar's *Issledovanija v oblasti russkogo narodnogo stixosloženija*, *Južnoslovenski filolog.*, XXI (books 1–4, 1955), 335–63.

Timofeev, L. I. *Teorija stixa.* Moscow, 1939.

—— *Problemy teorii literatury.* Moscow, 1955.

—— *Očerki teorii i istorii russkogo stixa.* Moscow, 1958.

—— "Sillabičeskij stix," *Ars Poetica*, II, 37–71.

—— "Vol'nyj stix XVIII veka," *Ars Poetica*, II, 73–115.

Tomaševskij, B. *Russkoe stixosloženie. Metrika.* ("Voprosy poetiki," installment 2.) Petrograd: "Academia," 1923.
—— *O stixe. Stat'i.* Leningrad: "Priboj," 1929.
—— *Teorija literatury. Poetika.* 6th edition. Leningrad, 1931.
—— *Stilistika i stixosloženie.* Kurs lekcij, Leningrad, 1959.
—— *Stix i jazyk. Filologičeskie očerki.* Moscow-Leningrad, 1959.
—— "Problema stixotvornogo ritma," *Literaturnaja mysl'*, II (1923), 124–40.
—— Review of B. O. Unbegaun, *Russian Versification, Voprosy jazykoznanija*, III (1957), 124–40.
Toptiev, A. V., I. A. Figurovskij, and V. L. Čenakala, eds., *Letopis' žizni i tvorčestva M. V. Lomonosova.* Moscow: U.S.S.R. Academy of Sciences, 1961.
Trubeckoj, N. S. *Die russischen Dichter des 18. und 19. Jahrhunderts.* Sketch for a history of development, published from a Russian manuscript by Rudolf Jagoditsch. Wiener Slawistisches Jahrbuch, supplementary volume III. Graz-Köln: Herman Böhlaus Nachf., 1956.
—— "O metrike častuški," *Versty*, No. 2 (1927), pp.205–23.
Trzykadłowski, Jan. "Rytmotwórcza funkcja akcentu w wierszu staro-polskim." Introduction to Karol Wiktor Zawodziński, *Studia z wersyfikacji Polskiej*, Breslau, (1954), pp. xxvi–xlvii.
Tvorčestvo Majakovskogo. Sbornik statej. Moscow, 1952.
Unbegaun, B. O. *Russian Versification.* Oxford: Clarendon Press, 1956.
—— "Les Débuts de la Versification Russe et La Comédie D'Arta-xerxès," *Revue des Études Slaves*, XXXII (1955), 32–41.
Vinter, E. "I. V. Paus o svoej dejatel'nosti v kačestve filologa i istorika (1732)," *XVIII vek*, IV, 313–22.
Virši. Sillabičeskaja poezija XVII–XVIII vekov, edited by P. N. Berkov, with an introduction by Iv. N. Rozanov. Moscow: Sovetskij pisatel', 1935.
Vostokov, A. X. *Opyt o russkom stixosloženii.* 2d edition. St. Peters-burg, 1817.
Zawodziński, K. W. *Studia z wersyfikacji Polskiej*, edited by Janina Budkowska. Breslau: Zakład imienia Ossolińskich, 1954.
Žirmunskij, V. *Rifma, ee istorija i teorija.* Leningrad: "Academia," 1923.

Index

STUDIES OF THE RUSSIAN INSTITUTE

PUBLISHED BY COLUMBIA UNIVERSITY PRESS

THAD PAUL ALTON, *Polish Postwar Economy*

JOHN A. ARMSTRONG, *Ukrainian Nationalism*

ABRAM BERGSON, *Soviet National Income and Product in 1937*

EDWARD J. BROWN, *The Proletarian Episode in Russian Literature, 1928–1932*

HARVEY L. DYCK, *Weimar Germany and Soviet Russia, 1926–1933: A Study in Diplomatic Instability*

RALPH TALCOTT FISHER, JR., *Pattern for Soviet Youth: A Study of the Congresses of the Komsomol, 1918–1954*

MAURICE FRIEDBERG, *Russian Classics in Soviet Jackets*

ELLIOT R. GOODMAN, *The Soviet Design for a World State*

DAVID GRANICK, *Management of the Industrial Firm in the USSR: A Study in Soviet Economic Planning*

THOMAS TAYLOR HAMMOND, *Lenin on Trade Unions and Revolution, 1893–1917*

JOHN N. HAZARD, *Settling Disputes in Soviet Society: The Formative Years of Legal Institutions*

DAVID JORAVSKY, *Soviet Marxism and Natural Science, 1917–1932*

DAVID MARSHALL LANG, *The Last Years of the Georgian Monarchy, 1658–1832*

GEORGE S. N. LUCKYJ, *Literary Politics in the Soviet Ukraine, 1917–1934*

HERBERT MARCUSE, *Soviet Marxism: A Critical Analysis*

KERMIT E. MCKENZIE, *Comintern and World Revolution, 1928–1943: The Shaping of Doctrine*

CHARLES B. MCLANE, *Soviet Policy and the Chinese Communists, 1931–1946*

JAMES WILLIAM MORLEY, *The Japanese Thrust into Siberia, 1918*

ALEXANDER G. PARK, *Bolshevism in Turkestan, 1917–1927*

MICHAEL BORO PETROVICH, *The Emergence of Russian Panslavism, 1856–1870*

OLIVER H. RADKEY, *The Agrarian Foes of Bolshevism: Promise and Default of the Russian Socialist Revolutionaries, February to October, 1917*

OLIVER H. RADKEY, *The Sickle Under the Hammer: The Russian Socialist Revolutionaries in the Early Months of Soviet Rule*

ALFRED J. RIEBER, *Stalin and the French Communist Party, 1941–1947*

ALFRED ERICH SENN, *The Emergence of Modern Lithuania*

ERNEST J. SIMMONS, editor, *Through the Glass of Soviet Literature: Views of Russian Society*
THEODORE K. VON LAUE, *Sergei Witte and the Industrialization of Russia*
ALLEN S. WHITING, *Soviet Policies in China, 1917–1924*

PUBLISHED BY TEACHERS COLLEGE PRESS

HAROLD J. NOAH, *Financing Soviet Schools*

PUBLISHED BY PRINCETON UNIVERSITY PRESS

PAUL AVRICH, *The Russian Anarchists*
JOHN M. THOMPSON, *Russia, Bolshevism, and the Versailles Peace*
LOREN R. GRAHAM, *The Soviet Academy of Sciences and the Communist Party, 1927–1932*

RUSSIAN INSTITUTE OCCASIONAL PAPERS

PUBLISHED BY COLUMBIA UNIVERSITY PRESS

Russian Diplomacy and Eastern Europe, 1914–1917 (Collection of articles by Alexander Dallin, Merritt Abrash, Gifford D. Malone, Michael Boro Petrovich, James M. Potts, Alfred J. Rieber)
RIMVYDAS SILBAJORIS, *Russian Versification: The Theories of Trediakovskij, Lomonosov, and Kantemir*

PUBLISHED BY THE RUSSIAN INSTITUTE

S. M. SCHWARZ, *Sotsial'noe strakhovanie v Rossii, 1917–1919* (*Social Insurance in Russia, 1917–1919*, with an English summary by Abraham Ascher)